CW00339262

LIGHTNING
UP

For Caroline, Julia, Victoria, Max,
Gemma and Nicholas

LIGHTNING UP

THE CAREER OF
AIR VICE-MARSHAL ALAN WHITE
CB AFC FRAeS RAF (Retd)

ALAN WHITE

Pen & Sword
AVIATION

First published in Great Britain in 2009
By Pen and Sword Aviation
an imprint of
Pen and Sword Books Ltd
47 Church Street
Barnsley
South Yorkshire
S70 2AS

ISBN 978 1 84884 021 8

Printed and bound in England
by the MPG Books Group

Pen and Sword Books Ltd incorporates the imprints of
Pen and Sword Aviation, Pen and Sword Maritime, Pen and Sword
Military, Wharncliffe Local History, Pen and Sword Select,
Pen and Sword Military Classics and Leo Cooper.

For a complete list of Pen and Sword titles please contact
Pen and Sword Books Limited
47 Church Street, Barnsley, South Yorkshire, S70 2AS, England
E-mail: enquiries@pen-and-sword.co.uk
Website: www.pen-and-sword.co.uk

Contents

Preface

This book is not an autobiography. I did not set out to write one. It is simply a record of a career in the Royal Air Force of a pilot who happened to be fortunate enough to fly fighter aircraft, and survive an occasional brush with Lady Luck.

I was not destined to fire my guns, having been too late for the Korean War and too old for the Falklands, and involved with little in between other than with some aspects of the Cold War and with a couple of minor dust-ups in the Far East. There was a time when I would have welcomed an opportunity to engage in aerial conflict. But one grows wiser with experience and time, and that foolishness passes.

I retain the greatest admiration for those who did – and do – find themselves flying in hostile skies, often with the odds stacked against them. Their courage humbles those who, like me, merely flew.

Acknowledgements

I am greatly indebted to my good friend Don McClen for encouraging me to write this book and for continuing to do so after he had ploughed through my first draft. His candid criticisms and helpful suggestions provided the essential catalysts for its successful completion.

I should also like to record and acknowledge the considerable help I have had in quite a variety of ways, from the confirmation of some of my hazy recollections, to the provision of facts, the sourcing of photographs, and the drawing of maps. The following acquaintances and friends all have my gratitude:

Hugh Alexander, National Archives, Kew
Peter Biddiscombe, old pal on 247 Squadron
Richard Calvert, friend and former squadron commander
Sebastian Cox, Head of Historical Branch (RAF)
Bill Duffin Hon Sec of the Independent Researchers' Association
Paul Jackson FRAeS, Editor in Chief, *Jane's All the World's Aircraft*
Norman Roberson, Honorary Secretary, 20 Squadron Association
Henry Roberts, amateur cartographer
Mick Rogers, Honorary Secretary 247 Squadron Association
Stewart Scott, author
Jerry Seavers, friend since 20 Squadron days
Eunice Wilson Archivist to 247 (F) Squadron Association

CHAPTER ONE

Just Out for a Spin

Sitting on the top-deck of a Belfast City bus one miserably wet afternoon in January 1953, peering through its condensation-steamed windows, I found myself wondering what the hell I thought I was doing. I was on my way to Sydenham, now Belfast City Airport, to have my first experience of flying – my 'familiarisation trip' with Queen's University Air Squadron. The rain was pelting down. The heavy dark cloud looked menacingly low. It had all been so totally different a few days earlier when I, and several other undergraduate would-be aviators, had spent a happy afternoon meeting the squadron instructors, having an introductory briefing, and being shown over the aircraft on which we were to be taught to fly. The prospect of flying had then been very appealing. In the present conditions it had no attraction at all and I seriously hoped that my trip would be cancelled.

About an hour and a half later, worrying weather notwithstanding, I was briefed and kitted out. I had fur-lined boots on my feet, a leather flying helmet and goggles on my head, and I had been handed a 'Mae West' – a bulky yellow flotation jacket – to put on. I had been supervised as I trussed myself tightly into the harness of a parachute-pack shaped to fit in the aircraft seat and, with that pack swinging awkwardly below and behind me, I shambled out from the dry comfort of the squadron's accommodation to one of its four Chipmunks.

Climbing cumbrously into the front cockpit I was somewhat relieved to see that the rain was slackening and that the gloom was lightening away to the west – but at that moment even a totally cloudless sky might not have dispelled the apprehension I felt about going up in this mini-machine whose cockpit hardly fitted me and which, besides, smelled slightly of sick.

Oddly, although I had been impressed by an older cousin who had come to spend a few days with my parents in the mid-1940s, proudly displaying Flying Officer's tapes and pilots''wings' on his uniform, I can't recall feeling any great urge to follow in his footsteps. At school I had been fired with the idea of making a career in the Army but I had been armlocked by my father into deferring that ambition in favour of reading for a degree; he had even set me up with a meeting at the home of a friend of his, a professor at Queen's, whose task was clearly to persuade me that a university education would be a much better bet than an immediate plunge into a military career.

While it would be wrong to say that I had had no interest in aeroplanes or in flying, I had never really given any thought to the possibility of getting airborne. My interests were elsewhere and, the moment I was old enough, I had joined the Territorial Army. The idea of the University Air Squadron (UAS) came three years later and owed more to the persuasive patter of a friend than to a burning desire on my part to learn to fly. And I doubt that his enthusiasm was initially any greater than mine as his principal argument for attempting to join was that: 'They have a great Mess and it's open on a Saturday night long after the pubs in Belfast close.'

UASs were set up – the first at Cambridge in 1925[1] – while the RAF was enjoying a brief period of modest expansion. As the then Chief of the Air Staff[2] put it, by encouraging undergraduates to fly the UASs would be '…. a great means of enabling the spirit of aviation to spread…', and they would '… give the brains of the country a chance of being used for aeronautical purposes….' They were also a means of encouraging undergraduates to consider careers in the various Branches of the RAF, and the free flying lessons provided by them was the bait for all potential officer recruits, not just for potential members of the flying, or General Duties, Branch. But the cost of providing such lessons, even with simple aircraft, had to be justified[3] and anyone applying to join had to display both the aptitude to cope with flying lessons and the qualities that the RAF was seeking in its own recruits. We thus found that joining wasn't simply a matter of presenting ourselves as keen applicants for membership of a university club.

The first hurdle to acceptance was the medical examination, a fairly lengthy affair that covered everything from the history of our health, through its current state, to possible future infirmity. During the course of it I was asked if I ever got sick in cars or on buses and this gave me a momentary twinge of concern; I had been sick every time I got into a car when I was a child, but I didn't volunteer this last, hopefully irrelevant, piece of information as I had long since grown out of the tendency. Besides, as rough seas and boats didn't bother me I reasoned, optimistically, that aircraft would be unlikely to do so either. Happily, we were both pronounced fit and able to see and hear to the required standards.

The next hurdle was the Aptitude Test. This required the would-be aviator rapidly to interpret a series of diagrams and photographs briefly displayed to him. The diagrams, designed to test the applicant's ability to solve general mechanical and mathematical problems, were in the format of a standard Intelligence Test. The photographs, which showed the standard flight instrument panels of RAF aircraft doing just about everything except flying straight and level, focussed the testing process more precisely. I had no idea how I scored on the Intelligence Test but I was relieved, and indeed smugly pleased, to find that I could read the instrument panels without difficulty.

The real test, however, was the Interview Board. My Board comprised a heavy, red-faced, wing commander flanked by two squadron leaders, all well decorated with World War Two medal ribbons and, as a group, just a little intimidating. They were seated side by side behind a table in front of which stood a solitary chair. 'Sit down please,' said the wing commander, waving his hand impatiently in the direction of the chair. Clearly not one to waste time on pleasantries, or putting the interviewee at ease, he went on without a pause: 'Why do you want to fly?' I felt it might be imprudent to confess that the idea had only recently entered my head so I told him what an influence my cousin had been; and, actually, thinking about it now, that may not have been a totally inaccurate answer.

A range of questions followed, designed and refined by long use, to determine whether one was a good prospect as a future member of the RAF. Were you a prefect at school? What games do you play and to what standard? What are your interests and hobbies? What books are you reading? Do you take an interest in current affairs? And so on. Each answer widened the scope of the questioning and raised the risk of exposing any attempt by the interviewee to claim more knowledge, abilities, or qualities than he actually possessed. In answer to a question from one of the squadron leaders I had volunteered the information that I was keen on sailing, and the wing commander immediately asked what relationship I saw between sailing and flying. I waffled about the handling skills that I felt were needed in order to get the best out of both boats and aircraft in the media in which they were operating. 'Really,' he snorted, 'I think you said you were reading Mechanical Engineering. I would have thought that someone doing that would have heard of Bernoulli.' I had, of course, heard of Bernoulli and knew that he had shown that water accelerating through a restriction in a pipe caused a pressure drop at the restriction, but I had not had the wit to connect restrictions in pipes with the shape of sails and wings. My questioner took obvious delight in explaining the connection and, to cover my resultant discomfort, I said that I had not expected a trick question. Preparing to deliver the *coup de grâce* he went on without hesitation: 'Let me sum you up, White. You are a practical man rather than a thinker. You prefer out-door activities to intellectual pursuits. For example, I doubt that I could have a conversation with you about literature.' At that point I wouldn't have bet on my chances of being accepted for the Air Squadron but I desperately hoped that I might yet prevent them dropping to zero. So I bit my tongue and began rapidly formulating a tactful reply. I felt that I ought to say something like: 'I believe that we could indeed have a conversation about literature but I imagine that you would find plenty of gaps in my reading and perhaps some weaknesses in the level of my understanding of complex works.' However, to my horror, it didn't come out like that and I heard myself saying, as if it were someone other than me speaking: 'If we did have such a conversation I imagine that we would soon discover how little you know.'

Perhaps the interview was coming naturally to an end at this point but that stopped it abruptly. 'Thank you White,' the wing commander said, dismissively. 'Good day – and, by the way, we don't need to ask trick questions in order to find out what we need to know about you.' That, I thought, is the end of any hope I might have of flying with the QUAS. Then, as I got up to go, I caught sight of the squadron leaders exchanging grins and my pessimism lightened. Six weeks later I learned that I had been accepted as an officer cadet in the Royal Air Force (Volunteer Reserve), and two weeks later I was kitted out and ready for my introductory flight. I must have said something right after all. Sadly my friend with the late night thirst had not.

'We'll climb above this cloud,' said the voice of Flight Lieutenant Dave Bennett from the back cockpit as we taxied out, 'and try and find a decent bit of blue so that you can have a go at the controls.' I didn't have the faintest idea how high the clouds might stretch or to what altitude a Chipmunk could climb. However, the confident voice in my earphones conveyed the conviction that blue sky was there to be found and I began to shed a bit of the apprehension that I had felt earlier. We lined up on Sydenham's main runway, tested the brakes briefly and were off. As we left the ground my attention was held more by what I could see outside the cockpit than by what was going on inside it; I was a nervous spectator rather than an attentive novice pilot. I had time to take in the fact that the airfield was littered with Sunderland flying boats, gathered post-war back to their principal place of origin, and to note the uncomfortable proximity of the cranes and gantries of the shipbuilding yard below us. But I had no idea what our take-off speed had been, what speed we were climbing at, or what our rate of climb was.

We went into cloud at what, retrospectively, I think was about 500 feet and climbed steadily, turning as we did. The lowest layer of cloud was not in fact very thick and we were soon in a clear space, albeit with more cloud above. The air was smooth, without a ripple of turbulence, and I began to relax and enjoy the sensation of being airborne, even though there was no horizon to focus on, and in spite of the fact that the new oxygen mask strapped to my face – not because we were going to need oxygen, but because the mask incorporated a microphone – smelled unpleasantly of rubber and was mildly claustrophobic.

We continued climbing through and above the next layer of cloud before levelling out. I can't recall how high we went, and probably didn't note it at the time but, thinking now about the Chipmunk's capability, and the total time we were airborne, I think it can't have been much more than 4,000 to 5,000 feet. Having levelled out, and performed what he described as a clearing turn, Dave Bennett invited me to 'follow' him through on the controls. This meant, and means throughout the flying-training world, the student lightly holding the control column, with his feet on the rudder pedals and, possibly, with a hand on the throttle, while the instructor continues to fly the aircraft explaining as he operates the controls what he is doing and why. We did this for a few minutes, climbing, descending, and turning, with me trying to respond in a manner that suggested I fully understood what I was being shown. I was then told, in a phrase that was soon to become very familiar 'you have control'. I can't recall that I felt a surge of delight as I took it, more a touch of nervousness about what I might be expected to do. My first impression was that the 'stick' was remarkably light and the controls much too responsive for my indelicate touch. After about five minutes of pushing and pulling with a bit of gross over-controlling to try to maintain a constant altitude I managed to make myself begin to feel somewhat seedy. I was therefore not at all unhappy to hear Dave say that it was time to head back and to let him take control again. However, I was totally unprepared for his next move. With a cheery 'keep your hands and feet clear of the controls while I get us down the quickest way' he put the Chipmunk into a spin.

I had no idea then what a spin was – but quickly concluded that it was a manoeuvre for masochists. To produce a spin the aircraft has first to be stalled. That is, the angle between its wings and the airflow (the angle of attack) has to be increased to the point where the layer flowing over them becomes turbulent and breaks away. This can be achieved by reducing airspeed and increasing the angle of attack to try to maintain the lift necessary to hold the aircraft's chosen flight path at the lower speed. Or it can be induced by pulling into a turn at a constant speed, vertically or horizontally, thereby requiring the wings to produce more lift to counter centrifugal forces. If the rudder is harshly applied at the point of stall the aircraft begins to roll, pitch, and yaw, concurrently – and lose height. The motion can be disorientating in a clear sky, and very disconcerting to a newcomer in cloudy conditions.

I was totally disorientated by it but, as it didn't turn my self-induced seediness into anything more serious as we descended, I can't believe that Dave can have done many turns before bringing the aircraft out of the spin and 'levelling off'. What mattered to me at the moment the world righted itself again – for clearly a tiny doubt had remained in my mind as a result of the question about buses – was that I had been thrown about in the air and had not thrown up.

We were back on the ground a matter of moments later. The entire trip, from take-off to landing had lasted just twenty-five minutes and, apart perhaps from the gyrations of the spin, I had enjoyed the experience. My early uncertainty had been replaced by enthusiasm – and I wanted more.

I got airborne for a real working flight eight days later. The man in the back, once again Dave Bennett, did the take-off and climb to height. As we levelled off, he launched immediately into a practical demonstration of the things that he had covered on the pre-flight briefing: the effect of elevators, ailerons, and rudders, and how engine power settings and speed affected the balance of the aircraft. He then handed control to me, as on the familiarisation trip, and invited me to do things for myself. This time, however, he was clearly determined that I should try to be precise in what I did, and not just move the stick about tentatively. I had to move it positively and continue doing each thing he tasked me with until he was satisfied that I had got the message. He was also insistent that I try to maintain rudder balance as I varied throttle settings, reminding me constantly to 'keep the ball in the middle'. He was not too fussed initially about height and speed-keeping but as the trip progressed he wanted these too. So I sweated away, anxious to show that I could do it and, unsurprisingly, came nowhere near giving him the accuracy he was asking for. His insistence on what appeared to me to be perfection was my introduction to the ethos of the Central Flying School (CFS), the *alma mater* of all RAF flying instructors.[4]

I flew again the following day, eager for more, but it was another three months before I achieved what I really wanted: to get off the ground on my own. The squadron's flying was done mainly at weekends, and good weather conditions were very much needed for the instruction of the inexperienced; not many Belfast winter weekends produced the right conditions and the consequent lack of continuity stretched out the pre-solo syllabus of stalling, spinning, 'circuits and bumps' and emergency landings over-long.

From my third trip, and for the rest of my time on QUAS, my instructor was Flight Lieutenant Harry Dodd. Harry was a small constantly cheerful man who taught with a happy combination of patience, gentle persuasion and insistence on precision. I later realised that this was true of most of the graduates of CFS – but not all.

The day for 'going solo' eventually arrived. I had an early Saturday morning trip with Harry and then went up with the squadron commander, Squadron Leader John Brignell, expecting nothing more than a progress check. However, when we landed and taxied in he told me to keep the engine running, got out, did up his seat straps, pointed to the sky and walked away. I mumbled through the pre-taxi checks, rather as one might recite a prayer, rechecked the tightness of my straps, tried to make my voice sound nonchalant as I called for clearance to taxi, and set off for the take-off point. I wouldn't say that I was exactly nervous about getting off the ground on my own for the first time but, as I opened the throttle and began to move down the runway, I was afflicted for a moment by a sudden irrational crisis of confidence: the thought that I might not be competent enough get the plane safely back on the ground.

The sheer elation when I did, one circuit and a landing later, was intoxicating. And, of course, there was the splendid thought that I would now be free to go off on my own without the voice of precision and discipline constantly correcting from the rear cockpit. This was not, of course, exactly how it was going to be, for solo flights were interspersed with instructional dual trips, and also with periodic checks by the chief flying instructor and the squadron commander.

We were required to concentrate during our solo trips on practising and consolidating what we had been taught on the duals and warned not to go off on frolics of our own. But, initially at least, it was difficult not to stretch the bounds of discipline a little to indulge in a bit of showing-off. For we newcomers this mostly involved nothing more than arranging to be overhead a particular place at a particular time, the hey-mum-look-up-it's-me moment of glory. Some months later, however, the risks inherent in the casual infringement of flight discipline were brought home to all of us by the death of one of the more experienced members of the squadron, Brian McClay, a close friend in my year in the Faculty of Applied Science. He had joined the squadron when he first went up to Queen's and had just qualified to fly the one Harvard on the unit's strength. He stalled it while circling at low level and rather too slowly over his girlfriend's house, spun, and went into the ground without recovering. Oddly, the loss of the Harvard seemed to matter more to the experienced members of the squadron than the loss of one of their number. I recall wondering at the time whether this apparent indifference to death was just undergraduate bravado or something that we thought was expected in a Service that had learned to live with heavy losses during the War.

The Harvard looked – and sounded – rather more interesting than the Chipmunk but it was also more of a handful as it was heavier, had a higher stall speed, and among other traps for the inexperienced, had a retractable undercarriage and a constant speed propeller. The Chipmunk, on the other hand was ideal as an initial – or in the jargon of the Service, *ab initio* – training machine as it was virtually viceless. Its Gipsy Major engine was reliable; its fixed pitch propeller speeded up and slowed down in simple direct response to throttle movements; its fixed undercarriage was a boon for the potentially forgetful; its gentle landing speed of 45 knots (52 mph); and its light and responsive controls could hardly have been bettered. While it might not have won any major aerobatic competitions it was fully aerobatic and, in those days, cleared for spinning. There was enough rudder control to allow good slow rolls to be accomplished – that is, holding a precise height while rotating slowly around the aircraft's longitudinal axis – and loops, barrel rolls and stall turns were all readily performable.

In August we went to RAF Biggin Hill for a fortnight for the squadron 'summer camp'. At the time this former Battle of Britain Station was commanded – very appropriately – by a distinguished fighter pilot, Wing Commander 'Splinters' Smallwood, DSO, DFC. It had one resident RAF fighter squadron, No. 41, equipped with

Meteor Mark 8s. It was also the home base of the two City of London Royal Auxiliary Air Force squadrons, Nos 600 and 615, also equipped with Meteor Mark 8s. The members of the Auxiliary outfits, most with war-time experience, back in the atmosphere of planes and flying, and away from their professional lives in London for the weekend, created a splendidly lively spirit in the Mess – well led on a Saturday night by 'Splinters' – and gave Biggin back something of the feel one imagined it had during the '40s. And, of course, apart from sharing in the 'operational' atmosphere of the Station, there was the pleasure for us of getting airborne several times a day, every day, over the summery countryside, exploring it, throwing the aircraft into aerobatics distinguished more by exuberance than by precision, soaring and zooming – and wondering as we did what it must have been like for those who operated out of Biggin in very hostile skies not so many years before.

I greatly enjoyed all of this, the flying, the comradeship and, not least, the apparent promise of pleasurable sociability as exemplified by the jolly crowd in the Biggin Hill Mess on a Saturday evening. That I was so taken by the whole package was perhaps naïve, but having seen what I assumed to be a fairly representative sample of Service life I decided that I wanted more of it. I had happily taken the UAS bait and was hooked. One month later, tossing aside without regret all thoughts of a career in engineering, I resigned from Queen's, and applied to join the RAF.

Notes

1 Ultimately there were seventeen.
2 Sir Hugh Trenchard. Created Baron in 1930 and Viscount in 1936. Widely acknowledged as 'The Father of the Royal Air Force'.
3 It was decided in 2005 that this cost could no longer be justified. While there 'remained the need for UASs to retain links with Universities both to allow the RAF to influence future graduates and to nurture recruitment', the need to provide flying was discounted. However, all UAS members would 'on a voluntary basis' continue 'to have access to 10 hours flying instruction per year'. Commanders' briefing Note, 15/05.
4 The Central Flying School is actually older than the RAF. It was formed at Upavon in Wiltshire in 1912 and tasked with training the UK's first military pilots.

CHAPTER TWO

Commissioned – But Perhaps Not Quite

Nothing happened for several months. Then, in February 1954, I was summoned by letter to attend No. 1 Central Medical Board in London at a week's notice. Enclosed with the letter was a warrant for a third-class ticket for the journey by boat and train, but no offer to meet any of the likely expenses of the thirty-six hours that I would have to spend getting to and from London. I assumed that this parsimony was normal Air Ministry practice, exchanged the warrant, paid a supplement to convert my ticket from steerage to first-class for the overnight boat-trip to Liverpool – an upgrade that was absolutely essential to ensure any degree of comfort on that journey – and set off for a medical examination that I hoped would be no more searching than the one I had had for QUAS.

The morning of my examination was one of the coldest of that winter, and I was well chilled by the time I found the Board's location in Cleveland Street. Things started promptly, and I had hardly time to thaw out before being called for the first round of tests. By mid-morning, with everything apparently going well, I was beginning to feel relaxed about the outcome. However, it had been noted that I had the inherited skin condition Ichthyosis – which made my hide extremely dry and flaky, particularly in low temperatures. The medical officer collating the results of the various tests suggested that this might well be a bar to my being accepted. 'With that skin you will never be able to serve in the tropics,' he said. I had never been anywhere hotter than France in mid-summer but I was sure that this opinion was wrong. I had put up with the physical discomfort of my skin condition for as long as I could remember, and had suffered not a little embarrassment at school because of it, and now here was a doctor threatening my future hopes by apparently straying beyond his field of knowledge.

'Before you make any decision about that,' I said vehemently, 'you had better consult a skin specialist, for your opinion conflicts with my experience. I've lived with this skin and I can assure you that it gets better the hotter the weather is. I don't like icy conditions but I can tolerate them. My skin has never held me back in any way.'

I don't know whether he was swayed by any of this or whether he did consult a specialist but a month later I was informed that my application to join the RAF as a pilot had been accepted.

On 17 March 1954, after another night on a boat from Belfast, I was on a cross-country train bound for RAF Kirton-in-Lindsey in Lincolnshire, to join a course of Officer Cadets at No. 1 Initial Training School, medically graded A1G1 Z1 – absolutely all right for functioning in the air and on the ground, and with no climatic restrictions on where I might serve. I had been given the rank of Acting Pilot Officer on an eight-year short service commission, to take effect upon my arrival at Kirton. The fact that nothing was assured after the eight years had expired did not worry me at all. I was doing what I wanted to do and I was happy to leave aside for the time being all thoughts of how I might deal with the longer term.

For the next three months the course was instructed in the ways of the Service, tested on leadership skills, and endlessly marched up and down the drill-square (as an officer, and already well-practised in drill courtesy of the TA, I was allowed to loiter indolently on its edge and watch). We were advised how to behave as officers and how to try to be gentlemen. We became fit as never before from multiple sessions in the gym, cross-country running, 'escape and evasion' exercises, and a lot of rugby in my case. I found the three months surprisingly enjoyable but like the rest of the course I was eager to move on, the others because it meant commissioning and a start to flying, and me a return to the latter.

We were all posted to No. 6 Flying Training School, at RAF Ternhill, Shropshire, at the beginning of July, becoming No. 109 Course there. As we checked into the Officers' Mess on the afternoon of our first day we were handed an information folder containing a variety of orders and instructions. Among these was a direction to present ourselves outside the Mess at 1800 hours in the flying kit that we were to pick up beforehand, to be photographed in the two flights into which we had been allocated as per the instructions.

We did all this, and again as instructed, we changed after the photographs into our best uniforms and assembled in the Mess bar where we were welcomed by a group of officers who introduced themselves as our instructors to be. As the party progressed we were subjected to a number of odd questions and a lot of deliberately frightening stories about what lay ahead. We should have realised that it was all a joke and that the 'instructors' were in fact members of the senior course in borrowed uniforms. However, the penny didn't drop until we had paraded, again as per the written instructions, outside the Mess at 0700 hours the following morning in PT kit to jeers, laughter and applause from the members of the other courses packing the Mess windows. And to compound our discomfort we later found the photographs that had been taken the night before, suitably captioned and pinned on the Mess notice board.

Later that morning we were marched to 'Ground School' by a real member of staff, told in outline how the next nine months would be spent, learned that one 'pupil pilot' flight would fly in the mornings and one in the afternoons. The flight not flying would be engaged in 'ground training', which would comprise a wide variety of things – lectures, physical fitness activities, initiative exercises, and so on. The first fortnight would be spent entirely in Ground School. We were also told that although we were all now officers we would be required to march everywhere as a body, salute all commissioned staff members and in the air, were to address all instructors, commissioned or otherwise, as 'Sir'. These measures, and the aggressive manner in which we were informed of them, suggested that we were not going to be viewed at Ternhill as quite the fully commissioned officers we thought we had become, and an incident in the Mess a few days later rather confirmed this for me.

The dining room in the Mess stretched out on either side of the double doors opening into it. Tables to the right of the doorway were reserved for the permanent staff and, at breakfast, newspapers were spread on a side-table nearby. To the left of the doorway was a similar side-table on which the same number of newspapers was laid out for the pupils. Because there were many more pupils than staff living in the Mess the papers on the left-hand table had invariably gone a few minutes after breakfast started. Seeing none to the left on my third morning, but plenty to the right, I went and picked one up from there. I had barely done so when a Mess waitress ran after me shouting 'Ere! You can't take them; them's officers' papers'. I couldn't help wondering at this point if I had gleaned a rather too rosy impression of Service life from my brief spell at Biggin Hill.

After our briefing in Ground School on the first day we were marched down to the 'flight line' to meet our real instructors, be shown over the accommodation there, and have a look at the aircraft. No. 6 FTS was equipped with the Provost T1, the aircraft that was then the RAF's basic trainer. It was, we were told, as we were shown over an aircraft in the hanger, 'easy to fly' – it got off the ground at 65 knots and landed at 55 – and its 550 bhp Alvis Leonides radial engine was a splendidly reliable piece of machinery. This last piece of information was good to know, and we all fastened on to it, but my main thought as I looked at the engine was that it would probably be a bit difficult to see around when taxiing; even an aircraft with as small an in-line engine as the Chipmunk, and fitted with a tail-wheel, required a fair bit of weaving about when moving on the ground in order to see what was ahead. However, that was a small problem and, after a walk around the Provost, and a brief sit in the cockpit, I was happy with the thought that this aircraft was going to be easy for an ace with 121 Chipmunk hours under his belt!

While we were having our look around an opportunity was offered to two members of the course to get airborne as passengers in a nine-ship Provost formation that some of the instructional staff were about to fly. Names were put in a hat and, in due course, the two winners went off to have their introduction to flying. The rest of us watched from outside the pupils' crew-room as the nine Provosts started up, taxied out and took off. Some thirty minutes later we went outside again to see them as they returned, flying over the airfield in a diamond formation. As they crossed in front of us the propeller of the aircraft in the middle of the formation chopped the tail off the aircraft in front of it. Shocked, we watched the tail-less Provost plough into the ground about a hundred yards from us. It was very obvious that there would be no survivors. A little later we learned that one of our course members had been in it. The following day our number went down further when, given the option in the aftermath of the accident, two of our fellows decided to transfer to another, non-flying, branch of the RAF.

A fortnight later, we had learned all about the innards of the Leonides, plus details of the Provost's electrical circuits (24-volt generator and batteries), its fuel system (32 gallons), its engine-driven compressor (supplying air at 450 lbs/square inch for flaps, air intake shutters, windscreen wipers, and at 150 lbs/square inch for the brakes), the functioning of its constant-speed propeller, and its six-shot cartridge starter system. We had also covered air traffic control procedures, radio communication procedures including the Morse code, aircraft emergencies, aerodynamics, aviation medicine, meteorology, and had been enjoined to follow the principles of 'good airmanship'. We were ready to graduate in earnest to the flight line and begin flying.

When we started I found myself allocated to a real gentleman of an instructor, a Sergeant-pilot from Belfast named Dalzell, another Harry Dodd type. His sympathetic and friendly approach to instruction was absolutely right for me and made my transition from Chipmunk to Provost straightforward and swift. His approach to instruction was also very suited to the side-by-side cockpit seating in the Provost as he made much – and effective – use of pointing, gesture and head movement while he spoke from behind his oxygen mask. All of this was a great improvement on the disembodied voice from the back cockpit and I quickly became a devotee of side-by-side seating. Sadly, Sergeant Dalzell, whose first name I never thought to ask, was posted from Ternhill shortly after he sent me solo on the Provost, and I never came across him again in what was still a large Air Force, compartmentalised by its division into specialist Commands.

He was replaced as my instructor for the rest of the course by a lugubrious Flying Officer who handled the Provost as if he was still dodging flak in one of the bomber aircraft that he had flown during the War. On our first trip together, while demonstrating how to make a short landing at a nearby grass airfield used by the FTS for 'circuits and bumps' and first solos, he appeared to be aiming directly at what looked like an old grassed-over bomb crater right on the airfield boundary. In the snapshot view that I had of this depression as we hit its edge I could see that it was not more than a couple of feet deep. I fully expected the Provost to catch its wheels, nose over and lose its propeller. However, we bounced clear without the slightest damage. There was no time to be alarmed by the incident before it was past; I simply hoped that none of the instructors I saw sitting on their parachute packs by the air-traffic caravan as we careered past it thought it was the pupil who was doing the flying – a shameful bit of vanity on my part. He was a conscientious and considerate instructor but he was predominantly a 'straight and level' man and I, arrogantly enjoying an easy introduction to the Provost, did not initially warm to him. As a result we sat politely with each other on trip after trip during the early phases of the course without developing anything approaching camaraderie.

The syllabus progression was much as it had been at QUAS except that we were now being introduced to extras such as instrument flying, cross-country navigation and, towards the end of the course, to night-flying. Until we could be assessed as fit to fly in cloud we were dependent on good weather for our solo flying and so, to get us on the way to a qualification for flight on instruments, we were introduced to 'simulated' instrument flying practice well before the end of the summer. This took place in clear skies, with the instructor on alert for collision avoidance. The world outside the cockpit was totally obscured for the pupil by a combination of goggles with purple lenses and orange screens fitted temporarily inside the cockpit windows. The first time I tried the goggles I wondered how I was going to cope as I could barely see the instruments. I assumed without question that this was deliberate obscuration in the interests of intensifying the value of the practice.

And so, through full instrument panel practice, through 'partial panel' when the main flight instruments were covered by card secured by sticky tape, and on to 'unusual positions' where the aircraft was put into either a spiralling climb not far from the stalling point, or some other unattractive position requiring immediate corrective action, I persevered, peering desperately at barely readable instruments, and not doing at all well. I knew that my lack of progress would be written up in the dual-sortie reports kept on each pupil and so I wasn't too surprised to find myself scheduled to fly on an instrument dual with the CFI. Before we got airborne he gave me a very thorough briefing on instrument flying but it was not until after take-off that enlightenment came: the purple goggles he had handed me were transparent; I could see the instruments clearly and, suddenly, what had been difficult became very straightforward. I wasn't privy to what may have been said to my instructor after we landed but he had a new set of goggles to hand me the next time we flew together on instrument practice. All the airborne instrument work, supplemented by more simulation in a rather rudimentary bit of kit on the ground, the Link Trainer, culminated in a test that qualified us to do limited flying in cloud.

The Link Trainer[1] was essentially an enclosed windowless cockpit (with seat, control-column, and standard instrument panel) mounted on a pedestal. Bellows inside the pedestal could move the cockpit through 360 degrees horizontally, and to 50 degrees of pitch and bank, a range of motion sufficient even for the simulation of spins and spin recovery. Electo-mechanical linkages converted control movements into instrument readings repeated at an instructor's console. The console also had a chart-table on which a pen-recorder could move to show how the occupant of the cockpit was coping with various air traffic procedures involving ground beacons, airfield approach aids, runway approach aids, and the like.

The aids that were available to us at the time included the Voice Rotating Beacon. This device consisted of a constantly rotating aerial that transmitted two signals on a VHF frequency, one a continuous tone, and the other an announcement of the reciprocal bearing of the beacon every 20 degrees, heard by an aircraft only when the associated aerial was directed towards it. Then there was Radio Range, a beacon that broadcast signals designed to indicate to the pilot which side of the beacon's narrow beam he was on. And there was Direction Finding, where an operator on the ground would manually rotate an aerial to enable him to find an airborne transmission's loudest signal and hence the direction from which it was coming; this was in the process of being automated to produce, on a cathode-ray tube, an instantaneous presentation of the direction (CRDF) of a VHF, and later, a UHF transmission.

One solo flying activity that was particularly popular throughout the course was 'practice forced landings', possibly because these provided a personally competitive test of developing skills. Or, perhaps, because they allowed us to fly close to the ground long before we were considered ready for low-flying. Practice forced landings involved chopping the power back to minimum boost, usually in the middle of another exercise, looking around for a field large enough to land in, and near enough to glide to, and manoeuvring to get over its boundary at a speed and height that would allow a safe landing within its confines. Once it was clear that this ideal pre-landing position was – or was not – going to be achieved, a fistful of boost was selected and the aircraft climbed safely away. One of the essential requirements for climbing away was to ensure that the constant-speed propeller had been pre-selected to fine pitch. Coarse pitch was great for achieving economy in straight and level flight, rather like a fifth gear on a car, and it reduced drag from the propeller sufficiently to extend the glide if a real engineless forced landing had to be made. Fine pitch was essential for an effective bite at the air when manoeuvring; it was always used for take-off and landing. One of our fellow pupil pilots got rather too close to the ground on his first solo forced landing practice without remembering to select fine pitch and, in spite of selecting maximum boost for the over-shoot, touched down in his chosen field. Air Traffic Control at Ternhill heard a faint distress call on the emergency frequency and, as is standard procedure, asked the sender for his position. 'I'm upside down across a hedge,' was the reply. As the cockpit of the Provost always smelled strongly of high-octane fuel, even when the right way up, and as one of the required actions prior to a real forced landing was to switch off all electrics, including the radio, the rest of us felt that he might have been wiser to have switched off and waited for someone to find him.

We started night-flying towards the end of November by which time we were sufficiently familiar with the Provost to take the new experience in our stride, and after a couple of dual sorties most of us were sent solo. There were little things to be wary of that hardly mattered during daylight, given that we were not going to be required to take off in cloud, such as the false reading that the artificial horizon gave as the aircraft accelerated. And there were little bits of wisdom to be learned such as the value of carrying torches against the possibility of the loss of electrics and therefore of cockpit lighting. However, by now we had all come to accept that the Provost was reliable as well as robust, and it gave none of us any serious reason to be nervous about going off alone in the dark, or thumping down on the runway as we returned. Night cross-country trips were conducted largely by following a triangular course from airfield identification beacon to airfield identification beacon and, provided these were not obscured by bits of clouds when we felt we should be seeing them, navigation sorties caused no concern either.

Early in the new year we moved on to simple formation flying and a lot more navigation trips, including some low-level ones. Low level for the courses meant nothing below 500 feet but it was a new and vastly more interesting experience than cruising along at higher level, often something close to full-throttle height.[2]

The first week in March, 1955, the final week at Ternhill, contained little more than the 'Final Handling Test' and, for some of us, a flight with an instructor who had the task of judging our attempts to compete for the 109 Course Aerobatic Trophy. I had been putting together what I hoped might be a winning five-minute aerobatic routine, practising it at odd moments over the previous fortnight. The finale of my routine was to be a 'falling leaf', a manoeuvre that I had seen performed at an air show but really knew nothing about. The general consensus among the instructors whom I questioned about it was that the manoeuvre was simply a matter of inducing an incipient spin with rudder hard over one way and, before the spin had a chance to develop, slamming the rudder hard across thereby generating an incipient spin the other way. One then continued from one incipient spin into another for as long as height allowed. This did seem to work and I felt sure that it would look good from the ground. However, the judge was not watching from the ground and I don't think that he was greatly impressed by having his head slammed from side to side by the erratic motion induced by my falling leaf.

The results of the aerobatic competition were announced, along with various other awards, at the formal dining-in night held to mark the end of the course. I didn't win that trophy but quite unexpectedly found myself presented with the 'Eustace Broke Loraine Memorial Cup', awarded to the 'Best All Round Pupil'. I mention this, not from lack of modesty (after all I had had a 121 hour head start on my fellow course members), but to make a point that I was shortly to learn: success can be a transitory thing.

Of the original twenty-six members of 109 Course, nineteen graduated. Apart from the one who had perished before we started, and the two who had thought better of it, one went quickly when he was found to have poor depth perception and could not judge his height well enough to round-out for a three-point landing, another could not conquer air-sickness despite a brave and prolonged attempt to do so, and two just did not come up to scratch in one way or another. All nineteen were posted for training on jet aircraft – eighteen on the Vampire and one on the Meteor.

Notes

1 The Link Trainer was the invention of an American, Edwin Link. He patented it in April 1929. He is credited with being the founder of the modern flight simulation industry.

2 To achieve maximum range an aircraft must be flown at its best lift/drag ratio. Piston-engined aircraft should also be flown at a height where the power required for the best lift/drag ratio entails the throttle opening fully. For light piston-engined aircraft with normally aspirated engines full throttle height can be as high as 12,000 feet.

CHAPTER THREE

Smooth – At Least with the Canopy Closed

Most of us had been given a flight in a Vampire T11 when we were about three-quarters way through the Ternhill course, four instructors from No. 5 FTS, RAF Oakington, just outside Cambridge, flying across for a day specifically for this purpose. The contrast with the Provost was marked. Apart from an impressively better performance, the way in which the jet aircraft slipped through the air was dramatically different. With no reciprocating engine vibrations this was smoothness itself and one could almost sense the fluid nature of the airflow.

Our course at Oakington began towards the end of March 1955. We started with the usual concentrated instruction in Ground School, plus this time, an introduction to ejection seats and to the use of oxygen in the air. Flying began with a gentle forty-five-minute sortie to give us a feel for the aircraft, a look at the general area around Oakington, and some familiarisation with local air traffic procedures.

It was very apparent from the outset that the atmosphere at No. 5 FTS was going to be more pleasant than that which had prevailed at No. 6. Whether the differences were due to personalities or to principle I can't say but we had clearly achieved some subtle change in the level of our acceptability and were now 'students' as opposed to 'pupils'. And for me there was another gain; I had the good fortune to be allocated an instructor whom I liked immediately, Flying Officer Paul Gray. Paul was younger than was the norm for QFIs and was, in fact, one of a small number of pilots who had been especially selected to undergo instructor training at CFS immediately after getting their 'wings'. The idea behind this was that they would have a clearer and more sympathetic understanding of their students' difficulties, and perhaps more patience, than those who had had a spell on front-line squadrons. Paul was my instructor throughout the course and we became good friends.

Before we went any further with the flying however, we had to be shown the effects of anoxia and have our ability to withstand very low atmospheric pressure tested. Both were done in a mobile decompression chamber positioned at Oakington for a few days for each course. This looked like a modification of the thing in which, in half-remembered films, one had seen deep-sea divers being treated for the bends. It was a large cylinder with portholes, divided into a main chamber seating eight, and a small subsidiary chamber that could function as an air lock. For our needs the air had to be progressively sucked out of the chamber in order to simulate increasing height. I wasn't very enthusiastic about getting into this mildly menacing device, not because I was in any way claustrophobic but rather because I didn't like the idea of being time-locked into it. As it happened the experience was not entirely unpleasant. The routine was to take us first to a simulated 15,000 feet with our oxygen masks off so that we could experience the effects of mild anoxia. To illustrate these to us we were told to write down the figure 1,000 on a pad before reaching 10,000 feet and then to subtract 4 from this and from each subsequent answer until, finally, we were helped to put on our masks again by the safety monitor who was in the machine with us. When we had the masks on, and had had a few sucks of oxygen, it was quite a revelation to see the rubbish that we had written while believing that we had remained fully alive to what was going on. Getting our masks on and breathing oxygen was in fact doubly welcome as it was becoming very obvious as we 'ascended' that reducing atmospheric pressure very greatly encourages flatulence.

To complete the session in the chamber we were taken on to a simulated 25,000 feet, paused there to check how everyone was faring, and then taken to 37,000 feet where we were kept for an hour, presumably to check if any of us were likely to be afflicted by the bends while we were 'up' there, or ear or sinus problems on the way down.[1] That sorted out, and everyone cleared, we were ready to tackle jet flying.

The Vampire T11 was not a pretty aircraft to look at. A development of the single-seat version of the Vampire family, it had lost something in the reshaping process needed to accommodate side-by-side seating. Still, it was a lot more capable than anything that we had been in before. Its Goblin Mark 3 engine, producing 3,200 lbs of static thrust at sea level, gave it a maximum speed of 455 knots and a reasonable rate of climb to 40,000 feet. It got off the ground at 105 knots, stalled at 90 clean (85 with wheels and flaps down), and its 330 gallons of internal fuel gave it an average sortie length in the training role of an hour's duration. For anyone who really wanted to squeeze time out of it in the air it could be flown at its 'endurance speed' of 160 knots when it would burn fuel at a rate of 110 gallons an hour at 30,000 feet (or 180 gallons an hour at sea level).

After two sorties of 'general handling' we concentrated on pounding the circuit in preparation for going solo and soon found that the smoothness of the jet aircraft posed a small handling problem that we had not had to think about before: getting rid of speed. All that one had to do in a piston aircraft was to throttle back and the drag of the propeller in fine pitch acted like a brake. And, there was a new technique to be learned with the engine: because of the relative slowness of the Goblin to pick up and produce power it was necessary to anticipate the need for more throttle before the speed started dropping too low; indeed, Pilot's Notes warned us not to reduce power below 6,000 rpm (full power was 10,600 rpm) on the approach to land. Pilot's Notes also warned us that 'movement of the throttle should normally be made slowly to avoid engine surging and high JPTs'. But these were minor matters and my logbook records a twenty-minute solo flight in the T11, immediately followed by forty minutes in the Vampire F5, after three and a half hours' dual instruction in the former.

The single-seat Vampire entered service as the F Mark 1 with No. 247 Squadron in the air defence role in 1946. The F Mark 3, referred to more commonly as the F3, followed in 1948. The F5, a version of the F3 adapted for the ground attack role with strengthened wings, followed swiftly and served widely with front-line squadrons at home and abroad. By the time we were climbing into the F5s at Oakington the Vampire had almost completely gone from the front-line but was still in service with ten of the twenty then existing

RAuxAF squadrons. We were all pleased to discover that most of the solo flying that we would be doing at Oakington would be in the F5s, as these former operational machines represented to our minds a real advance from the pure training aircraft that we had been flying previously. The F5 was also a more rewarding aircraft than the T11 in which to perform aerobatics, as it was lighter and more responsive. And, there was something slightly not right about the feel of the T11, possibly nothing more than the fact that one was sitting off the centre line, or possibly because widening the fuselage had distorted the original design concept somewhat. Certainly, I had not found the off-centre position in the Provost to be any problem at all; but then, that aircraft had been designed from scratch to be a side-by-side seater.

The entire repertoire of standard aerobatic manoeuvres could be done well in the F5, and the aircraft was forgiving enough to allow a fair amount of scope for experimentation. None of us were anywhere near skilled enough to produce anything really new, but we did try. I had given up falling leaves in favour of trying to perfect a vertical, climbing, slow roll followed by a stall turn. I tried for a long time to get it right but I was up against the aircraft's advertised maximum speed – which I never did quite coax out of the Oakington aircraft – and invariably found myself running out of upward momentum before I could achieve the stall turn. That required just enough forward speed, and therefore airflow, to allow the rudder to turn the aircraft around its vertical axis. If it was done just right the aircraft rotated as it ran out of speed and fell around its axis into a vertical dive.

For the rest of the month we did a lot of circuit work, culminating in what were known as 'bad-weather circuits'. These were flown for practice at 500 feet as opposed to the normal 1,000 feet down-wind and, because anything below the normal circuit height would involve a flatter turn from down-wind onto the runway heading, thereby raising a risk for the unwary of stalling on finals, it was felt that they justified some instruction and practice. We also did a lot of aerobatics sorties, and started onto instrument flying in the T11. In May we moved on to limited panel instrument practice, aerobatics and navigational cross-country flights (all at 30,000 feet), and 'high speed runs' at 40,000 feet dual, and at 35,000 feet solo. Neither the

Vampire T11 nor the F5 could reach anywhere near the speed of sound, but sonic shock-waves were created by the acceleration of the air over their wings.[2] In the T11 the first signs of compressibility caused by the shock-waves occurred at Mach 0.78. The purpose of 'high speed' flights was to let us experience these and their discernible effects on the aircraft.

The T11 was cleared for practice spinning for up to four turns and, from an early stage of the course, we were made well familiar with spinning and the techniques for recovering from spins. That is, upright spins where, in spite of all the bucking, yawing and rotating the aircraft remains basically the right way up. However, on an instrument practice trip, when trying to recover from an unusual position that had been thrown at him, one member of the course managed to get into an inverted spin. Neither he nor his instructor could get the aircraft out of it and, as a result, they had to use the ejection seats while upside down. Even when sitting firmly upright in a seat the acceleration induced by the explosive cartridge that moved it could cause compression fractures of the spine – a problem that the later rocket-propelled seats almost totally eliminated. And, as it was almost impossible to get the seat straps tight enough to avoid hanging a little way from the seat-pad when one was upside down, the seat could be moving damagingly rapidly by the time it connected with its occupant's buttocks. Fortunately, on this occasion, neither pilot suffered permanent injury.

We were introduced to low-flying in June and graduated into low-level cross-country map-reading trips – all of this highly popular with most of the course. As June slid into July we began to tackle formation flying, first in pairs and later in threes, first at 15,000 feet and ultimately, at 30,000 feet where the thinner air made engine response noticeably slower and less effective and thus good station-keeping a matter of keener anticipation on the throttle. The later formation sorties included 'tail-chasing', an enjoyable and safe approximation of formation aerobatics for the novice in which each pilot in a formation hung on the tail of the one in front at 200 yards distance while the leader manoeuvred about the sky.

Formal dinner-nights were held on Friday evenings at least once a month throughout the course. The dress was Mess-Kit for those who had it or No. 1 uniform with dress shirt and black tie for those who didn't. The evening started at 1930 hours with sherry in the Mess anteroom, where we chatted reasonably politely until 2000 hours when we filed into the dining room. Dinner was served, decorum was preserved and, when the last dishes were cleared, port was passed around the table and glasses filled. At this point the most junior member of the Mess, 'Mr Vice' (President), was invited by the President of the Mess to propose a toast to Her Majesty. This over, coffee was served and smoking was permitted. The opportunity was then taken by the President to say farewell to any staff member who was leaving the station. No one could leave the table until the President did so.[3] Everyone then moved back to the Mess anteroom and, inevitably, at some stage we would get around to playing the games that had been played in Messes during World War Two, and perhaps for years before it. Some of these were quite painless: the Schooner Race, for example, where teams vied with each other to be the fastest at sinking pints of beer, each player having to down his pint before the next one could lift his glass off the table. Others were rough, such as Mess rugby and 'Highcockalorum'. The latter required a team, usually eight strong to form a line, each person bent over and with his head between the legs of the one in front. The opposing team would then run one at a time at this human centipede, aiming to pile up on some unfortunate's back somewhere in the middle of the line, and hope to win by causing it to collapse under them. On one evening I got the bulk of the opposing team on top of me and, trying to hold them, tore a muscle in my back. When everyone piled off I found I couldn't get up and was half-carried off to bed by concerned, inebriated, friends and dumped there. The Station junior medical officer came up, just a little the worse for wear himself, looked at me stretched out on the bed, and went off promising to return with some painkillers. He didn't return until Saturday evening. Meanwhile, I had managed to drag myself – twice – to the bathroom, but that was so painful I gave up all thought of doing anything further except lying flat on my back. I stayed that way until Monday when I felt sufficiently recovered to get myself to work. Things were not too good for about a week thereafter but I managed not to miss out on any flying. The thought did cross my mind on the odd occasion, however, that ejecting might be a bit painful.

We were judged ready for Instrument Rating Tests in August, to qualify us for our 'White Cards'. These were the first in a series that went through 'Green' to 'Master Green' as experience was gained, and increasingly precise instrument flying standards were demanded and displayed during annual rating tests. The ratings qualified pilots to fly in specified 'Instrument Meteorological Conditions'; among these, and the most significant for us, was the level down to which a pilot was permitted to fly on an instrument approach. White Cards allowed their holders to descend on an approach to 500 feet above the published minimum for the approach aid being used, or for the aircraft being flown, whichever was the higher.

I failed on the first go at the rating test having made a complete cock-up of a 360-degree turn at 30,000 feet, but happily passed without problem the following day. Both trips were with the same examiner, Flight Lieutenant Ben Unwin, our flight commander, a man known for an uncompromising approach and an intimidating manner. However, it was not intimidation that produced my first test's result but my own lack of meticulous attention to what was happening. The T11 had enough power at high level to allow a turn to be sustained at the 45 degrees of bank required on the test, provided it was flown smoothly, and height and speed were precisely held. If either was lost it was impossible to get them back without first coming out of the turn. I let the height slip.

We began night-flying in mid-September and, as Paul Gray was away for a week, my first three sorties to the solo stage were with Ben. He was a man who cared little for social chatter and on the second sortie, in an endeavour to break the uncomfortable silence in the cockpit that I had experienced on the first, I remarked on the wide and varied lacework of lights that pointed up the spread of towns and villages across the countryside below. This seemed at the time a reasonable try at a bit of conversation. Taking a sneak look the following day at what had been written about my second night sortie – we all tried to see the notes made on us after dual sorties when an opportunity arose – I saw to my great irritation and that I had been recorded as being 'confused by the lights below'. Vanity again.

The following night Ben sent me solo and I have often wondered what he wrote about me after that flight, for I failed to lock my aircraft's canopy as I taxied out for take-off. The T11's canopy was a clam-shell, hinged at the back, motored up and down electrically, and locked in the closed position by a handle located centrally at its front end. I had closed the canopy but did not complete the locking action. As I reached take-off speed, and was easing off the ground, the canopy lifted in the airflow, ripped away with a startling whoosh and disappeared behind me. I felt like a total fool, but there was no time to worry about the likely later consequences of my carelessness. The immediate need was to decide whether to put down again or to continue the take-off and sort things out in the air.

The problem with trying to stop in these circumstances is the likelihood of more damage to the aircraft if there is not enough runway left to stop on and it careers off the end. It is sometimes better to get airborne and sort things out in the air – but not always. I wasn't entirely sure that I could stop but, as I had no way of knowing what damage the disappearing canopy might have done to the tailplane, stopping and staying firmly on the ground seemed the better option. I shut the throttle, hit the ground, applied the brakes, transmitted 'aborting take-off', and managed to stop with a yard or two of runway to spare. I expected Ben to have a few choice words to say when I was delivered back to the crew-room, but that was to come later. Once the runway had been checked for fragments of the canopy, and swept clean, he allocated me another aircraft and told me to go and complete my solo trip. I never again forgot to lock a canopy, or indeed skimped on completing any checks on the ground or in the air.

Only a few sorties were left to be completed over the remaining days of November, including a navigation test, an instrument flying test and the final handling test – and the course was over. The eighteen who had started it finished it and, on 30 November 1955, we were formally awarded our 'wings'. My final interview was not entirely comfortable and its message could be summed up as 'could and should have done better'. A bit of a drop from Ternhill, but at least I was deemed worth a posting to the fighter world.

A few months before the course was due to end I had proposed to my girlfriend from university days, Esmé Magowan, and had suggested a date for a wedding to coincide with the leave that I expected to have at the end of the course. She had agreed and we had gone ahead with the necessary arrangements. When I applied formally for permission to be married, a requirement that I thought was simply a matter of courtesy, I was interviewed by the CFI and told quite firmly not to be a silly ass. In his opinion, and this view was still shared by many who had served before World War Two, no one should seriously contemplate marriage much before the age of thirty. Besides, he pointed out, an officer did not qualify for a Marriage Allowance or for a Married Quarter before the age of twenty-five. I felt, with all the arrogance and confidence of the inexperienced, that at the age of twenty-three I was perfectly capable of making up my own mind about marriage and about my ability to cope both with a young wife and with my responsibilities within the Service – and of course I did not acknowledge any connection between concerns about marriage arrangements and forgetfulness in the cockpit. And, I didn't entirely share the view – held mostly by those who had graduated through age and rank to live in Married Quarters – that a young officer should necessarily be with his fellows in the Mess.

I was not refused permission to go ahead with my plans but it seemed more than a coincidence to find, as I did a day before the course finished, that I alone of its members had been posted to begin the next stage of training three days later. The other seventeen members were off on four weeks' leave. When I went to say farewell to the man in charge of Station rugby, Flight Lieutenant John Malloy, a friend as a result of my immersion in the game while I was at Oakington, I mentioned my predicament, more as a conversational grumble than as a plea for help. I didn't expect any favours and didn't intend to ask for any. However, John, who was also the station Adjutant, got quite indignant about 'a bit of an underhand deal' for one of his team and went stomping off to speak to the Station Commander. Later that day a grinning Malloy sought me out in the Mess to tell me that everything had been sorted out and that I would be getting the same spell of leave as the rest of the Course.

That night we had the customary end of course dining-out night and, after the formal bits, we relaxed in the bar in splendid celebratory style, challenged to far too many Schooner races and other damaging games by the junior courses. However, we went to bed happy, me particularly so because of the eleventh hour amendment to my leave schedule. The following morning, in spite of one or two sore heads, we paraded smartly before an audience of relatives, friends, and the visiting Inspecting Officer, our recently bestowed 'wings' proudly pinned to our chests. After lunch with our guests and a final round of farewells we were off. I left accompanied by three close friends from the course, John Carter, Jacko Jackson, and Paddy Foyle, all heading for the Liverpool to Belfast boat, and my wedding.

Notes

1 On an aviation medicine course at RAF North Luffenham (in 1968) the course members were subjected to an 'explosive decompression' in a similar chamber. We were taken to 37,000 feet, kept there for an hour, and then by means of an instant evacuation of air, we were subjected briefly to the effects of a much greater height. I mentioned this in conversation with an aviation medical specialist several years after the event. He was incredulous that this should have been done saying it was much too risky; however, it happened.
2 The curve of the wing on an aircraft flying at a high subsonic speed can cause the air flowing over it to accelerate beyond Mach 1. As this supersonic flow slows to match the subsonic flow conditions at the trailing edge of the wing a shock-wave will form. The sudden increase in pressure across the shock-wave will slow the layer of air closest to the wing's surface (the boundary layer). If the boundary layer actually reverses direction, and starts to move forward, the main flow will separate from the wing surface, increasing the drag already caused by the shock-wave, and cause increased buffeting and loss of effectiveness of controls at the trailing edge
3 This formal sequence was still being followed, with minor changes, some thirty years later when I was retiring.

CHAPTER FOUR

Aspiring Fighter Pilot

At the beginning of January those of us from Oakington destined to fly the Hunter, plus a few others from elsewhere, reported to RAF Chivenor, near Barnstable, to become No. 10 Hunter Course, at No. 229 Operational Conversion Unit. At first sight Chivenor was unimpressive. Before World War Two it had been the site of the North Devon Airport, a grass strip. Work was started in May 1940 on fields just to the west of the original grass area to lay three 1,000-yard runways. In October 1940 the airfield was re-designated as RAF Chivenor and became a Coastal Command Station. We had all hitherto been living in the Lutyens-designed Officers' Messes that had gone up on Stations built during the expansion of the RAF in the middle to late 1930s, all solid structures providing a fair degree of creature comforts, and lacking little other than the sound-proofing that would have been a boon for light-sleepers subject to aircraft noise, particularly jet aircraft noise (and the radios, gramophones, and – later – the music-centres, of next-room neighbours!). We were now to experience quasi-wartime conditions in huts that had not been designed to last for more than 'the duration'.[1] The walls were flimsy. The bedrooms were tiny. Heating in them was by small coke stoves that had to be stoked to maximum capacity and constantly refilled if they were to have any effect. And washing and bathing were catered for in an unheated hut, centrally situated among the others but separate from them. All that said, although I didn't fully realise it at the time, Chivenor had something about it that made course after course of aspiring fighter pilots warm to it, and remember it with fondness long after they had left it.

We were at the OCU to learn to use fighter aircraft as weapons and, in particular, to qualify to fly the Hunter. We started on

Vampires, the familiar T11 and the F5, doing much as we had done in our final weeks at Oakington. We were then introduced to battle formation, flying first in pairs about 500 yards apart, graduating as we got the hang of it to fours where numbers two and four in the formation flew in a swept back position some 100 yards behind their leaders. The idea of battle formation was to enable each element of the formation to 'clear' the other element's tail, and hopefully warn in good time of the approach of an attacker. In the missile era the distance between pairs went out to something like a mile, but to manoeuvre such a widespread formation successfully took a lot more skill than was appropriate for OCU students.

Battle formation was such a basically sound idea that one wondered why it had not been adopted before the 'Battle of Britain' period. The close formation flying that was the norm when the War started, and not dropped soon enough, forced wingmen to concentrate on tucking in on their leaders' wings to the detriment of lookout, manoeuvrability and, too often their survivability.

Before we had finished this phase I had found a house to rent and had moved out of the Mess. The house was at Woolacombe, some twelve miles from Chivenor, and just above what was probably the best beach in the south-west. It was an improvement on the Mess – but only just. As it was normally a holiday let there was no provision for heating in it other than via an Aga in the kitchen, and that winter was very cold. To defray costs, as we were all impecunious, Esmé and I shared the house with John Carter and his wife – not a very comfortable arrangement as it turned out for they were not entirely happy with each other. I had acquired a car, a 1937 model Standard which, although virtually time-expired, was adequate for the journey to and from work each day. At least, it was, until we took part in a treasure hunt organised by the Mess on a very frosty Sunday afternoon in late January. We met a Land Rover on a patch of ice on a single-vehicle width Devon road. Neither vehicle could stop and, although neither was travelling at more than about 20 mph, the impact wrote off the old Standard. For the next month, and until his wife decamped in it, we used John's car. When he moved back into the Mess I had to catch the steam train that then plied between Ilfracombe, Barnstaple, and beyond, stopping at Chivenor *en route*. There was more than an odd moment or two when, trudging the mile and a half between house and railway station, I wondered if I would not have been wiser to have deferred marriage until at least this course was over; and I am sure that Esmé must have wondered at times why she had exchanged the comforts of her family home for a rather lonely existence in an isolated, cold and under-equipped house.

The next phase of the course introduced us to 'cine' practice, where we flew in pairs, each taking turns to hold the gunsight on the other while filming our efforts via the trigger-activated cine-camera mounted on the gyro-stabilised gunsight. The sight projected two images, a fixed cross and a 'pipper', onto a small glass screen in such a way that the images appeared to be at a distance and hence the pilot had no problem focusing between sight and target. The cross indicated where the aircraft's weapons were pointing. The gyro-stabilised pipper was what one put on the target. It comprised an aiming dot and a ring of diamonds that could be moved in and out by means of a twist-grip on the throttle. By setting a target aircraft's wingspan on a scale at the base of the sight and moving the diamonds to precisely encircle the target's wing tips, its range from the fighter was fed into the sight. This used both range and the acceleration due to gravity, or 'g', to compute the amount of 'lead' required. The position of the fixed cross in relation to the pipper was an indication of the amount of lead being asked for. In straight and level flight lead would simply be an allowance for the pull of gravity on the rounds during their transit from the firing aircraft to the target. Against a turning target, centrifugal forces, expressed in increments of g, would be a significant factor in determining lead.

From simple tracking exercises we progressed to 'ranging and tracking'. This required us to close on the aircraft ahead, holding the pipper on it while moving the twist-grip appropriately. From this we went on to 'quarter attacks', which involved positioning abeam and above the target aircraft, turning towards it and then reversing to approach it from its stern quarter. The long-established conventional view was that a curving closure on an armed bomber would give the bomber's guns a more difficult tracking task and the fighter a higher chance of survival. It was also an excellent lead in to air-gunnery.

We graduated to this in our second month. The target was a fabric 'banner', six feet tall and thirty feet long, its front end attached to a metal bar weighted at one end to keep the banner upright in flight. It was towed on a 300-yard cable by one of the OCU's Target Towing Flight Mosquitos. The firing aircraft were required to set up a quarter attack that would allow a firing burst from 300 to 200 yards at an angle off the target of not less than 10 degrees. Each attack was filmed and, for the safety of the towing pilots, the 10-degree rule was sacrosanct. Following a dual instruction sortie in the T11 we were sent off in an F5 for a cine sortie on the flag. If this showed no breaches of the 10-degree rule, four live-firing sorties in F5s were to follow.

On my cine sortie I wasted twenty minutes chasing around, in and out of cloud, under the directions of the firing-range radar positioned at Hartland Point before I sighted the towing Mosquito. I joined on the 'perch', above and abeam of it and got in one quarter-attack before the next pilot turned up, on time, and I had to yield the flag to him. That meant my having to go up on a second cine flight, which, as it turned out, left me with only three firing sorties.

The F5 had four 20-mm British Hispano cannon, only one of which was loaded for a Chivenor firing sortie, and only with fifty rounds. Each of four pilots was allotted his twenty minutes on a flag in succession – twenty minutes to settle down, get the angle-off right, make the odd shaky non-firing pass, and achieve enough steady ones to fire out the fifty rounds in short bursts to good effect. I found this timing very tight. My principal problem was positioning myself at a consistent distance out from the towing aircraft before turning in for the curving quarter-attack. As a result, I was getting too little angle-off on some of my passes and too much on others. As the pressure on time built I wasted rounds by firing on the passes I was getting roughly right even if the pipper was not rock steady in the centre of the flag as it needed to be for maximum effect. And, towards the end of my twenty minutes I took to getting rid off my rounds in long rather than the recommended short bursts, which meant that I was firing a proportion of them before I was in effective range. My scores were abysmal.

The air-firing phase marked the end of the thirty-five-sortie

Vampire section of the course. We moved on with a mixture of eager anticipation, and a tiny touch of apprehension, to tackle the Hunter F Mark 1. We started this with five sessions in a mock-up of a Hunter cockpit to familiarise us with the various knobs, switches and instruments of the real thing, and to allow us to practise the various checks that were needed to get the real thing started, airborne, and safely back on the ground. The mock-up was fixed to the floor and did not move, unlike later aircraft simulators, or even the long-in-the-tooth Link Trainer, but it was animated in the sense that when the electrics were switched on the instruments erected, and various things in the cockpit indicated the correct response to the occupant's actions. As there was then no two-seat version of the aircraft, and thus no possibility of an introductory dual sortie, we took our work in the mock-up very seriously indeed.

While we were in the midst of these pre-flight exercises the news began to flash around Chivenor that a number of Hunters, on an eight-ship sortie out of an airfield in East Anglia, had crashed. This was bad news – but for most of us on the course, eager to fly the aircraft, and impatient to do so, it was someone else's bad news. This was shamefully unsympathetic perhaps, but the main emotion we felt was hope that we were not going to learn of some fault in the Hunter that might cause it to be grounded and our opportunity to fly it lost for the time being. As it happened, this was not the case. It was, rather, a sad cautionary tale about pressing on too hard against the odds.

The aircraft involved were from the Day Fighter Leaders' Course at RAF West Raynham, something that none of us had heard of at that stage of our training. Two members of the DFLS staff together with six students had got airborne in very doubtful weather conditions. They had barely climbed to height when they were recalled to base as the weather was getting worse. They got back overhead West Raynham with about twenty minutes of fuel remaining and, learning that the cloud-base there was down to 400 feet above ground level (agl), and that the visibility had deteriorated to 800 yards, elected to divert. Their options were to go either to RAF Marham at 10 nm (12 miles) from West Raynham, or to RAF Waterbeach at 30 nm (34 miles) where the weather was somewhat better. Although Marham, a Canberra bomber base, had recently had its very up-to-date Ground Controlled Approach equipment transferred to Fighter Command, and had had this replaced by an earlier and inferior model, the formation leader chose to divert there.

The formation descended at thirty-second intervals between pairs to 2,000 feet overhead West Raynham and set heading for Marham. However, during the few minutes it took the first pair to cover the 10 nm between the two airfields, fog was forming at Marham and disaster became a certainty. Having descended it was too late to opt for Waterbeach. The first pair somehow managed to land; another pilot luckily saw the runway at 150 feet above ground level and touched down just as his aircraft ran out of fuel; one was killed when he crashed out of fuel; and the rest ejected.

At Chivenor, we took aboard the thought that the Hunter Mark 1 was not exactly flush with fuel. In fact, it carried 334 gallons (or 2,570 lbs, the units in which fuel was now beginning to be shown on aircraft fuel gauges), which I note from my logbook gave us, in the fairly good weather conditions we were allowed to fly in at the OCU, between thirty and forty-five minutes airborne depending on what we were doing.

The Hunter was a real step-jump for us in terms of power, speed, fuel management and, not least, powered controls. And it was our first chance to fly a current front-line fighter;[2] the Vampire F5 was totally eclipsed by this magnificent beast. Powered by a Rolls-Royce engine, the Avon R.A.7,[3] it could reach 40,000 feet in seven minutes from take-off, and once there it could maintain a speed of Mach 0.93. This was impressive stuff for us.

We were all given twelve general handling sorties on the Hunter, graduating from circuit work, through aerobatics, flight with powered controls switched off, handling at maximum height, and a high speed run. These trips were then followed by four formation and two cine sorties – a total of just over eleven hours on the aircraft. Thus qualified as aspiring fighter pilots, in my case albeit as an 'Average' one, with a rating in cine exercises of 'Low Average', and in air gunnery of 'Below Average', we received our postings to Hunter squadrons up and down the British Isles and in Germany. I went to No. 247 (China British) Squadron at RAF Odiham, Hampshire, along with Chris Lansdell whom I had first met at

Kirton – and who, incidentally, had won the aerobatic trophy at Ternhill. He left Chivenor with a total of just under 300 hours; I left with just over 400. Thinking retrospectively, I have little doubt that if any of us had been required to fly the Hunter in hostile skies directly after passing out from the OCU, most of us would have been shot out of them, like many of the inexperienced kids forced prematurely by circumstances into Spitfires and Hurricanes sixteen years before.

Notes

1 No. 229 OCU moved to Chivenor in March 1950. For the next twenty-four years nothing was done to improve the accommodation on the Station. In fact there seemed to be an extraordinary reluctance to accord the airfield a long-term future. It was finally – and completely – rebuilt in 1979/80.

2 No. 43 Squadron, the first to be equipped with the Hunter Mark 1, began to receive the aircraft in January 1955. By June 1955, Nos 222 and 247 Squadrons had also got them.

3 The Avon engine also powered the Comet and, later, the Lightning.

CHAPTER FIVE

First Squadron

No. 247 Squadron was equipped with the Hunter Mark 4 when I arrived in April 1956.[1] It also had a Vampire T11 on its strength for simulated instrument flying and dual checks, and a Meteor T7 for target towing, a mix that was pretty standard equipment for Hunter squadrons at the time. The Mark 4 was basically the Mark 1 with an upgraded engine, some extra fuel giving a total of 414 gallons, and a 'follow up tailplane'.[2] I was allocated to 'B' Flight, commanded by Flight Lieutenant David Craig. I was welcomed, shown around and then taken to meet the 'Boss', as squadron commanders were and are, traditionally nicknamed. The Boss, Squadron Leader Charles Laughton, mentioned nothing about my poor showing at Chivenor on cine and air-gunnery, though he would have had my report from there, but I rather got the impression that he was not over-enthusiastic about my potential as a squadron pilot. Although my belief in my ability as a pilot had been dented by the episode with the T11 canopy and by my poor weaponry performance at the OCU, I felt no serious doubt about being able to hold my own on the squadron. Maybe nobody else shared my confidence. But, so what, I thought; surely all that was required was to show willing, and avoid being careless.

I started badly, however. The squadron currently had a thing about flying battle formation without transmitting any orders or instructions. Formation members had to watch the leader very closely and act instantly when he began to turn, particularly if he was turning away. Near the end of my second battle formation practice, flying about half a mile down sun from Flight Lieutenant Bob Poole, one of the 'old hands' on the squadron, I thought I saw him turn towards me. I immediately began to turn away from him, expecting to see him appear shortly on the inside of the turn. However, he was going the other way and, as a result, I lost sight of him completely. Probably to teach me a lesson the hard way he beetled off back to base and I got a rasping when I returned alone. Two weeks later I again lost my leader, Ted Skinner, this time during a tail chase. I had been hanging on at about 150 yards as he hauled us around above and among a bunch of cumulus clouds, and I lost him when he rather mischievously dived into one and was nowhere in sight when I emerged from it. I didn't mind this little bit of one-upmanship at the time but I can't say that I was very happy about it later when Boss Laughton suggested that if I couldn't stick to my leader I had no right to be on a fighter squadron.

Esmé was meanwhile in Ireland, with her parents. I had parked her there during the short spell of leave I had after Chivenor, to stay until I could find accommodation for us in the Odiham area and, as soon as I had an opportunity, I started looking. Also, on leave I had bought a replacement car, a 1947 model Armstrong Whitworth Hurricane coupé. It would have been a lot better if I could have found something cheaper to run but the coupé was on offer at the relatively knock-down price of £250, probably because there was very little demand for a second-hand luxury model that did only 13 mpg. I reckoned that I if I didn't run it too frequently or too far, I could afford it. However, as I drove around the local area looking at houses, and discovering how much I was going to have to pay to rent one, this rationale was a little undermined. A house that was reasonably cheap to rent and close enough not to break the bank on petrol costs was not easy to find. In the end I took on a dilapidated seventeenth century cottage, five miles from the airfield, at four guineas a week[3] and felt that I might just be able to remain solvent.

A few weeks later the squadron deployed for a fortnight to RAF Horsham St Faith, now Norwich International, to hold the southern day-fighter readiness commitment. This required a pair of Hunters to be held at cockpit alert from dawn to dusk, relieved for the dark hours by a pair from a night-fighter squadron. Pilots were nominated to take their turn in the cockpit, or as back-ups to come to cockpit alert should the prime pair be 'scrambled'. I was scheduled on the third day to hold alert as number two to the Boss. Because the weather was pretty poor – rain and solid cloud from a few hundred feet above the surface to over 30,000 feet – none of us seriously expected that we would be required to fly, a presumption reinforced by being stood down to holding alert from the crew-room. However, our complacency was suddenly shaken by an order to come to cockpit alert and, in time-honoured fashion, the Boss and I sprinted to the aircraft, some 150 yards away on the parking apron. I was so puffed, or possibly so apprehensive about taking-off on the Boss's wing on my first operational scramble, and in rain and low cloud, that my legs had a touch of the trembles as I hastened to do up my straps and concurrently have a check around the cockpit.

I had hardly completed strapping in when the air defence radar controller's voice came over the tele-brief – an open telephone line to the pilot via a cable plugged into the aircraft below its tail, tensioned to self-release once the aircraft started to move – ordering us to 'scramble'. We started, taxied, lined up as a pair, and were off, entering cloud at about 400 feet with me in close formation on my leader's wing. We broke cloud into clear blue sky at 33,000 feet only to be told within a few minutes that our 'target' had been identified as a civil flight deviating from its notified flight-path. We were directed to return to base and were guided back towards overhead Horsham. As we approached the overhead we were handed over to Horsham Approach Control and given the standard descent instructions. I had by this time closed from battle formation and was determinedly tucked into close formation for the ride down through cloud, conscious that my White Card rating did not qualify me to land back at Horsham other than on my leader's wing. Down we went, on the reciprocal of the runway in use, turning inbound at half the height from which we started, minus 2,000 feet, a routine designed to bring the descending aircraft to 2,000 feet agl, roughly in line with the runway and 10 nm from it. At 2,000 feet we were given continuous directions to steer, continuous readings of range from the touchdown point, and advice on the heights we should be at with each mention of range. This was the 'earlier and inferior' model of GCA mentioned in the previous chapter.

We came partially out of cloud at about 500 feet, able to see the ground directly below but not much ahead. I was still tucked in, holding formation, and at the same time trying to get glimpses out of the front windscreen. We had already put our undercarriages and flaps down in preparation for the landing and I expected that we would see the runway approach lights at any moment. 'Cut! Cut!'

yelled Boss Laughton over the radio – the standard aircrew brevity code for 'close the throttle'. I did so, assuming he had the runway in view. Almost immediately he yelled 'Buster! Buster!' – the standard code for 'apply full power'. I did so, still maintaining close formation on his wing. Sneaking another look ahead and down I could see a runway, now very close underneath, but there were no lights on it and it was strewn along its length with what appeared to be chicken coops – it was the disused wartime airfield of Rackheath. Almost at the same moment we picked out the lights of Horsham not far ahead and the drama was over. I thought it best to say nothing at the debriefing about chicken coops – and I never had another harsh word from Boss Laughton.

Practice Interceptions, or PIs, were an everyday routine on fighter squadrons. Pretty straightforward for the pilots, they were what kept the fighter controllers busy in their bunkers at the air defence radar stations. There were still a number of these spread around the country at sites once selected to defend against the *Luftwaffe*. The Odiham-based squadrons worked variously with radars at Box in the Malvern Hills, Ventnor on the Isle of Wight, Sopley just north of Bournemouth, and Beachy Head. The continued existence of these in 1956, and the number of fighter airfields still active in southern England, sometimes raised a question in the bar as to whether or not we entertained serious doubts about the French.

As far as the Hunter pilots were concerned, PIs were simply a matter of being directed by a fighter controller onto a target, generally the other Hunter of a pair, and controlled into line astern of it. We would track, range, and film our efforts on the way in. A skilled controller could bring the fighter to where the pilot simply had to complete a curving approach to gun-firing range; an unskilled one might put it into a lengthy stern chase.

Most of our PI practices were conducted with the fighter flying at 40,000 feet with occasional sorties at 45,000 feet. The Hunter Mark 4 flew quite nicely at Mach 0.9 at these heights with a top speed, straight and level of Mach 0.94 when pushed. Mach 0.9 – or, strictly, Mach 0.89 – was in fact both the Hunter's best climb speed and the best manoeuvring speed at high altitude. If speed was allowed to drop below this optimum the only way to get it back in the thin air at those levels was to dive, regain Mach 0.9 and climb up again. If the target was below the fighter to begin with gravity could be used to tighten the turn while maintaining speed. If it was above, and sometimes we would get a Canberra bomber flying as target at around 48,000 feet, the pursuit was more interesting; the Hunter could be pulled up in a poor approximation of a zoom climb in the hope of getting within a plausible 'firing' bracket behind the target before running out of speed.

The bread-and-butter routine of PIs was of course relieved by other things – solo aerobatic sorties, cine quarter practice, some pulling around the sky trying to stay on an opponent's tail, 'boom' flights, formation flying, practice diversions, the odd flight at night, and by periodic air defence exercises organised by Fighter Command during which we could expect an abundance of varied targets and a lot of scrambles.

Boom flights were simply authorised dive accelerations to above the speed of sound and were normally remarkably unsensational in the Hunter. Shortly after I joined the squadron I was despatched by another of the old hands, Mike Norman, to carry out a supersonic flight with the briefing that I was to turn the aircraft upside down at maximum height – I managed 47,000 feet – and to pull through. I found this sufficiently sensational to cause me to wonder if he had been having the new boy on: although I had the stick pulled fully back in an attempt to pull out of the resultant near-vertical dive the tailplane was completely ineffective until I had lost about 30,000 feet when thicker air, increasing the speed of sound and raising the indicated airspeed, began to give it a bit of bite. The surprising thing, given the later objections lodged against Concorde's supersonic booms, is that nobody in Britain in the 1950s seemed fussed about the ones that fighter squadrons were dropping pretty well on a daily basis.

Landing from an aerobatic sortie one day I noticed a couple of Hunter wheels lying in the hut from which routine servicing on the flight line was organised and supervised. The aircraft log-books for the serviceable aircraft that the engineers in the hanger sent out to the 'line' were laid out in the hut for signature by flight line servicing crews and by the pilots before and after flight. The log for each aircraft, the Form 700, held a record of everything found wrong with it, and what had been done to put things right. The tyres on the wheels that I spotted were new but both had patches where the tread was worn completely away. Someone had managed to defeat the Maxaret anti-skid units momentarily, perhaps by applying the brakes on the point of touching down. Our new and very recently arrived successor to Boss Laughton, Squadron Leader Steve Carson, landed shortly after me and spotted the tyres as he entered the '700 hut'. He asked which aircraft they had come off, and looked in its Form 700 to see who had been the last pilot to fly it. As it had been me he assumed that I had done the damage. A further word or two with the line chief would readily have elicited the information that they had been taken off the aircraft before I had been in it. He stormed into the crew-room and in front of most of the pilots told me that he would not have me on the squadron if I could not land an aircraft properly. I didn't say anything because I couldn't be entirely sure at that moment what the true story was but, convinced that I was taking the blame for something that I particularly took pride in not doing – landing too fast and braking too hard – I went out to the 700 hut and asked the obvious questions. I was also getting rather tired of being the subject of the 'give-a-dog-a-bad-name syndrome'. My tyres were in perfect condition. My immediate reaction was to find Boss Carson and point out his mistake to him, but I didn't; attacking the squadron commander did not commend itself as a sensible action by an irritated junior pilot, so I decided just to take his rebuke on the chin and leave things as they were. However, David Craig had also asked the appropriate questions and sometime later pointed out to the Boss that he had jumped to the wrong conclusion about the tyres. A couple of days after the incident I got a grudging apology which, in the circumstances of the poor reputation that seemed to have attached to me since I joined the squadron, was very welcome.

We deployed to Biggin Hill in September 1956 for a week for the annual autumn air defence exercise. This reproduced very largely the atmosphere that must have prevailed in the autumn of 1940 – lots of sitting around on the grass in the sunshine outside the squadron offices, being scrambled from dawn to dusk to intercept a variety of target aircraft, many of them from European bases coming in over the south coast at high level. Only two things were different: we were not being shot at; and we were operating at much greater heights and speeds than was the case in 1940. I don't recall having any briefings on the squadron about likely Russian tactics, but the conventional wisdom of the day was that Soviet bombers would have to fly as high as possible to achieve maximum range and therefore a low-level threat could be discounted.

Odiham had five hangers, three large solid pre-war ones and two smaller corrugated iron jobs that had been added sometime later. Our sister squadrons on the base, Nos 54 (Hunters) and 46 (the first squadron to be equipped with the Javelin night-fighter), each had one of the large ones. No. 247 Squadron had one of the latter, positioned as far away from the main area of the Station as it was possible to get. The other small hanger housed the Station Flight whose purpose was to look after visiting aircraft and the Vampires and Meteors belonging to ourselves and the other squadrons, an old Anson that could occasionally be misappropriated for a visit to the Channel Islands (for cheap booze), and a splendidly polished DC3 kept on standby for use by a near neighbour, Field Marshal Montgomery. Because of 247 Squadron's poor accommodation we were viewed with mild pity by the other squadrons but we more than compensated for any disadvantage – which we didn't really feel – by making our presence felt in the Mess and in the local area. It may of course simply have been coincidental that there was a particularly happy bunch of people on the squadron at the same time but it didn't take much to spark a party. And every Saturday night started without fail with the pilots – including our NCO pilots – and all the wives and girlfriends, meeting in the King's Arms in Odiham village, the pub that we had adopted as our own. And there were sorties to other pubs in the surrounding area sometimes ending in mild mishap, such as on the night twelve of us went out to a pub in the very ancient Rolls-Royce owned by Ian 'Bungers' Whittle, the highly intelligent but mildly impractical son of the man who had developed the jet engine in Britain, Sir Frank. On the way back Bungers somehow managed to drive off the narrow Hampshire byway we were on and into a flooded ditch. We had a few beers from the crate we were carrying for emergencies, and thought about how we might extricate the car. Only Ginger Bosley initially showed any initiative, spending about an hour in a nearby field unsuccessfully trying to persuade a horse to let him attach a towrope to it. In the end there was nothing for it but for eleven of us to get into the water up to our waists and shove.

In March 1957 the squadron began the process of re-equipping with the Hunter Mark 6. This aircraft was an improvement on the Mark 4 in several respects, the most significant being the introduction of hard points, ancillary pipe-work and wiring to enable four 100-gallon drop tanks to be carried. Two drop tanks instantly became the standard fit for routine flying on Mark 6 outfits, giving scope for longer sorties – hitherto, with the Mark 4, we seldom managed more than forty-five minutes at a time in the air.[4]

In April, in anticipation of a deployment to Cyprus scheduled for the end of June, we started flying long-range cross-country sorties with four drop tanks fitted. On landing from these, the fuel we had used was carefully recorded. The new B Flight commander, Brian Cox, slide-rule and graph-paper at the ready, took charge of the collation of the figures we produced, and as the results emerged, became increasingly enthused with the idea of making an attempt to fly from Odiham to Malta non-stop. This would have been, at the time, a record-breaking distance for the Hunter and, as it seemed well worth a try, a request for permission to do it went from the squadron up the chain of command to the Air Ministry.

In March, also, I reached the magic age of twenty-five at which I both qualified to receive Marriage Allowance and go on the Married Quarters List. As Married Quarters had never been provided in sufficient quantity to meet demand for them, and I had no hope of qualifying for one at Odiham, I set about looking for the next best thing, a Hiring – a rented property taken on by the Station for which the occupant paid a subsidised rent to the Government. I found a rather good flat in Odiham village and life began to look up. On 28 May Esmé gave birth to a daughter, Caroline, in the military hospital at Aldershot. She had a difficult birth, not a very pleasant time in the hospital, and was not at all happy about either the new baby or my coming absence with the squadron. Although we had moved out of our ancient hovel and closer to the Station, and she could therefore be more readily in contact with squadron wives, she decided that she would be happier with her parents while I was away. She knew and accepted that I had no grounds for trying to get out of the coming trip and put no pressure on me to do so. However, she was beginning to suffer from what I now know to have been post-natal depression, and it was not a good time to desert her. I was therefore more than relieved when her mother came over in the middle of June and took Esmé and baby under her wing and back to Belfast.

The first twelve of the squadron's sixteen aircraft left Odiham for the Cyprus detachment towards the end of June. They were headed for RAF Nicosia, then the main airfield in Cyprus, landing for refuelling stops en route at the French Air Force base at Istres in the Rhone valley, and RAF Luqa in Malta. Four of us, with Brian Cox straining at the leash, waited behind for permission for the non-stop flight to Malta to come through.

For reasons that were not disclosed to us, permission was refused. We got the message late on a Friday afternoon – just before desks were cleared in London for the weekend. Perhaps the fuel consumption figures that we had assiduously collected were not accepted. Or perhaps it was thought that the Hunter's lack of serious navigation equipment would make a flight with marginal fuel reserves imprudent. As we had nothing more than map, compass, stop-watch and a bit of equipment showing distance from ground beacons (where they existed), the DME, or Distance Measuring Equipment, and would have had to rely on the accuracy of the forecast wind strengths and direction plus, possibly, the odd steer from French Air Force radar, the Ministry's lack of faith was not too difficult to understand. Brian was so annoyed by the refusal that he decided that instead of trying to break a record at high-level we would fly the Odiham to Istres leg of our flight to Cyprus at low-level.

We set off early the following morning, flying in battle formation at 250 feet, with me in the number four slot. The weather was perfect as we coasted out just east of Brighton, dropping even lower over the sea, creaming along at 360 knots, and feeling that this was the sort of thing that we had joined for. We hit the French coast to the west of Dieppe and sped on south-eastwards in bright sunshine and excellent visibility, not in the least concerned that we might be disturbing a multitude of French citizens enjoying a Saturday morning lie-in. Over the Puy de Dôme the visibility began to deteriorate and, dropping down into the Rhone valley we found ourselves in quite a thick haze, its effect made worse by the fact that we were looking into sun. I hoped that Brian knew exactly where we were as I was getting rather low on fuel by this stage. Istres is normally not difficult to spot as it is close to the western shore of a reasonably large body of water, the Etang de Berre. However, we didn't see it and burst out over the Mediterranean at the mouth of the Rhone, the tail-end men slightly disorientated as we had just passed another body of water on our starboard side. Luckily Brian ignored that, turned port onto north, climbing a couple of thousand feet to make both visual and radio contact with Istres more practicable, and made both within the next few minutes. I should like to assume that he had as carefully calculated the feasibility of the low-level trip as he had the hoped for high-level one but, from the quantity of fuel put into our aircraft after we landed it was clear that three of us had touched down with little flying time left. We flew the remaining legs of the trip to Cyprus at high altitude, and without drama.

The next three months in Cyprus were a delight, with flying during the mornings and 'dinghy drill' as our excuse for driving up to Kyrenia in the afternoons, our revolvers strapped to our waists in case any EOKA terrorists attempted to interfere with our visits to the beach. The principal reason for our being on the Island was to maintain an air defence readiness state there and this involved us, in turn, spending hot hours in a stone-built, tin-roofed hut beside two armed aircraft on a remote part of Nicosia airfield. The flying itself provided an interesting departure from the normal routine at home with a number of army-cooperation exercises allowing us to become familiar with visual reconnaissance work and with simulated ground attacks. We were also introduced to air-to-ground firing. This was done, diving against 10 feet square targets, on an air-to-ground range on which Larnaca Airport has since been built. This was a highly satisfying exercise as it is a lot easier to put cannon shells into a static ground target than is the case with an airborne one. Unfortunately we had only a couple of live air-to-ground sorties each so our appetite for it was hardly satisfied. In fact, we didn't do very well at all for firing practice on 247 Squadron: apart from the bit of air-to-ground in Cyprus, I had a total of just three air-to-air firing sorties during my time on the squadron – but enough to lift me to 'Average'.

Between flying in the mornings (the working day was still the long-established British hot climate one of 0700 to 1300 hours, and the Airmen's meal at 1300 hours was still referred to, as it had been in India, as 'tiffin'), afternoon trips to Kyrenia, and evenings spent in the bar drinking brandy-sours at gloriously cheap duty-free prices, our time in Cyprus went by very pleasantly indeed. Initially, we didn't venture out after dark for, although there was something of a lull in EOKA terrorist activities while we were there, going out at night was not recommended. However, as time passed and we persuaded ourselves that we were becoming aware of what was sensible and what was not, we became a little more venturesome. We went into town mostly in pursuit of a change from Mess food, and just occasionally to sample a cabaret that had been mentioned as worthwhile. Not that there was much in Nicosia to attract one to take risks; the food would hardly have won any culinary awards, and the nightlife was pretty downmarket. We did enjoy one cabaret, however, but that was because it featured, along with the usual performances by scantily clad 'artistes', a monkey on roller-skates, and only then because the monkey took exception to the Boss and bit him.

No. 54 Squadron replaced us in Cyprus in early October and we started home with mixed feelings. The flying had been varied and good, and most of the squadron had thoroughly enjoyed the detachment. I found a whole range of odd things appealing about it and, specifically, about Cyprus. For example: bringing my aircraft to readiness in the cool of the dawn and watching the sun spectacularly lighting the Kyrenia mountain range as it came up; relaxing with tea and a sticky bun in the Mad Hatter's tea shop in Kyrenia at the end of an afternoon spent in the sea; the balmy warmth of the evenings; the scent of the local vegetation; and, in fact, just the middle-eastern foreignness of the place. However, it was time to get back to families and pick up again where we had left off.

The trip home was totally uneventful apart from a rather hairy descent into Malta through a cluster off towering thunderclouds, typical of that time of in that part of the Mediterranean. As Luqa was unusable owing to strong crosswinds we had to land on the slightly shorter runway at the Naval Air Station at Hal Far – a runway which, I recall, started alarmingly close to the edge of a steep cliff. We stayed overnight in Malta, and took off in brilliant sunshine the following morning, refuelled at Istres, and set off on the final leg as a formation of fifteen (we had left one of our aircraft for 54 Squadron). The Boss's aim was to arrive over Odiham in some style and we did so. We flew across the airfield a couple of times in three diamonds of four and a 'vic' of three in close formation line astern, finally running in for a 'break' in echelons line astern. Waiting to welcome us, and totally unmoved by our display of formation flying, was a clutch of seven customs officers who fell on us like hungry piranhas as soon as we taxied in.

We had heard before we went to Cyprus that the squadron was likely to be disbanded as part of the cuts presaged by the then Minister of Defence, Mr Duncan Sandys, in his 1957 Statement on Defence. Scientific advances, Mr Sandys had said, were going to 'fundamentally alter the whole basis of military planning'. Missiles, he predicted, would in the future provide air power. Accordingly, provisions would be made for the V-force to be 'supplemented by ballistic rockets', and the fighter force would 'in due course be replaced by a ground-to-air guided missile system'. I don't recall that, at the time, any one of us was thinking much beyond how 247 Squadron's demise was going to affect us personally. We were a happy, companionable bunch, who enjoyed being on the squadron, and the shared experiences of three summer months in Cyprus had made us wish all the more that life could continue as it was. Some even vainly hoped that what they saw as a very successful overseas deployment might be recognised as a reason for an eleventh hour reprieve. However, the Air Ministry was working on other considerations – factors such as the length of time each squadron had been in existence, whether or not it had been awarded Colours, where it was based, and so on. No. 247 Squadron was too far down the list to have any chance of survival as a flying unit. By the end of December the Duncan Sandys Axe, as the culling instrument came to be known, was swung against us and the squadron ceased to be.

We were not alone in getting the chop. The process had started in March with the disbandment of all twenty RAuxAF flying squadrons. This was followed by a progressive reduction in the twenty-eight RAF fighter squadrons that had constituted the strength of Fighter Command at the beginning of 1957. The same happened to the twenty-three RAF fighter squadrons in 2TAF.[5] By 1962, when the situation had stabilised somewhat, the number of fighter squadrons left in Fighter Command and in RAF Germany was eleven and five[6] respectively.

There was initially quite a number of redundant fighter pilots, many of whom found themselves posted to jobs that made no sense of the cost of their training, such as those of Married Families agents on Stations, or range safety officers at remote bombing ranges. I was very lucky to be posted to another flying appointment, albeit not one that I would have asked for under more fortuitous circumstances: target-towing on Meteors at Chivenor.

Esmé and I had made a wide circle of friends at Odiham, both on and off the Station and I was sorry that she was not present for the squadron's final few weeks. The farewells were numerous and prolonged, and just a little sad. However, following the squadron's disbandment parade and final formal guest night, there was nothing for it but to pack up and depart on our various ways. Mr Sandys had seriously disturbed the even tenor of a happy existence.

Notes

1 Deliveries of the Mark 4 began in early 1955. It eventually equipped nine squadrons in the UK and thirteen in Germany,

2 Movement of the elevators by the pilot activated the tailplane trim motor to act in conjunction with them.

3 My daily rate of pay as a flying officer was nineteen shillings and sixpence (97.5 pence), supplemented by flying pay of eight shillings (40 pence). Four guineas (£4 and 20 pence) was not quite half my weekly total, but not far off. Happily military rates of pay were greatly improved later that year.

4 The Mark 6 was fitted with the 10,150 lbs static thrust Avon 203 or (later) the 207; it carried 3,000 lbs of internal fuel; had an AVPIN (isopropylnitrate) fuelled starter system (replacing the cartridge systems of the earlier Marks); had leading edge extensions added to cure the mild pitch-up tendency from which earlier Marks had suffered; was fitted with a multi-channel UHF radio; was capable of Mach 0.94 at sea-level; could reach 45,000 feet in 7.1 minutes from take-off; and had a maximum practical operating ceiling of 47,500 feet. Nineteen squadrons in the UK and Germany were equipped with the Mark 6; four others were equipped with the Sapphire-engined Mark 5 in much the same time-scale.

5 A 'Tactical Air Force' was formed within Fighter Command in June 1943 in preparation for the invasion of Europe. It initially comprised two of Fighter Command's existing Groups, Nos 83 and 84, plus No. 2 Group, which was moved over from Bomber Command. The TAF was renamed 2TAF in November 1943 when it achieved Command status. Its HQ was established in Germany in April 1945. In July 1945 2TAF was renamed BAFO (The British Air Forces of Occupation), becoming 2TAF again in September 1951. Some scope for (more) confusion was created in February 1952 when NATO's Allied Air Forces Central Europe (variously referred to as AAFCE or AFCENT) subdivided into 2 and 4 Allied Tactical Air Forces; 2TAF became part of 2ATAF. It was renamed RAF Germany on 1 January 1959.

6 Supplemented by ten Bloodhound surface-to-air missile squadrons – of which No. 247 Squadron was one.

CHAPTER SIX

Chivenor Revisited

During my final few weeks at Odiham I had organised myself a short introductory course on the 247 Squadron Meteor T7 and had managed to notch up twelve hours on it before I left. I wanted to get a little ahead of the game by being able to report to my new job at Chivenor as a fully functioning Meteor pilot. Besides, it was something productive to do in the dying days of the squadron when the emphasis was more on preparing the Hunters for despatch elsewhere than on producing a flying programme.

I got to Chivenor about tea-time on 30 December 1957. It was an odd sensation seeing the place again so comparatively soon after passing out from it in such an undistinguished way. All the familiar things were there to remind me of my last time at it – the dunes behind Braunton Sands just beyond the airfield boundary, the ramshackle hutted Officers' Mess just off the main runway, and the wartime make-do sleeping accommodation. But there was one important difference: last time I had been a member of a bunch of hopefuls nervously anxious to satisfy the requirements of the course and successfully graduate. This time I was back, not quite with a full tour under my belt, but at least as a reasonably competent Hunter pilot, comfortable in the knowledge that, finally, I had been accepted as such on 247 Squadron. I was on the staff of the OCU, even though on the supporting fringe.

The Target Towing Flight was part of one of the two Hunter Mark 4 training squadrons now at Chivenor. Both had been given Reserve Squadron status, an attempt, I suppose, to make the effect of the Sandys' cuts seem less severe. No. 145 (R) Squadron had the TTF as an appendage; the other, No. 234 (R) Squadron, had the Vampire T11s, still in use only for check rides of one sort or another, instrument tests, and dual instruction on cine and the flag. New and effective Hunter simulators had been installed in the twenty-one months that I had been away, and these were proving their worth in getting the courses started smoothly on their three-month training period on the aircraft.

I had checked into the Mess on arrival – looking in the local area for a house to rent would come later – and started off the following morning by reporting to the man in charge of the TTF, Flight Lieutenant Sid Cooper. Sid was also responsible for the Visiting Aircraft Flight and the two entities shared a hut on the northern fringe of the airfield. He was one of those officers who tend to end up in the various nooks and crannies of the Service where responsibility is not acute and life is relatively undemanding. His welcoming words contained the subliminal message that he was content not to be at the cutting edge of things and wanted his pilots to be relaxed, happy, and just do the job without making any waves. This made the flight sound like more of a backwater than I had expected and, as I wasn't quite ready to sink into an easy-chair in the crew-room and indulge in bridge in preference to flying, I had a slight passing doubt about how I might fit in. Sid then took me to meet the squadron commander who, to my mild surprise, turned out to be my former flight commander, Brian Cox. Brian had left 247 Squadron in September while we were still in Cyprus, and while I was aware that he had been posted to Chivenor I had lost sight of that fact while waiting for my own posting. I was not unhappy to find a familiar figure in charge.

Later that day I went up in the Meteor T7[1] for the mandatory dual check given to all new arrivals on any RAF flying unit. And, over the course of the next week, I was introduced to the target-towing version of the Mark 8 by way of three familiarisation sorties, and then sent off to do my first tow.

I found a bungalow to rent in the village of Georgeham, perched on a hill about four miles from Chivenor and settled mother and child into it. As Esmé had not made any attempt to learn to drive, it was a little isolated for her but, as there were always a few students and their wives renting houses in the village, this was never a serious problem. The students also provided a ready source of baby-sitters and so we did not, over the time we were there, ever have to miss out on the Chivenor social life.

As well as flying the target-towing Meteors the pilots on the TTF were responsible for taking turns at the end of the runway to see that the flags were properly laid out on the ground and for attaching them to the towing aircraft. Basically, the flag was laid flat with the tow cable in lengthy loops beside it. The towing Meteor was then taxied onto the runway and stopped about fifty yards ahead of the flag. The pilot on flag duty then attached the cable eye to a hook at the back of the Mark 8's ventral tank, checked with the Meteor pilot that the release mechanism was working, reattached the cable and signalled to him that he was clear to go. The aircraft was then accelerated down the runway in the normal way, lifted off steeply to get the flag clear of the ground cleanly, and climbed away at 125 knots. Air Traffic would tell the tow pilot if the flag was in good nick and flying upright. It was always a nuisance if the cable snapped or the flag failed to fly properly on take-off as there would not necessarily be another Meteor immediately available as a replacement.

The firing aircraft were loaded, as had been the standard practice when I went through on the course, and probably long before, with inert-headed ammunition pre-dipped in one of four colours of paint. The colours allowed the four pilots that were normally scheduled to fire on each flag to pick out their own scores afterwards. It was a source of anguish and irritation to those who had already fired on a particular flag if a subsequent firer hit the cable and lost the flag in the sea.

Once successfully off the ground the towing pilot headed for the designated range area just beyond Lundy Island, checking in as he did so with Hartland Point radar. He then flew up and down the range, as directed, at a steady 180 knots. This scintillating task, enlivened from time to time by the odd student whose pattern on the flag suggested that his rounds might hit the Meteor rather than the target, normally lasted for about forty minutes (the students were by now firing in pairs). However, slippages in the programme could drag it out to the point, usually an hour, when fuel usage made it prudent to think about heading back. I found that even the thought of adding up to an hour and a half per trip to my log-book total did nothing to offset the excruciating boredom of towing, and it was always a relief to get back to the airfield, drop the flag, and have a few minutes in the air without the drag it produced. I did keep reminding myself, however, that towing was certainly better than having to sit out the immediate aftermath of Mr Sandys' cuts in a makeweight ground job.

Forty-three days into this routine things took a distinct turn for the better. Brian Cox decided that he could use another Hunter 'tactical instructor' and moved me into this role. 'I'm giving you a chance to fly the Hunter,' he said, 'but if you put one foot wrong – even if I see you taxiing too fast – you'll be back on Meteors.' And so, short of the experience of my fellow instructors, all of whom had done at least one full tour on a fighter squadron, I had to turn overnight into someone capable of persuading the students that I knew what I was doing.

I started off by flying as number three on four-ship battle formation sorties with students flying as numbers two and four, and was leading four-ships within a couple of weeks. And a month after my move onto Hunters I found myself thrust into leading twelve aircraft in a battle and close formation sortie – the sort of thing that occasionally happened as a collective celebration of freedom by the instructors between courses. Because 247 Squadron had not had any first-tourists for some time before Chris Lansdell and I arrived together, had received very few after us, and was used as a holding post for experienced pilots in the run up to its disbandment, we newcomers had not been given an opportunity to lead more than a pair on it. We were the perpetual number twos. In fact, it took the experience of being on the staff at Chivenor to bring home to me how casual some of the more senior members of the squadron had been about teaching newcomers the tricks of the trade, or indeed arranging anything approaching a progressive training programme for new pilots. There was, without doubt, a splendid spirit on the squadron but, in retrospect, I think it would not be unreasonable to liken the atmosphere on it more to that of a flying club than an operational squadron. Of course, certain fundamentals were always covered before a trip: we were briefed on call signs, radio frequencies to check in on, told what we were going to practise in the air, and told what fuel states to report to the formation leader as the trip progressed. We didn't quite have to contend with a 'kick the tyres, light the fires, and we're off' attitude, but the new boys had largely to learn for themselves whatever way they could.

And so life went by at Chivenor with me learning more in my first two months as a tactical instructor than I had picked up on 247 Squadron in twenty. Close and battle formation and cine sorties with the students were interspersed with the usual individual aerobatic and practice emergency trips, the occasional PI, some air-to-air firing, air-tests after major servicing, large staff formation sorties between courses, and a Fighter Command autumn exercise in my first year when the reserve squadrons deployed to other airfields, 145 Squadron to RAF Strubby. And, from time to time, just as a fill-in when help was needed, I flew the Meteor – mostly on towing trips but occasionally with someone who needed to practise instrument flying in the aircraft.

It was on one of the latter sorties that I had the only 'flame-out' in all my years of jet flying. I had just given a group captain student an unusual position leaving him, slightly mischievously, spiralling steeply upward at 30,000 feet with the throttles closed. When I asked him to recover I saw the throttles slam forward so fast that they were almost a blur. The engines couldn't take it and extinguished – so much for my being slightly unkind to the man. The initial action needed in this situation was to get all the unnecessary electric services off swiftly in order to conserve battery power for an attempt to relight. It was then necessary to exercise patient restraint until one had glided down to thicker air to maximise the chances of getting this. I could almost feel my passenger willing me to get on with it – that terrible desire of the older, more experienced, and more senior in rank, to over-ride the actions of the junior, or at least offer advice, even if the junior is the nominated captain of the aircraft. However, to his great credit, he did neither, and we had two engines running again by 10,000 feet. Later jet-engine design very largely eliminated the risk of flame-outs and I only know of one example on the Hunter – when Mick Rogers, one of 247 Squadron's more spirited characters, managed to do it when pulling up into the vertical in pursuit of a high-flying Canberra.

There was a considerable amount of friendly rivalry between the two Chivenor squadrons, mostly manifested on formal dining-in nights through the medium of the traditional after-dinner games. Some of it seems pretty silly in retrospect but, at the time we all participated happily, sometimes at the expense of our quite costly Mess-Kits, feeling that it was all part of a rich tradition. About a couple of months into my tour Brian Cox proposed to the 145 Squadron staff that we equip ourselves with water-pistols for the next dining-in night and, at a signal from him we should all stand up and let the 234 Squadron lot have a blast from them. The Mess dining room at Chivenor was quite narrow and, for such occasions the room was laid out with two long tables running its length, with about six feet between them. A 'top table' for the Station hierarchy joined one end of the long ones together. In this set-up even the short reach of water-pistols could be quite effective. On the night we all sat patiently through the meal, our water-pistols concealed, until the toast to Her Majesty had been drunk, the coffee served, the brandy and liqueurs passed around, and the Mess waiters and waitresses had withdrawn. We then rose as one man and whipped out our pistols. No. 234 Squadron reacted by also arising as one man and, producing hitherto concealed stirrup-pumps, totally outclassed us in firepower. For anyone not old enough to have been around during World War Two it is perhaps necessary to explain that stirrup-pumps – which were issued widely to the populace hopefully to help cope with bomb-induced fires – were hand-pumps that were designed to suck water from a bucket. A leg was attached to the pump in such a way that it projected outside the bucket. On the base of the leg was a plate on which a foot could press as a steadying influence thus leaving hands free to work the pump-handle. Stirrup-pumps could deliver a volume of water far in excess of the output of any water-pistol. We had clearly had a mole in our midst, our plot had been known about, and the tables had been decisively turned on us.

Starting that year, and lasting until March 1959, Chivenor had the task of tutoring several courses of Iraqi pilots. Iraq had bought Hunters, and part of the deal between the two Governments had been that the RAF would train a small number of experienced pilots who would then go home and convert their fellows to the aircraft. It didn't take us long to discover that our part in this would be no easy task. Most of the Iraqis were enthusiastic about the learning process but a minority clearly felt that taking instruction from us was either beneath their dignity or too much of a bother. Also, none of them was very happy about flying in the cloudy conditions that the rest of us accepted as normal. Accordingly we nursed them along, gently trying to make them feel part of the RAF scene in general and the Chivenor family in particular. But there were limits to what could be achieved and even close nursing could not cover everything. One member of the course suffered a partial engine failure one morning, misjudged his approach, hit a low sea wall some 150 yards short of Chivenor's runway, and tore off his undercarriage in such a way that the aircraft was slewed through 180 degrees. I caught a snapshot view of it emerging from behind a building 'flying' backwards at about ten feet above the runway. It remained in the air for just a few seconds before hitting the ground perfectly flatly and coming to a halt almost immediately. The pilot sat in the cockpit, dazed, until pulled out by the fire crew. He was uninjured, but didn't want to continue with the course. Another forgot to put his undercarriage down before landing. When the ambulance and fire crew reached his aircraft, which had ground to a halt not far from the Officers' Mess, he was nowhere to be seen. After a search he was found in the Mess, in his best uniform, sitting reading a newspaper. When asked if he was all right he said: 'Of course, why do you want to know?' He protested that he had not been flying and that the wheels-up landing was nothing to do with him. When it was pointed out that his signature was on both the Authorisation Sheet and the Form 700 he demanded to speak with his Embassy. He did not return to the course either and I have often wondered what happened to him when he got home.[2]

At the end of July I was offered the opportunity to train up to be one of three aerobatic display pilots that the OCU had been asked to provide that year and, whenever I had the opportunity over the next few weeks, I went off to work up a five-minute aerobatic sequence. I did four sessions of my planned display routine above 7,000 feet, the minimum height laid down for normal aerobatic sorties, before

I decided that I was sufficiently consistent to come lower. Oddly, although Chivenor had begun to receive the new dual-seat Hunter, the T7, as I was beginning my work-up, my performance was not checked by means of a dual sortie at this safe height, as had become the practice several years later when I found myself again performing solo aerobatics. I just lowered my height progressively on my own initiative to 4,000 feet, then 3,000, then 2,000. As I had a reasonably well-developed sense of self-preservation I practised at each level until everything I did, particularly the heights and speeds at various crucial points on each manoeuvre, was exactly as it should be. In early September I was practising down to 1,500 feet and I carried out the fourth flight at this level over Chivenor so that Dick Ellis, the Wing Commander Flying and CFI, could check me from the ground. Then, finally, just before appearing in public at RAF St Eval's Battle of Britain Open Day, I did a practice at 1,500 feet in a T7 with Mike Hughes, my (courageous!) flight commander, to be given clearance to come down to the display height of 500 feet.

I carried out most of my practices at the lower heights over the disused airfield of Winkleigh, about 20 nm to the south-east of Chivenor. I wonder now at the tolerance of the people who lived near it as no one registered a noise complaint during or after any of my low level and very noisy appearances there. Such tolerance was still the norm in 1958 but it lasted just long enough for the post-war generation to find their voices.

At the end of my first year on the staff at Chivenor I was assessed as being 'Above Average' as a pilot. This gently massaged an ego somewhat bruised by the assessment with which I had left the place on my way to 247 Squadron, and by the begrudging acceptance that I initially got there. It is just possible, of course, that all members of the staff were seen in these terms – something that could arguably be justified by the truism that there is no better way to improve in any pursuit than to engage in teaching it.

The Hunter sorties at Chivenor averaged forty minutes each and so, despite flying two, three, or even sometimes four times a day, my hourly total didn't mount as fast as it had been doing on 247 Squadron – once we got the drop tanks, that is. However, in April,

1959 I got another opportunity to fly with four drop tanks and to go further abroad in a Hunter than hitherto. The Indian Government had contracted with Hawker, via the British Government, to buy several squadrons' worth of Hunters and to have them delivered. The RAF undertook delivery and the task fell to the Ferry Flight at RAF Benson. As this unit didn't have anything like the number of pilots needed for it, reinforcements were sought from the Hunter outfits around the United Kingdom. Chivenor supplied two of the three pilots required for an early April four-ship delivery to be led by a Ferry Flight pilot. I was more than happy to be nominated as one of the Chivenor pair and both of us set off eagerly to Benson to embark on this new experience.

We were required to report there in time to spend a few days with the flight, being briefed, sorting out maps, and familiarising ourselves with the route we were to follow. When these preparations were complete, we went over to Hawker's factory at Dunsfold, picked up four Hunter F56s, as the Indian-destined aircraft were designated, and flew air-tests in them the following day. The air-tests revealed a few faults that required rectification before we could leave and it was not until late in the afternoon three days later that we got away. The plan was to refuel at the French Air Force Base at Orange and spend the first night at RAF Luqa in Malta, but the lateness of our departure from Benson, and the slowness of the refuelling process at Orange forced us to stop overnight there.

That was a mistake: we took a taxi into town, stayed over long in a pleasant little bistro drinking French beer, and much too late in the night had to walk the five or so miles back to the airfield. After too few hours' sleep we were up, getting briefed and planned for the next leg of the journey to Malta. We took off at 0800 hours, and one and three-quarters hours later we touched down at RAF Luqa where we were provided with a standard RAF Transport Command packed lunch box for breakfast: a pork pie, a cheese sandwich, an apple and a slice of fruit-cake. I list the contents of the package only because I always afterwards blamed the pork pie for how I felt later in the trip.

We took off as soon as we had been refuelled for a direct flight to RAF Nicosia. On the climb we passed through a wisp of cloud no more than a few hundred feet thick and I felt a touch of vertigo – a reminder perhaps of the effects of alcohol from the evening before on one's balancing mechanism, itself very susceptible to the accelerations that the body is subject to in the air. Fortunately the sky was clear at our cruising height, the visibility perfect, and so the effect was fleeting. About an hour later, however, as we passed abeam RAF El Adem in Libya I was not feeling at all well. When our leader asked if all was in order with fuel states and oxygen adding that, if we had any problems, we could divert into El Adem, I thought that I would like nothing better than to divert and get on the ground as quickly as possible. However, that wish was opposed by the thought that if I landed I might not have felt well enough to climb back into my aircraft for the final 500 nm to Nicosia until at least the following day. And that could have initiated an exposure of folly that I did not wish to court.

With some distance still to go to Nicosia I was feeling very decidedly unwell. As waves of nausea advanced and receded I alternated between optimism about being able to hold out until landing, and a feeling that neither hope nor resolution were going to save the day. I watched the cloudless coast of Cyprus, discernible from nearly 200 nm grow closer with a terrible slowness – my misery turning our cruising speed of 9 nm per minute into the slowest of slow motion. When at last we started the descent to Nicosia I knew beyond doubt that I was not going to make it. As no fighter pilot would dream of carrying a sick-bag the problem was how to be decently ill within the confines of the cockpit. I wondered if I could use one or both of my cape-leather gloves but threw the idea away as impracticable. I thought of using the outer shell of my helmet – we had a cloth interior housing earphones, and a separate hard outer 'bone dome' – but that would have been too difficult to get off with the canopy closed, and too difficult to hold while manoeuvring to land. Sadly there was no happy solution and I had no choice but to face the not inconsiderable embarrassment of handing my kit to the ground crew at Nicosia for cleaning.

We spent a quiet evening in the Mess there, all four of us interested only in getting to bed early – and were fit and ready the following morning for the next leg of the trip to Tehran. However, because of some difficulty in getting flight-clearance from the

Iranian authorities for our Indian aircraft we didn't get away until mid-morning on the next day. We were following what was known as the 'CENTO'[3] route, an agreed aerial path for NATO and CENTO military aircraft that went north out of Cyprus and almost overhead Ankara before turning right for Tehran.

The border between Turkey and Iran is about 170 nm long with Russia to the north and Iraq the south, and the CENTO route aimed for its middle. A belief was prevalent among military aircrews that the Russians interfered electronically with navigation aids in the area of the border but, as we didn't have any means of interrogating any aids there, this didn't worry us. With a reasonably accurate forecast of upper level winds we could be pretty sure of staying well away from hostile territory even if we could not see the ground. In fact, the sky was clear and we were able to pick out without difficulty from height, and against the general sepia-coloured background, unmistakable major features (such as large military airfields) and, most importantly, Lake Van, a very useful waypoint not far from the border with Iran.

We stopped overnight in Tehran, parking our aircraft in a military enclave within the civil airport. We were met by the British Air Attaché and driven into town to the hotel he had booked for us – and which he probably used for every transiting RAF crew. It was a dull dark place that smelled strongly of kerosene and stale smoke from eastern tobacco, and might just have ranked as one-star had it got into any hotel guide. None of us was in favour of eating in it that evening and so decided to go out to a restaurant and perhaps seek some local colour. We also wanted some warmth for it had got quite chilly as the sun went down, a phenomenon that had probably as much to do with Tehran's altitude of 4,000 feet above sea level as the time of year.

Unfortunately our Ferry Flight leader, who seemed to know his way about, was determined to set the itinerary for our evening out, and was clearly in no hurry to find an eating spot. He led us further into town and down some rather dubious alleyways to a stout wooden door set into a high wall. He knocked loudly on this and, almost immediately a small panel opened. A pair of eyes gave us the once-over and their owner, presumably concluding that we looked like reasonable prospects, opened the door and admitted us. Inside was a vaulted hallway that led to a fairly large room with a small dance floor, a three-piece band and a well stocked bar. The only other occupants at the time were two men and half a dozen girls. It didn't dawn on me immediately, nor on the other two temporary ferry pilots, that we were in a brothel, but when it did the only thing that prevented us from leaving hastily was the fear that we wouldn't be able to find our way out of the labyrinth of alleys and back to the hotel. Our leader was totally relaxed. 'Best sort of place in Tehran to get a decent drink,' he said, taking one of the girls onto the dance floor. The rest of us clustered uncomfortably together at the bar, not at all sure of ourselves in this unfamiliar territory but trying desperately not to look too much like the proverbial 'innocents abroad'. Our demeanour, obviously not what was the norm in the place, eventually led one of the girls to approach us and ask if 'You no like Irani girls?' in a manner clearly intended to raise doubts about our manhood. By this time the room had got quite full of potential customers for the girls' services and the two men who had been in the place when we first arrived – two American oil-men as we had earlier discovered – were getting into a serious argument about the size of their bill. The appearance of hitherto unseen bouncers who were clearly not going to let them go without full settlement suggested that it really was time for us to leave. Our leader, by now, was lying on the dance floor calling on us to join him in looking up the skirt of the girl he was with. 'Look, no knickers!' he yelled at us. We grabbed him, lifted him to his feet, and beat a retreat without much dignity but with great dispatch. The hotel's food seemed quite adequate after that.

The following morning we left for Sharjah, another flight of one and three quarter hours' duration. With an absolutely clear sky and good visibility on the ground for the entire trip we had no worries about navigation. As we headed steadily south-south-eastwards we had a clear view from the comfort of our cockpit cocoons over a wide swathe of the land below, mostly comprising mountainous terrain, with peaks rising in places to over 12,000 feet, and most of it looking not at all like the sort of territory one would want to have to bale out over. We saw the Gulf – at the time variously known to the littoral states as either the Arabian or the Persian Gulf depending on local perspectives – long before we reached it and had no difficulty picking out the location of RAF Sharjah on the sandy shore some 50 nm across the Strait of Hormuz.

Sharjah was a bit of a shock for anyone used to landing on smooth tarmac. The runway surface was oiled and rolled sand, rough and really not well suited for high-pressure tyres filled to 400 pounds psi. The airfield buildings were in much the same style as those we knew at Chivenor, the only solid structure being the old fort that not very long before had provided accommodation for passengers disembarking for an overnight stop from Imperial Airways' flying boats en route for points further east and south. The heat and humidity were almost unbearably oppressive and we survived only by downing a few very welcome beers under one of the fans in a corner of the Officers' Mess hut. Overnight it rained heavily necessitating a re-rolling of the runway by the Station steamroller before we could even think of taking off.

Our next stop was the Indian Air Force base at Jamnagar situated on the southern shore of the Gulf of Kachchh about 120 nm south of the border with Pakistan. On arrival we were not permitted to open the aircraft canopies until we had assured the authorities, by spraying ourselves with cans of disinfectant that had been supplied to us in Cyprus, that we were not importing any infections. We were then handed a printed sheet giving us an up to date list of all outbreaks of notifiable diseases in the surrounding administrative area, and allowed to get out while the planes were refuelled.

From Jamnagar we flew low-level to Delhi, diverting more than a little from the direct route to help ourselves to an aerial view of the Taj Mahal. This privileged look at a spectacular monument would have been fine but for the diving and wheeling kites – birds large enough to do serious damage to any aircraft striking one – thick in the air over and around it. After a bit of fierce manoeuvring in the interests of bird avoidance we were more than delighted when our leader gave up his attempt to show the place to us and set off along the railway-line leading in the direction of our destination. Again the weather was ideal, and we had a magnificent view of the land we were flying over, close enough at a few hundred feet above the ground, and slow enough at 360 knots, to see it all in its dusty, occasionally colourful, and decidedly non-European glory.

We spent the night in New Delhi, this time in a rather good hotel as the Indian Government and not the Air Ministry was paying. And the following morning we flew the last few hundred miles to the Indian Air Force maintenance base at Chekari, just outside Cawnpore, to hand over the aircraft. Chekari was an extraordinarily interesting repository of aircraft old and new. Just about every piece of concrete around the edge of the airfield had aircraft parked on it, many of them of World War Two vintage. Inside the hanger that quickly swallowed our aircraft were dozens of French-built Ouregons, a post-war fighter-bomber already heading for obsolescence. Nothing much outside the hangers seemed to be in a ready-to-fly state, and there didn't seem to be a great deal to distinguish the place from an aviation museum such as Duxford has become at home.

We had reached Chekari shortly before nine in the morning and had completed the business of handing-over our aircraft by ten. We were informed that a DC3 – the redoubtable Dakota – was being prepared to take us back to Delhi and were told where to find it. By this time the sun was becoming hot and we were becoming thirsty. We found the aircraft and also a man with a bicycle who offered to go and buy some soft drinks for us. The DC3's port engine was being run and we could see that the ground crew clustering around it were not happy. Soon we saw why. What looked like a filter was taken out, examined, and small bits of metal were removed from it. While this was going on we sought a bit of shade and waited for the return of our emissary to the source of drinkable fluid. When he came back, proudly dangling four bottles of a pinkish liquid from his handlebars, we were rather put off by the suspicious-looking particles swimming in them. We took the bottles but didn't drink from them until late afternoon when we were feeling so thoroughly dehydrated that we were more than ready to dismiss the thought of rotten stomachs, or worse.

The engine-running test had got nowhere and, as afternoon merged into evening all work on the aircraft had been abandoned. We were left sitting by it wondering if we had been forgotten and trying to decide where we might find someone to consult about an alternative to the deserted Dakota. The Air Traffic Control tower seemed like a good bet and, to our relief, we found an Indian Air Force crew in the flight-planning room briefing themselves for a flight to Delhi in a C119, an American-built twin-engined transport, considerably more modern than the DC3. We attached ourselves to them, stuck close, and flew back to Delhi in the cockpit with them – a remarkably sizeable space and the only part of the aircraft where the engine noise was at a tolerable level. Four days later we were on our way back to the United Kingdom in an Air India Constellation – one of the last of the large piston-engined inter-continental airliners still in service.

When I got back to Chivenor I found a posting notice waiting for me informing me that I was going back to a front-line Hunter squadron, No. 19, and I was to join it on 19 May. This was extraordinarily good news and I was delighted, not least because I had always been slightly concerned that my employment as a tactical instructor at Chivenor lacked official sanction and could be rescinded at any time. However, this did not stop me thoroughly enjoying my second spell at the OCU. I had been lifted by it well out of the new-boy status that 247 Squadron had kept me in over-long. I had been recommended during it for a Permanent Commission by Chivenor's Station Commander (and had been awarded it by a Board held at the HQ of Chivenor's parent Group, No. 12); and, above all, I had been taught the value of a meticulously professional approach to fighter flying. I left, aware that I owed a great deal to Brian Cox for affording me the opportunity to escape from the backwater of target-towing and gain some very valuable experience on the Hunter instead.

Notes

1 The T7 was an unpressurised twin-seat version of the Meteor Mark 4. The Meteor first entered operational service in July 1944 (with No. 616 Squadron RAuxAF) and was employed briefly against the V1 'flying bombs'. The Mark 8, later modified for target-towing, was introduced in 1947 and was widely deployed both with RAF and RAuxAF squadrons. A night-fighter version, the NF 11, was in service with the RAF until the late 1950s. The Meteor 8 saw operational service with the Royal Australian Air force during the Korean War: ninety-three ex-RAF Mark 8s were procured by the Australian Government for use in Korea; fifty-two were lost in operations there.

2 Writing in the Station monthly log, the Form 540, at the end of March 1959 the Station Commander, Group Captain RAL Morant, recorded his considerable relief that the last Iraqi course had now completed its training at Chivenor. He went on to say: 'We have heard that their successors are now being trained in Russia and we wish the best of Russian/Iraqi luck to both parties.'

3 The Central Treaty Organisation (CENTO) was initially formed in 1955 as the Middle East Treaty Organisation, also known as the Baghdad Pact. The participating nations were Iran, Iraq, Pakistan, Turkey and the United Kingdom. Iraq withdrew in 1959 after the monarchy was overthrown. Iran withdrew after the fall of the Shah in 1979 and CENTO was dissolved.

CHAPTER SEVEN

Deputy Flight Commander

No. 19 Squadron was based at RAF Church Fenton, near Leeds, when I joined it, but was due to move to RAF Leconfield, outside Beverley at the end of June 1959, some five weeks later. Leconfield had been having a runway extension and a general sprucing up to become both a fighter base and one of the thirty-six V-force dispersal airfields that had been, or were being, set up around Britain and overseas. The week after I arrived the squadron deployed to RAF Acklington on the Northumberland coast for a fortnight's air-to-air firing. At the end of this it went directly to Leconfield and so my recollection of Church Fenton is rather hazy – except that I recall that the countryside around it lacked the kind of features that normally facilitate finding an airfield on a visual approach; an easy boob – that one member of the squadron made almost on a daily basis – was to find oneself lining up for a run-in and break at the nearby disused airfield of Sherburn-in-Elmet.

The detachment at Acklington provided a useful opportunity to get to know the members of the squadron. They were all there, living in the Mess, and free from the normal restraints of domesticity at home. As the newcomer I was prepared to fit in, keep quiet, and hope slowly to gain acceptance. However the Boss, Major Newall, a USAF officer on an exchange tour, presented me with a minor dilemma: he announced that he was going to appoint the 'instructor from Chivenor' to be a deputy flight commander. I didn't expect this, and there were others already well into their tours on the squadron who might have hoped that the vacancy that he wanted me to fill would have been theirs. I would have much preferred not to have been bounced immediately over the expectant heads of my new compatriots but I was reluctant to turn down a chance to have an executive role on the squadron – even though I knew that it was somewhat undeserved. I was being accorded much greater experience than I had; I was being treated as a second or even third tour pilot although my time on 247 plus my time at Chivenor merely added up to one full tour's worth. Someone from the OCU must have said something reasonably complimentary to the Boss before I arrived – a complete reversal from my first departure from Chivenor.

Our Acklington air-to-air firing programme was carried out off the coast of Northumberland under the surveillance and control of the GCI[1] Station, RAF Boulmer, but, as always, with responsibility firmly placed on the pilot for not firing if there were boats below that might be hit by falling shells or shell cases. This required us to be clear of cloud and enjoying good visibility – just one of the factors that made a firing programme difficult to run in the summer in Britain, never mind the winter. Add in aircraft unserviceabilities, gun stoppages, tow aircraft availability, the various problems with the flag, and it is easy to see that a bit of luck was invariably needed to give everyone a decent number of firing attempts – even during a fortnight-long detachment.

The Hunter 6 carried a small radar-set in its nose for the purpose of feeding target range into the gunsight. The alternative, for firing on the flag, was to set a fixed range on the sight by means of the control on the throttle and to fire at the moment that this was reached. The flags were especially fitted with a crude metal reflector to enable the radar to be used during practice firing. However, keeping the radars functioning was held by some to be a bit of an unnecessary effort and not every squadron tried to do it for air-firing programmes. The conventional wisdom was that it was entirely possible to judge the range at which to start firing the fleeting burst that there was time for before having to pull vigorously up and over the flag to avoid colliding with it. If we were about to go to war, that would be another matter. The alternative view was that the sight would predict bullet drop more accurately if the radar steadily fed in the closing range to the point of firing and therefore the set should be kept serviceable at all times. We didn't use the radar at Acklington and the squadron average over the detachment was a mere 16.7%. One pilot, Tony Park, dragged it up from something worse with a personal best of 78%, at the same time proving that quite decent scores were possible.

The first thing I did when I got to Leconfield was to investigate the possibility of getting a Married Quarter. A pious hope as a number of officers from RAF Patrington, the GCI Station at the mouth of the Humber, had been accommodated at Leconfield while the airfield was non-operational. They were allowed to stay and only senior Leconfield executives were housed. Eventually I found a rather crummy house in Hull, a town that I remember with little pleasure, and moved Esmé and Caroline up from Chivenor – where we had actually enjoyed the advantages of a Quarter during our last four months there. Years later, when house prices had surged, leading people to eschew Married Quarters in favour of buying their own homes, many within the hierarchy of the RAF were aghast at the exodus from the Stations. It was felt best that people should be on hand for emergency call-outs. I listened not long after the rush into house purchase had begun to a Deputy Commandant at the RAF College, Cranwell, describing what was happening as 'a cancer in our midst'. Having by then been forced more often than not to take whatever accommodation I could find off Stations I was unable to feel much sympathy with this point of view.

When the squadron had sorted itself out at Leconfield, and started routine training, I found, among other things, that the approach to PIs had changed at some point since I left Odiham. We still did the standard stuff that I knew so well, mostly with Patrington. However, there had clearly been some new thinking about how to cope with radar and communications jamming. It was by now assumed, given the massive Soviet investment in electronic warfare equipment, that there would be jamming by specialist aircraft, as well as by bombers, should a major airborne offensive be mounted against the United Kingdom. The Type 80 air defence radars that had begun to be installed as recently as the mid-fifties were felt to be unlikely to have enough power effectively to 'burn' through the jamming that a major Soviet attacking force was now thought likely to be able to produce.[2] And, of course, jamming of VHF and UHF radio transmissions and reception was almost unstoppable. We could even do it ourselves on a single radio frequency by pressing the radio transmit button and holding the channel open.

To give the fighter force some chance of intercepting a bomber stream in intense jamming, Fighter Command had devised a simple and surprisingly effective scheme. Known as the 'Lane System', this comprised a matrix of parallel lines – the 'lanes'. These were 10 nm wide, and ran out from 'start gates' about 60 nm from the east coast. Each lane was designated by a letter, and the whole was reproduced on charts about eight inches square upon which we could write with a chinagraph (wax) pencil. The charts, prepared for different slices of the system, slotted neatly into kneepads, which we strapped on in the cockpit. To enable us to position ourselves – at least at the gates – we drew range circles from selected DME beacons on the charts.

The standard operating procedure for the fighter force in war now provided for aircraft to be allocated to lanes by instructions passed over the tele-brief, given as much information as was available prior to any scramble instructions, and to be scrambled to specific gates with a 'start time' to set off up the lanes if nothing further was heard from the ground. If the fighter pilot had not spotted his target by the time that he expected to, calculated on the last given position of the bombers relative to the gate, he would turn about and start a sweep from one side of his lane to the other at an angle to the lane that, given his speed and the anticipated speed of his target, should have him moving landward in pace with the bombers. The Hunter pilot, without airborne radar, would thus have some chance of a visual pick up if visibility was poor or his target was veering slightly outside his lane. All of this would be backed up by a continuous broadcast by the main radar stations on all fighter frequencies giving 'hostile activity' in the lanes, or any other seriously pertinent information, in the hope that some of this would penetrate the radio jamming. No attempt would be made by individual fighter controllers to control specific fighter aircraft. And, as we really were 'the Few' by now, we would operate as individuals, not by formations, and not even as pairs.

There were refinements to the basic plan, designed by the optimists at Fighter Command HQ, which might or might not have worked depending on the weight of jamming. An example of one such refinement was a code word to swing the lanes onto another compass direction should the general heading of a bomber wave not be straight down the standard matrix. Optimism that the system would work was based on the fact that jamming was attenuated by distance and, as long as the bomber stream was a fair way from the United Kingdom, and the fighters were closer to the radar Stations, the enemy could be seen and the broadcast might well be heard.

We practised with the lane system on every air defence exercise, some with a few targets and some, when there was a major exercise, with numbers expanded by aircraft from other NATO air forces. The RAF had a small force of Canberras equipped to provide jamming for training purposes, and the V-force had some very useful self-defence jamming equipment including 'chaff'. While the jamming that could be produced on exercises was heavy enough to require designated radio and radar frequencies to be kept clear for safety purposes, and all civil-air radio and radar frequencies to be left unaffected, there was never anything capable of producing the effect that was expected from the Warsaw Pact. To give added reality, the radar Stations simulated the worst effects they thought they were likely to encounter, and the Canberra crews got a lot of pleasure from an otherwise tedious role in cocking up our communications quite effectively.

On paper the lane system looked a bit half-baked but it did work remarkably well. On one exercise, for example, I surprised myself by finding the target in the lane to which I had been directed some 140 nm out from the coast, and a high proportion of successful lane interceptions was not uncommon for the Hunter force, and pretty standard for the airborne-radar equipped Javelins. The continuing conventional wisdom, that the enemy would come only at high level, made life a lot easier for the defenders by minimising the likelihood of the bombers being cloaked in cloud and by allowing the fighters to operate at maximum fuel efficiency. Of course, this might not have been the case in reality.

An inescapable thing on squadrons was the 'Secondary Job'. This might be allocated by the squadron or by the Station and could range from the very minor, such as squadron entertainments officer, to the more onerous administrative tasks such as Mess Secretary or Officer in Charge of the Sergeants' Mess. There were also secondary jobs more closely related to one's primary role as aircrew such as the one I was given on 247 Squadron following a fortnight's course at the Survival School at RAF Thorney Island, that of Squadron Safety and Survival Officer. All of these secondary tasks, whatever their importance, gave squadron, wing and Station commanders, opportunities to comment in officers' annual reports on abilities and qualities beyond those displayed in their primary roles. This added refinement to the reporting system – and gave an opportunity to the ambitious young to get themselves noticed.

At Chivenor the Station Commander had called me to his office not long after I had moved from the TTF to tell me that he wanted to have a Station magazine and that I was to have the task of managing it. And I was to make enough money from advertising to enable it to be distributed free. I think the fact that he recommended me to be interviewed for a Permanent Commission after I had done this for nearly a year illustrates quite well the benefits that could come from secondary jobs. Now on 19 Squadron, the newly arrived Boss, Squadron Leader Les Phipps, decided that I was to become the squadron Instrument Rating Examiner. I already had a secondary job running the Station rugby team but becoming an IRE would give me a professional qualification of a kind much valued by junior pilots, and I was therefore more than happy to go to RAF West Raynham, the home of the Central Fighter Establishment, for the month-long IRE course. This involved some pretty intensive general instrument flying on full and limited instrument panels, a lot of recoveries from very unusual positions, dealing with aircraft emergencies including flying in manual 'in cloud', Air Traffic procedural flying and, finally, aerobatics on instruments. By the end of the course instrument flying came very naturally, accuracy and precision were watchwords, and its graduates were ready to be painfully and ruthlessly demanding of those they were now trained to test.

Back on the squadron life went on as normal: PIs and more PIs, formation flying, air combat, air-to-ground firing on Cowden range just twenty miles away, a lot of instrument rating tests, air-tests, the occasional flight at night – just enough to keep us qualified to do it – and, twice a year, a drive down to Chivenor for the newly inaugurated week-long 'Hunter Simulator and Emergencies' course.

The Hunter Simulator and Emergencies course arose out of the positioning of Hunter Mark 4 and, later Mark 6, simulators at the OCU – a cheaper option than providing all Hunter bases with them. The simulator, mounted on hydraulic jacks and capable of pretty impressive movement, enabled a full range of emergencies, air traffic procedures, and instrument practice to be carried out with a fair degree of realism. Certainly, the box of tricks made one sweat. The week also included dinghy drill, with all being thrown into the sea from the Bideford lifeboat and hauled out (after a an hour or two of chilly bailing and bobbing about in one-man dinghies) by one of No. 22 Squadron's rescue helicopters based at Chivenor. Apart from anything else this bit of sea bathing provided an opportunity to test the integrity of one's immersion suit. These rather uncomfortable two-piece garments were made of a rubberised material that was impervious to water but was (supposed to be) capable of allowing air to pass through. There was a rubber neck-seal and wrist seals, all of which gripped tightly enough to keep water out at those points. Rubber boots were vulcanised to the bottom of the trousers, and the top of the trousers and the bottom of the jacket each had six inches of rubber attached that one rolled together to form the final seal. We wore these when operating over the sea around the United Kingdom during the eight months or so when the water temperature was below 10°C – and they could be a lifesaver.

Air combat, which had not figured at all when I was on 247 Squadron, and was not on the syllabus at the OCU, was now a recognised training requirement. The Americans had learnt a lot of lessons during the Korean War about fighting in jet aircraft, and these by now had been passed to the RAF fighter squadrons. We would go up in pairs, and sometimes in fours and, from flying abeam at 40,000 feet, turn away from each other through 45 degrees, fly for a minute, turn inwards through 90 degrees, search for the opposition and try to get into a firing position behind him – or them. Pilot's Notes for the Hunter limited the maximum g that could be applied to $+7^3$ (and $-3^3/_4$), but achieving high g was impossible until one got down into thicker air. Manoeuvring at height required some delicacy, as trying to pull too hard simply caused drag to bleed the speed off, and thicker air was needed to give the engine the power required to overcome drag. Each combat inevitably involved a lot of turning, looking for an opportunity to trade speed for height advantageously, and the ultimate loss of a lot of height as tighter turns were pulled, with gravity used to keep at the optimum turning speed. There were lots of tricks of the trade to be learned either for gaining advantage or for turning the tables on an opponent. One such trick, for use if one suddenly realised that someone was behind and coming into gun-firing range, was to barrel roll holding a boot-full of top rudder (to skid the aircraft and give the pursuer difficulty in tracking), slamming the throttle closed and, perhaps, lowering some flap (the pursuer would have seen airbrakes go out) to help knock off speed; this could have the opponent hurtling past having failed to realise that his closing speed was building up into a liability. Its success, however, did depend on the opponent failing to spot soon enough how rapidly he was closing on his target.

The Hunter oxygen system could be selected either to supply 100% oxygen to the pilot or to provide an 'air-mix'. If air-mix was selected the system gradually increased the percentage of oxygen available to the pilot as the aircraft climbed until at a cockpit altitude of 22,500 feet only pure oxygen was being delivered. The idea was to produce economy in the use of the oxygen carried by the aircraft. At first it was standard practice to select 'air-mix' but some doubt was cast on the functioning of the system by an incident where a pilot reported that his number two was apparently suffering mild anoxia. By the time we were practising air combat on 19 Squadron the Hunter outfits had been instructed to select '100%' on the ground. One day Barry Pickering, one of the first-tourists on the squadron, came to me and said that he was getting worried about his hearing as he was waking each morning almost totally deaf. I was too, and so we asked around the crew-room. It seemed that most of us were experiencing overnight deafness after pulling a lot of high g on 100% oxygen. I don't think the Station doctor took us seriously for we never did have this odd but very real phenomenon explained.

One of our more colourful pilots, John (Jeff) Hawke was still living in York several months after the squadron had moved from Church Fenton, and commuting daily to Leconfield in an ageing Bedford van. Coming into the crew-room one morning looking slightly flustered, he grabbed the phone. 'Is that Beverley police?' we heard him ask. He went on: 'I wonder if you are likely to have a patrol-car travelling between Beverley and York this morning?' The answer apparently being yes, Jeff then asked: 'I wonder if you might task its occupants to look out for my car number-plate.' This appeared to elicit the response that a number-plate might be too small to spot readily from a passing car, for his next words were: 'That will be no problem, Officer, it's attached to the back-door of my van.'

This was very typical of a man who never took no for an answer and was not above mildly bending any rule for personal advantage. And yet he was among the more popular members of the squadron. I was not at all surprised when years later I came across him as an established trader in vintage aircraft, a one-time terrorist suspect having flown low over the White House in a World War Two B25 bomber that he had just bought, the owner of two Junkers 52s, and a provider of specially built aircraft for film-makers (for example, the mock 747 that he 'crashed' for 'White Knights', and the Gunbus that he had made for the film of that name). Sadly, he crashed and died in a Cessna 175 in Bosnia during the turmoil there, doubtless on some dubious mission.

In mid-November we deployed to Cyprus, taking our T7 with us, to take our turn at holding the air defence readiness state on the Island. We followed the old familiar route via Orange, Luqa, Nicosia, with no problems *en route*. The day after our arrival was spent settling into the equally familiar visiting-squadron accommodation at Nicosia – the yellow sandstone-built huts. The outboard drop tanks were taken off and the normal routine of aircraft servicing got under way. Two aircraft were moved to the readiness dispersal – still in the same position just off the remote end of the main runway – and their guns armed.

Flying began with the usual individual sorties for those who had not flown out of Nicosia before. The rest of us got straight away into

PIs with the local radars at Cape Gata and on Mount Olympus. Then, towards the end of the first week, we began a gun and rocket-firing programme at Larnaca range. I disgraced myself on my first rocket sortie by pressing the bomb-release button on the stick rather than the rocket firing-button as I dived towards the target. Unfortunately the bomb-release button was the means by which the drop tanks could be jettisoned and away went one of my two tanks. Oddly, the other one failed to release thereby giving me a minor asymmetric problem and a bit of a worry that it might drop off somewhere on the way back to base, or as a result of being jolted on landing. As I didn't want to be accompanied down the runway by a rupturing fuel tank my touchdown was exceedingly gentle. I expected Less Phipps to be a little less than pleased but, for a man who didn't take kindly to carelessness in the air, he was surprisingly sympathetic.

In early December I led four aircraft from Nicosia to El Adem to take part in a weeklong army co-operation exercise. When I contacted El Adem Approach Control at about 100 nm range I was told that the airfield was experiencing a 'bit of a sandstorm' that was reducing visibility. At that point it would have been an easy option to divert to Benghasi some 180 nm further west. However, I wanted to get down at El Adem if at all possible to meet the exercise deadline and so decided first to have a look for myself at the conditions there. When we got overhead at 40,000 feet and could see the airfield clearly vertically below, I decided to defer the idea of a diversion. We let down, and at 5,000 feet could still see the airfield fairly clearly as we passed over it. If we had climbed at that point we would still have been able to divert to Benghasi with some fuel to spare, but any further delay was going to rule this out as a safe option. Putting the formation into line astern at 500 yard intervals I let down into the circuit, levelled at 1,000 feet agl, and could see nothing but sand. Trying to remain cool I timed the downwind leg, flying the reciprocal of the runway direction on a compass heading, called for wheels and flaps, and started a descending turn onto the runway heading. I didn't find the runway.

Calling to the formation members to raise wheels and flaps I climbed once more out of the sand level and, with that sick feeling that comes with the realisation that one may have screwed up badly, looked back for the airfield. It was in fact inside the turn I had made onto finals and falling rapidly behind us. Fuel states were not yet critical and we had enough for a few more attempts to get down. However, the sooner we did, the better, and I was desperate to make the next circuit absolutely right. Moreover, I had to get the others down with me and not leave anyone alone in the air to cope by himself. This time I stayed at 3,000 feet downwind, timed with care to ensure that we were beyond the airfield before turning in, and began a gentle descent on finals. I could see nothing but sand as I rolled out on the runway heading but, just as I was about to call for another overshoot, I spotted a large whitewashed concrete block below and in front. This was one of a line of blocks that had been put down in the 1930s by the Italian Air Force for the very situation we were now experiencing. The white blocks led to the end of the runway and unquestionably saved me from a very dicey situation – entirely of my own making. Oddly, the other three members of the formation, following my imprudent lead with unjustified faith, had felt no panic at all.

The rest of the week was spent in finding and carrying out mock attacks on military targets in the vicinity of places one had first heard of when the Eighth Army was engaged with the Afrika Korps; places such as Tobruk and Derna. And we indulged ourselves to our heart's content in some really low low-flying. I found that ten feet or so over flat desert was comfortable – though not for everyone: once, while running along the North African east–west highway, I caused a long-distance lorry to flash his headlights at me in warning as I approached him at about cab height. The minimum permitted height for low-flying in the United Kingdom was 250 feet agl in the interests of minimising, to some extent, disturbance to those below, and possibly to minimise the risk of accidental encounters with such things as power-lines. We all recognised that in war we would have to be 'on the deck' if we were going to pursue the RAF's policy of attacking at low level, to reduce and hopefully eliminate the chances of being detected and fired at successfully. On this exercise we were in effect anticipating the concept and the authorisation of 'Operational Low Flying' training introduced within the RAF some twenty years later.

During our absence from Cyprus the rest of the squadron had redeployed from Nicosia to RAF Akrotiri, then just reopened following a major makeover to transform it into a main base capable of handling V-bombers and strategic transport aircraft. We joined them directly from El Adem on a new, very generously sized, concrete parking apron designated as the fighter dispersal. Unfortunately the hangar and office accommodation planned for the dispersal had not yet been started. There was no cover for the aircraft and thus all servicing had to be done in the open. The air and ground crews were accommodated in four interlinked marquees that leaked badly in the heavy winter rains.

The Mess at Akrotiri was a different matter. Attractively built in yellow sandstone, with a welcoming log-fire burning in the anteroom, it was a pleasure to escape to it from the marquees. Most evenings at Nicosia five of us had played poker together, and we took up this pursuit again at Akrotiri, nobody winning much but passing the time happily, constantly entertained by the repeated malapropisms of one of our number notorious on the squadron for producing them. Unhappily, Nigel Pickesgill, B Flight commander and one of the more gentlemanly members of the squadron, mislaid his wallet one evening and we spent an uncomfortable four weeks as he silently wondered if one of us might have misappropriated it; we were all very glad when he found it – where he had left it, on a ledge under the table in his bedroom where we had been playing.

The final few weeks of the detachment passed enjoyably in a series of army co-operation exercises and another session of air-to-ground gun and rocket firing. However, by mid-January, when it was time to go back to the United Kingdom we were all pleased to give up cold leaky tents and head for home. Cyprus in winter does not have the appeal of Cyprus in summer. However, southern Europe was much colder, as we discovered on the way home: we had to stay overnight at Luqa because of poor weather at Istres and icy conditions affecting Orange. Foolishly we had stuffed no kit for an overnight stay into the radio-bay – the only stowage space available in the Hunter – and, with nothing other than our flying overalls we had a miserable night in Malta, and shivered at Orange the following day while the aircraft were being refuelled.

Back at Leconfield we settled down once more to normal life – lots of the usual things but every day different, and always an extra bit of something to add spice. For example, I was off to the Royal Netherlands Air Force base at Soesterberg in early May with half the squadron on a fortnight's NATO exchange – memories of canals and dykes and polders, and of Captain Darrell Bjorkland, our US Marine exchange officer, and myself borrowing bicycles to ride around the airfield to a USAF enclave and finding it extraordinarily difficult to ride back with any dignity after the hospitality we received there.

Another out-of-normal event was the Queen's Birthday fly-past on 11 June. The squadrons taking part each deployed four aircraft and a spare to two airfields in Norfolk a few days beforehand. Our detachment was to RAF Stradishall. On the day of the fly-past the 19 Squadron aircraft made up the last box of four in eight boxes and it was a hell of a ride as the leader kept adjusting his throttle in the interests, I suppose, of getting his timing right over Buckingham Palace. Down the tail end it was necessary to pump the throttle through its full range from closed to maximum power simply to maintain station. He also seemed to have failed to take into consideration how far below his own level the back end of the formation would be stepped down, and I recall as we crossed the north-eastern approaches to London the ground flashing past very alarmingly close below us.

In July the squadron deployed to RAF Sylt in the North Frisian Islands for three weeks of air-to-air firing. Sylt was RAF Germany's armament practice camp, and as such was well prepared to provide the facilities for a firing programme that were such a pain to organise from home. It was my first experience of life in Germany, a RAF posting to which most pilots aspired. Sylt is a long thin island with about twenty-one miles of beach and dunes that would have been very attractive had it not been for the constant wind that blew off the North Sea. However, as it was also a nudist beach, few of the squadron's air and ground crews were deterred by the wind. Several of us, sunning ourselves in the dunes one day, trying to shelter from the chill breeze, were amused to see three of our fellow pilots, coming down the beach. They were obviously on the outlook for something prettier than the overweight and ageing *Fraus* that seemed to make up the majority of the females frolicking on the sands: Neddy Nicholls, a tall gangly lad trying to pretend that he was looking only at the quality of the sand but surreptitiously sneaking the odd look here and there; Pete Taylor, showing no such inhibitions, his head swinging continuously from side to side as if he was at a tennis match; and Ching Fuller, trying to cover his mild embarrassment at being with the other two by carrying his squadron boater (it was the thing on 19 Squadron to have boaters) strategically in front of his lower body.

The weather was ideal for flying on the range while we were there and the firing programme went extraordinarily well. I had twenty 'live' sorties – which doubled my total experience of air-to-air firing to date – and there is no doubt that this continuity was valuable as the squadron average reached 24.5 %. I was averaging 30% hits on the flag, with a best of 56%, a matter of little moment now, but a very important matter of pride to me at the time. Clearly the original OCU rating of 'below average' had stung.

We went to Sylt again – for a month – in January 1961, but this time we fell foul of the German winter and spent half of our time there snowed in and unable to fly. We did a lot of ground-training during the day and relieved the tedium in the evening in the Mess bar enjoying the relative painlessness of duty-free prices, and inevitably we fell into the practice of playing silly games for drinks. The most popular, and most destructive was 'horsing' for Sekt, the German equivalent of champagne. This required each member of the 'horsing' group to select up to three coins, or none at all, hold the amount selected in his closed hand, and guess at the total in the group. Anyone getting this right could relax. Eventually a pair would remain and the loser would buy the booze for the group. At five shillings (25 pence) a bottle for Sekt we tended to get through rather a lot, and as it was quickly intoxicating it stoked the evening from the outset. My final duty after a night in the bar was to search the snow between the Mess and the block in which our bedrooms were located for Tony Park, with whom I shared a bedroom. He had a marked tendency to fall asleep en route to bed.

I escaped for a week from all of this to go back to Hull where Esmé was giving birth to a second daughter, Julia, and to see how my mother was coping with Caroline. I got a lift over by air but had the odd experience of travelling back by the troopship that then still plied between Harwich and the Hook of Holland. I was sought out by the Duty Transport Officer at Harwich, who just happened to notice that I was destined for Sylt, to act as escort to an airman being returned there accused of assaulting an officer. There followed an interminable journey as far as Hamburg by military train, and then onward by a rather slow connection to Sylt town. I had always understood that prisoners had to be escorted by people of their own rank so that they could not compound their situation by striking a superior. I had made this point at Harwich but the DTO had pleaded with me in desperation and, grudgingly, I acquiesced. As it happened my prisoner had cooled down from whatever passion had previously afflicted him and he behaved impeccably throughout the journey. He was in fact quite an agreeable travelling companion.

Towards the end of the second Sylt detachment Boss Phipps decided that the squadron should give a drinks party for the Station personnel. This was to begin at 1900 hours but unfortunately most of the pilots anticipated the party by getting into the bar two hours before it, and 'horsing' madly for most of that time before stumbling off to change. Not everyone survived to return and the Boss was left rather unsupported to host the party. The following morning we could see that he was somewhat upset. Pete Taylor had pointed out months before that his lower lip turned down when he was angry. For some reason this had become known on the squadron as the 'Habsburg Lip' and the degree of anger was assessed by the level of its lowering. Irritation was labelled '40 degrees', the take-off flap setting in the Hunter, and real anger was 'full flap'. The morning after the discourteous failure of a fair number of the squadron officers to meet their hosting duties it was, justifiably, at full flap, and it stayed there long after he had expressed his displeasure to us.

The snow and the resultant reduction in firing sorties notwithstanding, the detachment was a success in terms of the scores achieved. After the first spell at Sylt Les Phipps had decided to ensure the serviceability of the radar ranging sets on all the aircraft for the second, and this unquestionably led to better scores. The squadron average was 29.7%. My best was 64%.

Shortly before we had embarked on this second Sylt spell the Boss had told me that he had nominated me to go on the next Day Fighter Combat Leaders' School course at West Raynham. The

DFCLS course had been formed by adding to the former DFLS course the content of the Pilot Attack Instructors' course, itself a casualty of the changes that had flowed from the Sandys cuts. I was naturally pleased to be going as the course was widely acknowledged to provide the best professional training available within the fighter world at that time, at least in the United Kingdom.

I went down to West Raynham on 1 March and began flying the following day. We started gently with battle formation at 45,000 feet and went almost straight away into cine quarters and ranging and tracking against an evasively weaving target at 40,000 feet. From there we went into an air-to-air firing phase – very different from what I had been used to in that we flew four aircraft in the flag pattern simultaneously rather than the normal pair. This required a pretty careful effort at continuous synchronisation to keep one aircraft on the perch, one halfway into the firing position, one firing, and one halfway out to the perch. But it actually worked surprisingly well, possibly because of the level of experience of the participants, and I found I was getting some very good scores – a best of 83%. Perhaps I was ready at last for seriously hostile skies!

We followed the air-to-air phase with an air-to-ground one, firing rockets and guns on Cowden range. After this came a fighter reconnaissance phase and, finally, a lengthy air combat one. The air combat phase started gently with pairs of students manoeuvring against a staff member, or a staff pair, and built up into formations of four students ranged against staff pairs or staff fours. Initially all combat exercises were flown with a starting height of 40,000 feet and were called off at 7,000 feet, but towards the end of the phase we were doing our stuff down to 1,500 feet agl.

Every sortie on the course, other than the single-aircraft FR ones, was student led with instructors flying in the number two or four slots in critical watchfulness. As a result we became rapidly adept at meticulous pre-flight planning and full but succinct briefings and de-briefings. The final test of our planning and briefing came when we had to prepare for a 'fighter sweep' to Germany. This was the culmination of the course, the grand finale. It involved getting a formation of thirty-two aircraft airborne, Hunters of the Day Fighter course and Javelins of the Night Fighter course that was running concurrently, forming them up into a planned spread of battle fours, and flying to Germany. Our destination was RAF Geilenkirchen, just over the Dutch border, about fifteen miles north of Aachen. The weather on the day chosen for the 'sweep' couldn't have been better, with hardly a cloud in the sky.

We levelled at height and settled into formation, spread out across a wide front, contrails streaming from all but the battle four that was flying deliberately below contrail height. As we were fair game for every available fighter aircraft based in northern France, Belgium, Holland and West Germany we expected opposition, and we got it. One moment there was nothing to be seen, the next, someone out on the starboard side of the formation called 'Pair, right, three o'clock, five miles'. With best steely British calm the formation leader, Jeremy Hall, instructed a pair on the starboard side of our grand gaggle to break away to engage them and thus allow the rest of us to fly serenely onwards. That is not how it happened, however. Within seconds of the first sighting aircraft were appearing from all quarters, and in no time our large and unwieldy formation was forced to break into smaller units. Very quickly, these disintegrated into pairs manoeuvring against pairs or singletons, pulling maximum g and spiralling downwards. One moment the sky was full of aircraft wheeling and turning. Then, suddenly individuals were breaking off their own private mock combat at a couple of thousand feet or so with none of the other participants in sight. I couldn't help thinking that it was fortunate that visibility was good for I wasn't entirely sure where I was when I levelled out. We had not left everything to chance, of course, and had spent a bit of time at the planning stage picking out possible diversion airfields and major identifying features along and well to the sides of our route. I didn't immediately see anything to help, and I didn't have the fuel to hang around, so I pulled up a few thousand feet to have a wider look at my surroundings. I was, in fact, about 20 nm to the east of Geilenkirchen with enough fuel for about 40 nm. We usually ended sorties on the DFCLS course with a little more than that, but not a lot. So I didn't sweat too much; just enough to be glad when the airfield came into view. About a third of the formation ended up spread around various other Dutch, Belgian and German bases.

The DFCLS course lasted until the end of May and it had been well worth every minute. When I got back to Leconfield bursting with enthusiasm to share what I had learned I found that I would shortly be moving again. I had been posted as a flight commander to No. 20 Squadron. Disbanded in Germany at the end of 1960, No. 20 was to reform at RAF Tengah on Singapore Island on 1 September 1961, and I was required to join the squadron commander designate at the Maintenance Unit at St Athan at the beginning of July to organise a plot to ferry its aircraft out there. I had flown 586 hours on 19 Squadron and had enjoyed them all. I had even become almost reconciled to living in Hull. However, the idea of going to the Far East and still flying Hunters was very appealing.

Notes

1 Ground Control Interception Station. The UK air defence radar system was originally based on separate reporting (or early warning) units and controlling units. Throughout the 1950s the system was subject to a number of projects and plans for change. The 'Rotor' plan of 1956, for example, involved the construction and installation of thirty-nine new radar Stations, thirty-four of which were to have underground bunkers. However, this plan perpetuated the old split concept and, in 1958, Fighter Command proposed a modified integrated system, based on eight 'comprehensive' or 'master' radar Stations plus ten 'satellites'. However, this plan was invalidated in turn by the development of a new and more powerful radar, the Type 85, and it was back to the drawing board.

2 The invention of the carcinotron valve, a new form of microwave oscillator, gave jammers a distinct edge over even quite powerful radars such as the Type 80. It was expected that the Type 85 would produce enough power to restore the balance. A contract for three Type 85s was placed in 1958 (to be sited at Boulmer in Northumberland, Staxton Wold in North Yorkshire, and Neatishead in Norfolk). Under a new plan these, plus five Type 84s, and two Type 80s at the northern extremities, were to provide United Kingdom air defence cover by the early 1960s.

3 The Hunter had a design load factor of 7.5 g; that is, it was to be capable of sustaining this value without suffering permanent distortion. It was also to be capable of sustaining 50% more than this (11.25 g) without structural failure.

CHAPTER EIGHT

Slow Trip in a Fast Jet

While I was at West Raynham another Hunter squadron, No. 92, had been deployed to Leconfield to join Nos 19 and 46 (a Javelin outfit). No. 92 Squadron was currently the RAF's formation aerobatic display team[1] One of its flight commanders, Richard Calvert, had been selected to be the commanding officer of No. 20 Squadron. When I met him he was enjoying the double pleasure of promotion and the prospect of a superlative assignment. We had both got the good news about our postings at roughly the same time and we used our last few weeks at Leconfield to become acquainted.

Six other pilots from the Leconfield Hunter squadrons had also been selected for 20 Squadron: Jim Farquharson and Don Marshall from 19, and George Aylett, Chips Carpenter, Derek Gill and Jerry Seavers from 92. Jim was an easy-going, good-natured South African who could be relied upon to take on any task thrown at him, and I knew he would be an asset on the new outfit; Don, similarly. I hoped that the other four, who had all been members of the 92 Squadron aerobatic team, would be able to accept that their spell in the heady atmosphere of display flying was over, and that they would be able to settle willingly back to normal squadron life – and do so under a Boss who had been on the squadron with them but not on the team.

Boss Calvert and I set off together from Leconfield, driving first to London to have a briefing at the Overseas Department of the Air Ministry, and then on to St Athan, a RAF Maintenance Unit near Cardiff. At that point 20 Squadron existed only as an Air Ministry intention, a laid-up Squadron Standard and, in a RAF depository somewhere, a collection of silver and other memorabilia of the squadron's service in locations as diverse as France in the First

World War, the North West Frontier of India in the 1920s, and Germany in the post World War Two era. It had to be recreated from scratch and we were to begin the process at the Maintenance Unit.

The RAF Command we were to be under, Far East Air Force, was being reinforced as part of a policy change dictated by growing concern over the stability of the countries of the former French Indo-China and of Thailand, and by a perceived requirement to be able to reinforce as far as Australia if the need arose. This was, after all, the era of belief in the so-called Chinese 'salami' strategy – the slicing off from western influence, through communist-led insurrections, of one East Asian country after another. No. 20 Squadron was to be an element of the reinforcements now being positioned on the fringes of possible trouble spots. Specifically it was to be on hand as a mobile and readily available British contribution to the South East Asia Treaty Organisation[2] should anything nasty threaten.

Our aircraft were to be Hunter FGA Mark 9s. These were, essentially Mark 6s, currently being refurbished by the Maintenance Unit, and being fitted with mounting points for two 230-gallon drop tanks, a braking parachute, a Marconi AD722 radio-compass, a third oxygen bottle to give the aircraft 3.5 hours' endurance, and an extra mass flow of air for air-conditioning. The Mark 9s would be marginally heavier than the Mark 6s but their performance was expected to be essentially the same. No. 20 Squadron's aircraft were scheduled to come off the Maintenance Unit floor in a steady trickle over the next three months. Dickie Calvert's instructions were to get the squadron to Singapore and to a fully operational status there as quickly as possible.

Within hours of our arriving at St Athan it had become depressingly clear that the first part of this task wasn't going to be easy. St Athan was geared to provide nothing but the bare aircraft. We were going to have to identify, and order from various elements of the RAF supply system, the wide range of items that we would need for the deployment. For example we would have to obtain Mae Wests and the emergency gear that would go in them; we would have to decide what survival gear we ought to have in our dinghy packs for the journey; and we would have to order maps and charts and details of all the airfields we would use, or might use as diversions. The list seemed endless, and we were unsure where to begin, as neither of us knew – or had thought we would ever need to know – a great deal about the RAF supply system.

We would also have to liaise with personnel staffs to arrange to get the pilots who had been nominated for the squadron to St Athan at the right time for the departure dates that we would have to plan for them. And we would have to arrange, among other things, to have them tested and certified as competent to undertake turn-round servicing on their aircraft, jabbed against cholera, yellow fever, and tetanus and, finally, checked out on dual sorties just before coming to us.

In the event it took us a little over a month to get everything organised and, on 21 August, we were ready for departure. We handed over a fully functioning ferry launch-pad to Flight Lieutenant John (Moose) David, the other appointed flight commander and, full of eager anticipation for what lay ahead, we climbed into our aircraft, shorts and khaki shirts under our flying-overalls and our scant kit for the journey stuffed into the radio bays of our aircraft. The Boss and I were each leading a pair, the two most junior pilots nominated to join the squadron, Flying Officer Barry Highgate and Flying Officer John Smith, flying as our number twos.

The morning we left St Athan we were talking to the crew-members of a Twin Pioneer, a slow short-range piston-engined aircraft designed for use on short landing strips. They were also about to depart for Singapore. We laughed when the navigator mentioned that they would be doing the journey in short hops, refuelling at thirty-five airfields en route, and taking a fortnight for the journey. With the 230-gallon tanks on the Hunter inboard pylons, and two 100-gallon tanks on the outboard ones, we had planned for just seven stops: Luqa, Nicosia, Tehran, Karachi, Delhi, Calcutta and Bangkok. And we expected to do the trip in eighteen flying hours spread over four days. We should not have laughed.

Our timing was thrown out from the first day. Instead of a simple hop of just over 50 nm to RAF Lyneham to clear Customs, we had to divert to the Naval Air Station at Yeovilton when Lyneham's runway was closed by an aircraft emergency as we approached to land. As a result we didn't get there until the following morning. However, day two went without a hitch and we got to Nicosia by the late afternoon. We set off for Tehran on day three, John Smith and I leaving as planned twenty minutes after the Boss's pair.

About twenty minutes into the trip I spotted two contrails approaching us on a reciprocal heading and, as they got closer, was somewhat surprised to identify the aircraft making them as Hunters. This was such an unlikely event in that part of the world that it was a fair assumption that it was our first pair. As they flashed past above us I pressed the transmit button and asked what was wrong, as something obviously was. The answer was enigmatic: 'We have had internal trouble; wait for us at Tehran.' We had to wait until the following morning for enlightenment when they caught up with us. Barry had had a bad attack of 'the runs' and, as Nicosia was the last RAF source of possible succour and supplies before we reached Singapore, the Boss had decided to return there and get him and his ejection seat some new kit.

Someone in the Air Ministry had decided that the cheapest way to support 20 Squadron on its ferry trip to Singapore would be to contract with the British Overseas Airways Corporation to refuel us at our various stops and to give us any servicing assistance that we might need. In support of this arrangement Hunter servicing manuals had been supplied to the BOAC resident engineers at each of our planned stops, and supplies of AVPIN had been pre-positioned (with great difficulty, as few carriers wanted to take the risk of handling this extremely volatile fuel). The weakness in the arrangement with BOAC showed up very quickly when the Boss's pair could not be refuelled on arrival at Tehran, but had to wait for an incoming BOAC aircraft to be dealt with first. That, and some difficulty in getting flight clearance for the leg to Karachi forced us to spend the night in Tehran – a second consecutive night in the same dismal hotel that I had stayed in on the Indian ferry trip, this time made even less pleasant by the presence of 'hostesses' in the bar in the evening, and by the tedious need to respond to the question 'You no like Irani girls?' Actually, many Iranian girls are strikingly attractive, but the ones in the brothel, and in our hotel on this trip, were decidedly not so.

The following morning Dickie Calvert's aircraft would not start. The resident BOAC engineer, trying to be helpful, but not having paused to see if there was any guidance in the servicing manuals, exacerbated the problem by running the starter turbine on mine in a vain attempt to determine from this what might be wrong with the Boss's; the result was that eventually my turbine refused to function as well. That led to yet another night in Tehran and, by the morning our number twos had both gone down with a bad attack of food poisoning. 'Don't eat anything in Tehran but well-grilled chicken,' was the post hoc advice of the doctor summoned for us by our Air Attaché. In the end, after two days of ineffectual attempts to get the engines going, Nicosia was prevailed upon to fly up a technician. Arriving as the sole passenger on a Hastings transport aircraft he cured the problem within minutes by the simple expedient of getting some boiling water and pouring it on the nozzle that fed the AVPIN fuel into the starter turbine. He explained that the system could be expected to give trouble at Tehran's altitude but was unable to say quite how boiling water cured it.

Finally, on the seventh day after setting out from St Athan, engines fixed and the poisoned number twos feeling well enough to climb into their cockpits, we were more than ready to leave Tehran with its discomforts and slight and constant undercurrent of menace. The Boss's pair started successfully watched by a large group of US servicemen who had been off-loaded from a transport plane nearby while it was being refuelled. Then, just as it looked as if the pair was going to get away in good style the braking parachute burst from the tail of the Boss's aircraft, raising a round of laughter and applause from the onlookers. He had inadvertently put the three-position brake 'chute switch to 'deploy' instead of to 'test' on his round of pre-taxi checks. I was so determined not to spend any more time in Tehran that I rather brusquely suggested that he and his number two stay in their cockpits while I grabbed the 'chute, stretched it out on the ground, repacked it as well as I could, and stuffed it into the small space available for it. When they started up again I kept my fingers tightly crossed until I saw them leave the ground and climb away.

John Smith and I started up twenty minutes later, and with the engines running, I called him for the standard radio check. He didn't answer but indicated visually that he could hear me. As conditions were good at Karachi, and forecast to remain so, I decided that it might be better to go rather than to risk stopping

New boys at Ternhill, duped by the senior course into posing in flying kit on their first night.

The author on the first day at Ternhill.

(Above) An Inspection at Oakington. The Vampire T11 clam-shell canopies can be clearly seen.

(Right) The author receiving the "Ground School Trophy" on passing out from Oakington. A minor recompense for a poor performance there.

(Below) Number 10 Hunter Course at Chivenor.

The Author looking very pleased with himself after a first flight on 247 Squadron.

September 1956, just before leaving for Biggin Hill for the autumn air defence exercise: Ian "Bungers" Whittle, Chris Lansdell and Ted Skinner on the wing; Pete Young, Pete Biddiscombe, the author and Ian "Izzy" Brimson standing. (Peter Biddiscombe)

247 Squadron aircraft at Hal Far, Malta, on the way home from Cyprus.

Cartoon by Chris Curtis, "A" flight commander, presented to the squadron pub, the Kings Arms in Odiham village.

247 Squadron pilots just before disbandment, 1957.

Line-up for an AOC's inspection, Chivenor 1958.

19 Squadron Officers, Sylt, 1960. Back row, left to right: Bob Turbin Ching Fuller, Jeff Hawke, Jim Farquharson, Major Moore USAF (SEngO), Roger Ouston, Neddy Nicholls, Pete Taylor, Don Marshall. Front row, left to right: Pete Bacon, Darryl Bjkorlund, Nigel Pickersgill, Boss Phipps, Chris Cristie, the author, Barry Pickering.

Hunters and Sabres at Butterworth. (Richard Calvert)

20 Squadron detachment at Korat. The front row comprises, left to right, an attached intelligence officer, the author, Boss Calvert, John Smith, Barry Hygate and Peter Blockey, the squadron adjutant. (Richard Calvert)

(Above) Trying to get organised on arrival at Bangkok (Left to Right) - Don Richies, Mike White, John David and Don Marshall. (Richard Calvert)

(Right) Squadron "offices" at Chiang Mai.

(Below) Consultation with the line-chief in the Operations tent, Chiang Mai. At the table, left to right, Bob Shields, the author, and Heinz Frick.

Open day at Chiang Mai. (Richard Calvert)

Giving one of our new pilots a check-out in the T7 along the Strait of Malacca. (Norman Roberson)

Flying along the coast of Sabah, December 1962. (Norman Roberson)

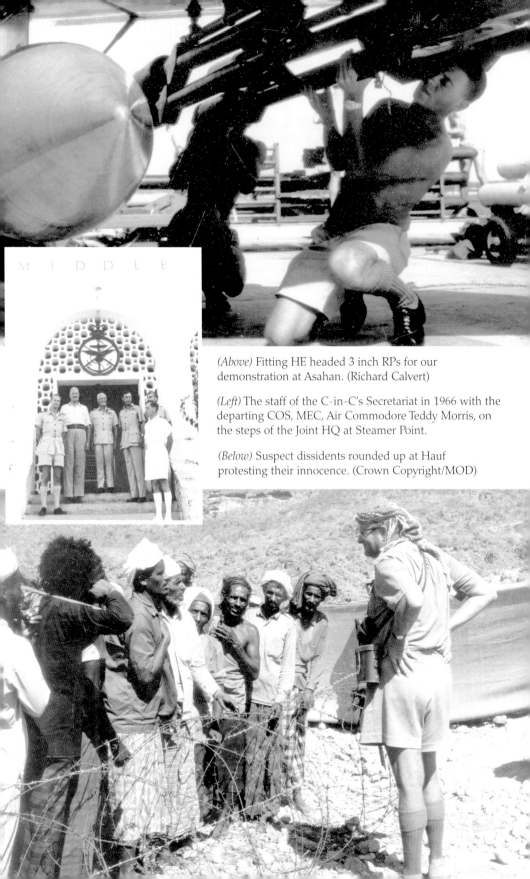

(Above) Fitting HE headed 3 inch RPs for our demonstration at Asahan. (Richard Calvert)

(Left) The staff of the C-in-C's Secretariat in 1966 with the departing COS, MEC, Air Commodore Teddy Morris, on the steps of the Joint HQ at Steamer Point.

(Below) Suspect dissidents rounded up at Hauf protesting their innocence. (Crown Copyright/MOD)

Good heavens, it never rains in Aden.

View of the naval storage tanks that were rocketed as families were being evacuated. The hairpin approach to the Main Pass road into Crater can be seen on the right-hand side of the photograph. (Crown Copyright/MOD)

About to take on a "real man's aeroplane". Number 41 Course at RAF Coltishall. From left to right: Mal Gleave, the author, Mike Streton, Don McClen, Peter Chapman, Dickie Wirdnam, Brian Carrol and Peter Carter.

Coltishall Lightning Mark 1A on display. (RAF Museum, Hendon)

The Lightning Mark 6 workplace. Described as an ergonomic nightmare, but comfortingly snug once its layout became familiar. The "dinky" radar joystick can just be seen, bottom left; the radarscope, hidden by the "boot" is at the top of the photograph to the right of centre. (Stewart Scott)

Two Mark 6s of 11 Squadron tanking from a Victor. (Stewart Scott)

The drogue up close (minus the Victor and hose!). (Stewart Scott)

Greeted by Gp Capt Phil Lagesen the Station Commander, Tengah, after a hairy ride from Gan, January 1969.

11 Squadron with over-wing tanks fitted for the return flight to the UK flying a Diamond 9 over Singapore's southern seafront. (Crown Copyright/MOD)

the engines again. I asked him if he would be happy to come with me without the ability to transmit. He gave a 'thumbs up', and we went.

I should have known not to push my luck – again. We got off the ground without problem, climbed to height and settled down for the leg to Karachi. Everything looked good, but within ten minutes my relief at getting away from Tehran was undone by a mini-drama. Looking up from dialling in the Ishfahan radio-compass beacon I saw John's aircraft coming fast towards me from the extended battle formation position he had been in a moment or two before. As he came close I could see his fingers scratching furiously at the rime ice that totally covered the inside of his cockpit canopy, trying to keep a small hole clear. His cockpit heating was obviously not working, and I wondered if he might also have lost some cabin pressurisation. His fingers pointed furiously downwards but I already had the message. There was nothing for it but to descend fast, burn off fuel, and return to Tehran. We levelled off at about 1,000 feet agl and buzzed around for nearly thirty minutes getting down to landing-weight. My unfortunate number two, briefly exposed at height to a temperature that was dropping rapidly towards the outside air figure of –46°C, got nicely cooked for a spell at low level at +35. I later discovered (with the help of the manuals, but not of the resident BOAC engineer) that the problem with John's aircraft had been caused by nothing more than a popped circuit-breaker – but it took me the rest of the day to find that out as the Hunter had a myriad of circuit-breakers hidden in various boxes in a variety of nooks and crannies. Oddly, his radio set worked perfectly after landing, and neither it nor the offending circuit breaker gave any further trouble for the rest of the journey to Singapore.

Fate smiled on us the following morning and we got away without any hitches, reaching Karachi in two and a half hours' flying. Visibility all the way was perfect and I had another exceptionally clear and extensive view of the totally inhospitable terrain that characterised most of that part of the world. However, our good fortune didn't last. We found the other pair still at Karachi, thwarted by foul weather at our next intended stop, Palam, New Delhi's international airport. We had come up against the effects of the south-west monsoon and had no option but to stay put.

The weather the following morning was only slightly better but, as we had already been delayed so much, the Boss decided to have a go at getting into Palam. With a full fuel load the Hunter Mark 9 had a range of a little over 1,400 nm and thus we could fly the 550 nm to Delhi and, as long as we remained at height, come back comfortably as far as Karachi if we needed to. The weather at Karachi was forecast to remain good. As usual John and I took off twenty minutes after the first pair and had an easy ride for the first 200 nm. Then we ran into very severe turbulence and electrical activity in the tops of closely packed thunderclouds, and John Smith had to earn his pay hanging on to my wing.

I contacted Palam ATC at an estimated 100 nm range and was given the information that it was not raining heavily and that the cloud-base was better than 500 feet agl. As this was reasonably encouraging, and we had heard the first pair reporting the beginning of their descent, we forged on. Unfortunately the electrical activity in the storm clouds all around us rendered our radio-compasses almost useless as homing devices, our DMEs had packed in sometime after Nicosia (only the Boss's had continued to work this far), and Palam was resolutely ignoring my requests for a DF check for overhead. However, I was reasonably confident that we were on an accurate course and timing for overhead Delhi as the forecast winds that we had been given for the climb out of Karachi and for the height we were to fly at were very light (15 to 20 knots). Moreover, I expected to be able to ease below cloud safely across a wide swathe around Delhi, and was happy that, once in sight of the ground the Yamuna (or Jumna) river and the tributary that joined it just south of Delhi, the Hunan, would provide unmistakable features that could be used to pinpoint our position. I deliberately flew for a couple of minutes – 18 nm – beyond the calculated overhead time just to make it a little more probable that we were past the overhead and could therefore make the final stage of our let-down more slowly and delicately than normal. I called Palam for clearance to descend and began a normal high rate of descent on a heading reciprocal to the runway in use. I levelled out briefly when we got to 2,000 feet, still in cloud, and then began to ease down gently looking for a sight of the ground. We broke out of the main cloud-base at 500 feet agl with about half-cover below, not to see the expected rivers but to see instead a vast flooded area that effectively disguised the rivers' whereabouts and made nonsense of any attempt to map read. That was disconcerting and all I could do was to continue in the direction in which I felt Palam ought to lie, and hope for the best.

Five minutes later – a very long time at low level in a Hunter when not entirely confident about position, and the fuel for a climb and return to a decent diversion is burning down rapidly – I spotted a civil airliner about 10 nm ahead, a Tupolev 104, not far off the ground and climbing. It was more than a fair assumption that it had taken off from Palam, so we were home and, despite the prevailing conditions, dry.

I called Palam to announce our exact position and got permission to make a straight-in approach to land. As we turned off the runway we were directed to a dispersal occupied by two squadrons-worth of Hunters belonging to the Indian Air Force and to a warm welcome from a bunch of IAF pilots. 'You have rewritten Noel Coward!' one of them cried out in greeting. 'How's that?' I asked. 'Well only mad dogs and Englishmen would fly fighters during the monsoon. We do not.'

We were at Delhi for five days, kept on the ground by incessant heavy rainstorms and low cloud both there and at Dum Dum, Calcutta, our next intended stop. This was no great hardship as we were housed in an excellent hotel, the Ashoka, whose air-conditioned comfort enabled us to escape from the oppressive heat and humidity of the monsoon each evening – after a relaxing afternoon cooling off in the British High Commission's swimming pool, very conveniently situated just across the road from the hotel. The only pain was journeying out to the airport each morning, complete with our kit, in the hope that we might find a sufficient improvement in the weather to allow us to get away. Every morning we spoke with the same Met forecaster, and every morning got the same bleak picture: closely packed cumulo-nimbus to 50,000 feet. 'Don't you ever change your forecast chart?' asked the Boss. 'No,' he replied, 'not until the monsoon is over.' There was nothing we could do until the weather improved, and it was somewhat exasperating to get a signal on the third day from HQ 224 Group in Singapore, via the High Commission, rather waspishly ordering the Boss to get a move on.

We got away from Palam at last, fifteen days after setting out from St Athan, bouncing along in considerable turbulence and electrical activity in virulent storm clouds all the way to Calcutta. My unfortunate number two had to hang on grimly on my wing yet again, this time for nearly two hours. The cloud-base at Dum Dum was only 400 feet above the surface but the flatness of the vast Ganges delta was an advantage as far as easing down and out of cloud was concerned and, thankfully, I had less of a problem finding the airfield than I had at Delhi.

One of the two booster pumps situated in the main fuselage tank had failed on the Boss's aircraft during the flight to Dum Dum. This necessitated him switching off the working pump and accepting the fuel feed provided by tank pressurisation and gravity. Normally a booster pump failure represented no great problem. Pilot's Notes recommended that the engine be throttled back to about 80% of maximum engine rpm and this was fine for level flight below 20,000 feet. It was a bit dicey for overshooting from a baulked approach, and was certainly not good enough for take-off – that last 20% of engine speed represented an important slice of power. So we bedded the four aircraft down for the night and set off in a bus, courtesy of the BOAC staff, for the Great Eastern Hotel in what was, coincidentally, a very dramatically flooded Calcutta.

As soon as we had checked in we used the hotel teleprinter to request a replacement booster pump from Singapore. This was delivered overnight by civil air and the following day, with the help of the local BOAC engineer, and a band of workers carrying away and dumping the 240 gallons of fuel that had first to be drained from the main fuselage tank, I managed to take off the failed pump and put on the new. This was well outside the authorisation that my simple servicing certificate gave me so it was perhaps just as well that the Boss got safely off the ground on his next take-off.

We got to Don Muang, Bangkok, without further drama on the seventeenth day after leaving St Athan, and reached Singapore on the nineteenth, stepping out of our cockpits into an atmosphere that was so moist that one could almost drink it. We were met by the Station Commander, Group Captain Tom Pierce, a rotund, bustlingly forceful man who, having welcomed us, conducted us straight away to the air-conditioned splendour of Tengah's recently completed V-force facility. This was very obviously under-utilised and, apart from the odd practice dispersal by elements of the V-force, was likely to remain so short of the outbreak of World War Three. We were grateful for the coolness inside it, and glad to sit down and enjoy a welcoming beer in it but, when the Group Captain, anxious to make some use of this splendid building, tried to sell it to us as the place to keep our flying-kit, we were presented with a dilemma. The hutted accommodation and dispersal that had been allocated to 20 Squadron were, as we were now discovering, almost a mile away. As the squadron would be flying the usual fighter programme of shortish sorties once we had established ourselves, perhaps up to three times for each pilot per day, we felt that we would be likely to waste a lot of time before and after each flight travelling between the two locations. However, as we didn't want to start off at Tengah on the wrong foot with the management the Boss agreed to give the Station Commander's scheme a try.

The rest of the squadron, another ten Mark 9s (two of which were to be Command spares) and a T7, coming out after the monsoon had run its course, made much better time than we had and, by 6 November, all aircraft had safely reached Singapore. A Javelin squadron, No. 60, deploying concurrently from the United Kingdom to Tengah, lost an aircraft on approach to Dum Dum during the monsoon so I suppose we first four could count ourselves lucky to have got through it with little more than a few nervous moments.

Notes

1 Number 111 Squadron, the 'Black Arrows', performed in this role from 1956 to 1960; beginning with four Hunter Mark 4s they graduated to displays with up to sixteen Hunter Mark 6s and, in 1957 delivered a show-stopper at the Farnborough air display by performing a formation loop with twenty-two aircraft. No. 92 Squadron, the 'Blue Diamonds', held the commitment in 1961 and 1962, also performing with up to sixteen aircraft. No. 56 Squadron, the 'Firebirds', held it in 1963 to 1965 with nine Lightning Mark 1As. It was then passed to Training Command, on the grounds of economy, and the 'Red Arrows' team was formed, initially equipped with the Gnat T1, getting the Hawk in 1980.

2 The South East Asia Treaty Organisation (SEATO) was formed in September 1955 mainly to provide for collective defence in South East Asia against communist subversion and possible aggression. It comprised eight member states: Australia, France, New Zealand, Pakistan, the Philippines, Thailand, the UK and the USA. By 1992 it had become 'inactive'.

CHAPTER NINE

Tengah and Other Places

No. 20 Squadron's role in the Far East was to be primarily ground attack, with air defence as a secondary responsibility. We were all happy with this as most of us had been in the air defence role for at least one tour, some of us for several, and the emphasis on ground attack offered a welcome change. But first, we had to decide how best to come to terms with our new environment, and how to train to operate effectively in it.

Malaya was extensively covered by dense tropical forest. Apart from the towns and villages, the swathes cleared for commercial crops ranging from rubber to palm oil and pineapples, the many scars of mining activity, and the numerous muddy rivers, there wasn't much other than an undulant sea of greenery. A railway line ran roughly north-west from Singapore, up the centre of the Malay peninsula, turning north at about 125 miles and heading for Kota Bharu on the east coast, where the Japanese came ashore in 1942; as it turned north a branch came off heading west for Malacca, running on northwards through Kuala Lumpur, and finally rejoining the other line on the Thai side of the border between the two countries. Metalled roads were mostly to be found up the western side of the peninsula, but one ran north-east from Johore Bahru to Mersing on the east coast, and then followed the curves of the coast roughly northwards, losing its metalled surface here and there along its length. North of Malacca the ground rose, initially in a relatively narrow range of mountains parallel to the coast with peaks of over 6,000 feet, before spreading more widely across the country and reaching heights of over 7,000 feet. We felt pretty certain that becoming competent at finding small targets in the Malayan environment should enable us to operate successfully anywhere in South East Asia.

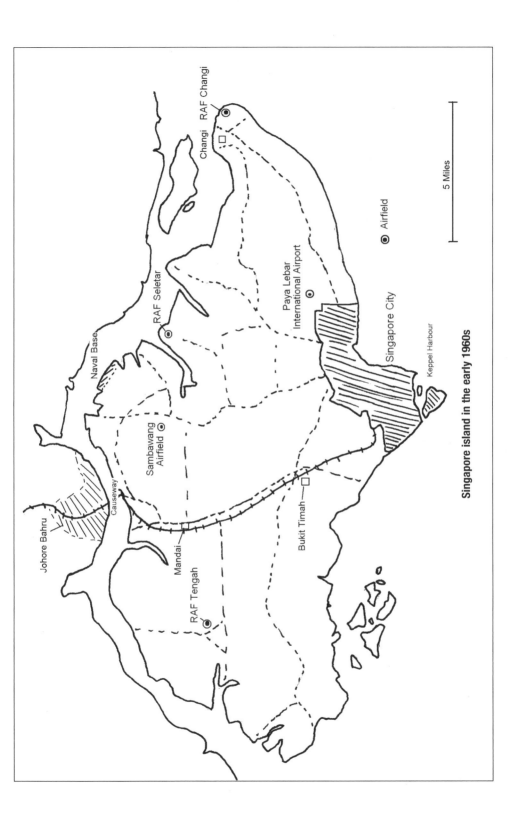

Singapore island in the early 1960s

The most obvious and pressing need was to identify some realistic training targets at a variety of distances from Tengah – hard to navigate to, and hard to find even close up. We started with a lot of low-flying within 100 nm from Tengah, with 230-gallon tanks fitted, looking for anything whose dimensions we could ascertain, or even guess at sufficiently accurately to enable us to assess the results of mock attacks via cine film. We found, photographed from the air, and went out and measured where this was practicable, a number of road and rail bridges, and small remote buildings on rubber plantations. Then we went further, looking for targets at the maximum range that we could expect to achieve carrying the 230-gallon tanks and a weapon load of 16 x 60-lb RPs, flying out high, letting down, and climbing again for the return trip – the 'hi-lo-hi' in pilot-speak. In that fit (although we didn't carry any rocket rails for everyday training) we worked on a radius of action of 285 nm for a hi-lo-hi, and 165 nm for a low-level run out and back, a lo-lo. The area around Kota Bharu, 300 nm north-east of Singapore, was well within our radius of action with just the 230-gallon tanks fitted. Almost as far up-country in Malaya as one could go before crossing into Thailand, it provided both an abundance of good targets and a reasonable test of navigation given the almost constant cloud cover at height. Consequently the local population there subsequently saw and heard more of us than they would probably have wished, in formations of two or four aircraft, and usually at dusk and at dawn.

We also liaised with the Army, working out methods of target-marking by Forward Air Controllers flying above the jungle canopy in Austers. And we worked with unseen FACs who floated tethered balloons up through the trees to mark a base point from which we could follow their target instructions.

We were also anxious to organise some gun and rocket-firing practice as soon as we could after settling in, if only to ensure that everything worked. Initially, we were forced to make do with live attacks on China Rock, a lump of stone the size of a small house sticking out of the sea off the eastern coast of Singapore island. It was of little value as far as the guns were concerned other than to provide something to keep the squadron armourers occupied. We had a go at plotting the fall of our three-inch rockets by positioning pilots as observers on the shore some distance from the rock but this was also of little value and we soon abandoned it. By the end of the first week in February, however, we got a proper air-to-air firing programme under way courtesy of the Canberras of Station Flight, RAF Seletar. We used the Hunter's radar-ranging and achieved a creditable squadron average of 21.5%. And in March we were in business with air-to ground firing when the Army agreed to let us set up targets on their weapons range at Asahan, some 80 nm up-country, and have regular access to it.

Meanwhile, the squadron pilots were being trickled through the FEAF Jungle Survival School, two at a time. The School's courses were a fortnight long. The first week was spent at RAF Changi being lectured to on how to cope if we found ourselves baling out over thick tropical forest. The second week was spent in the jungle clad in army tropical fatigues, wearing the jungle-boots that were standard flying kit in that part of the world, and carrying a scrap parachute plus some aircrew ration packs. We were there to experience the reality of chopping our way through undergrowth day after day, dealing with snakes and other nasties, building effective shelters for the night in advance of the inevitable afternoon downpour, and ridding ourselves of leeches by the end of each day's chopping expedition. The grand finale of all this was an escape and evasion exercise on the night we got out of the jungle, tired, and stinking from dirt and incessant sweating induced by the heat, hacking and hiking. We were dropped off on the Singapore side of the Johore Bahru causeway and instructed to find our way across the island to Changi trying to avoid capture (and hence interrogation) by the troops deployed to catch us. Oddly, I quite enjoyed everything until the finale: I could have done without the experience of falling into several ditches that smelled like cesspits as I tried to get undetected to Changi through a number of village areas in the pitch-black of the night.

In late March 1962 we deployed for a week to Butterworth, a substantial airfield on the coast abeam Penang. This was the Malayan base of two Royal Australian Air Force F-86 (Sabre) squadrons. The idea was to liaise and work with another element of a nominal SEATO force, setting up a tented camp and operating as we would from a forward site. We found, as we were to find on other occasions, that the Aussies of our own age group were very hospitable and a real pleasure to be with, but determinedly competitive in their approach to us. When we visited the squadrons' crew-rooms the first thing that struck us was how much more generous the Australian Government was than ours in providing for its servicemen; while we had had to club together to buy a fridge for our crew-room at Tengah, their crew-rooms were provided with fully-fitted kitchens with cookers, fridges and freezers. It may seem a little thing now but, as powdered milk, disgusting stuff, was the norm in Singapore, the fresh milk stacked up in their fridges made us very envious. And that emotion was compounded by seeing the ready availability of steaks, eggs and other such goodies supplied for between-flight snacks; our own Government's largesse ran to the modest daily chocolate-biscuit ration that had been medically advised at the beginning of the jet age as necessary to keep up the blood sugar levels of high-flying fighter pilots!

But that Butterworth detachment was memorable above all for the opportunity it provided to practise mock dogfights against an aircraft that had proved itself in combat in Korea. We flew with the two 230-gallon tanks fitted, while the Sabres flew with clean wings. This should have given them a distinct advantage, and it did until we got down to about 20,000 feet. The joint debriefings after each combat flight were characterised, as ever between fighter pilots, by hotly disputed claims; but the proof was in the cine film and, to our delight in that friendly but highly competitive Aussie versus Pom atmosphere, only the Hunters were assessed as having achieved successful 'kills'.

We met the Butterworth squadrons again the following month when we took five aircraft and eight pilots to Thailand for a SEATO exercise, quaintly named *Air Cobra*. A mixed force of Australians, British and New Zealanders plus, oddly, a squadron of Vautour light bombers that had flown out from France for the event, were positioned at the Thai air force base at Korat, some 85 nm north-east of Bangkok. A couple of USAF F-100 squadrons deployed into Takhli, the same distance north of Bangkok, and a US Army division, air-lifted in, was out in the 'field' to the east of us.

During the exercise, which mostly involved carrying out mock attacks on US Army vehicles in territory that resembled the African veldt, we worked with US FACs and found that they had a totally different approach to ground attack to our own. The RAF tactic was to go in at very low level from an Initial Point, or IP in pilots' jargon, at about 10 or more nm from the target, chosen because it could be readily identified. We would then climb steeply to 3,000 feet at a Pull up Point, or PUP, that had been calculated to give either a 20-degree dive for guns or 30 degrees for a rocket-attack, then look for the target, or be guided from the ground onto it. The US tactic was for the attacking aircraft to call the FAC from above 15,000 feet and be guided down from there. Our system was designed to give us a fair chance of getting to the target under radar and/or fighter cover without being spotted, hopefully keep us reasonably safe from missiles and, because of speed – 480 or perhaps even 540 knots – from anti-aircraft and small arms' fire. The Americans, usually with assets to spare, tended to rely on a protective fighter screen to enable their ground-attack aircraft to stay out of ground-fire for as long as possible. The RAF did not change to the high-level option until the first Gulf War demonstrated the hazards of running Tornados at low level against heavily defended airfields – and the introduction of the 'smart' bomb plus the availability of shared American assets opened up other possibilities.

We got back to Tengah on 30 April. Ten days later, listening to the breakfast-time news on Radio Singapore we heard the newsreader say'…bodies of Laotian insurgents have been reported crossing the river Mekong into Thailand….'At the squadron we learned that the Thai Government, long concerned about the activities of Pathet Lao guerrilla groups just across its border with Laos, had appealed to SEATO for help. By mid-morning HQ FEAF had directed us to prepare for deployment.

We stopped flying and put maximum effort into getting twelve aircraft serviceable to go. Outboard drop tanks were fitted and gun packs loaded with high-explosive rounds. Ground support equipment was packed, personal weapons were issued to the pilots, and rifles were drawn from the armoury for the ground crew. All was ready within twenty-four hours and most of us were itching to go. Meanwhile, in London, the news that the Cabinet had made a decision to send 'a token force' to 'Siam' was raising a great deal of heat among Labour Party backbenchers. The Conservative Prime Minister, Harold Macmillan, had announced the decision in the House and, when challenged, had refused to undertake to consult Members before the force was sent. Labour backbenchers tried to force a debate, the Member for Ashfield saying that the decision had been 'flung on the House at the shortest possible notice and might be carried out in the next day or two – perhaps in the next twelve hours', and that South East Asia 'was already a powder keg'. The Speaker, having refused a debate, changed his mind after an intervention by Mr Chuter Ede one of the Labour Party's most senior members and a former Home Secretary, and allowed a vote on the matter. This was defeated, but the row rumbled on.

We were happily unaware of all of this and were eager for the off. Naively, we wanted to go to war. However, it was interesting and instructive to discover that not everyone on the squadron shared this desire. One member of my flight came to me to ask that he be left off any deployment as he had just realised that he was out of currency on his cholera and tetanus jabs. He might have got some sympathy from the medical staff but all he got from me was an order to go and get jabbed in double-quick time and, even though this might not give him immediate immunity, he was going with us.

We were ready but Thailand was not. There were only six airfields in the country capable of supporting jet operations and only three were fully active. An Air HQ had been set up in Bangkok as a matter of urgency and, sensibly putting the cart before the cavalry, had allocated the active airfields initially to air transport. Four were nominated for later use by the 'offensive air', one each for the USAF, the USMC, the RAAF and the RAF. The French did not choose to join us on this occasion. No. 20 Squadron was allocated Chiang Mai, and on 25 May six of our Hunters were despatched from Tengah with orders to check in at Bangkok before going on northwards. We thought, and most of the pilots hoped, that we might be going to have a shooting war.

As it happened, our naive thirst for action was frustrated. While the six were on their way north the Thai Government announced that the initial identification of the intruders had been wrong: the incursion across the Mekong had been by Royalist Laotian troops retreating in some disorder from a Pathet Lao force. At Don Muang,

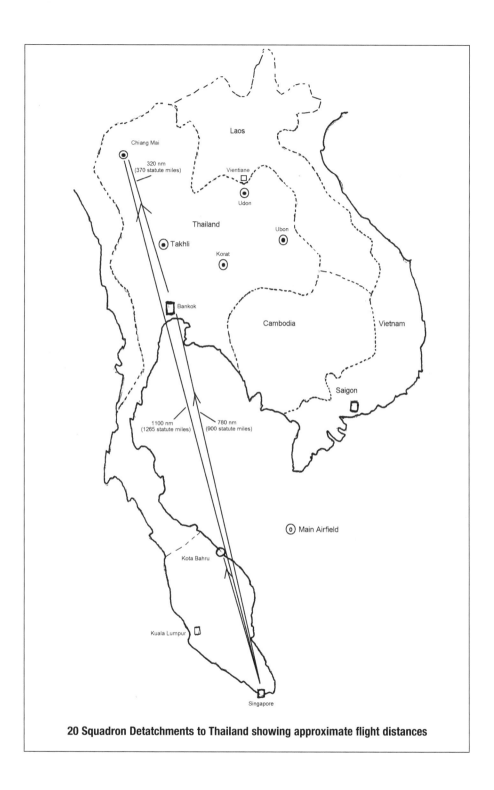

20 Squadron Detatchments to Thailand showing approximate flight distances

the pilots were told to await further instructions. A little later we discovered that it was just as well that we had not been required immediately in north-west Thailand as the bulk fuel-storage facilities at Chiang Mai had been found to contain some dubious stuff and would have to be drained, cleaned and refilled before there could be any hope of the squadron operating from there. Our advance party was already at Chiang Mai, setting up tents and other facilities, and its members were quite happy to have more time than they had anticipated to get organised with the camping gear provided – which included, as an example of how up-to-date we were, eight-man tents, marked 'made in Delhi, 1944'. And, once the disappointment of not getting instantly into action in Laos had receded, the pilots made the most of the period, luxuriating in the King's hotel in Bangkok and flying formation sorties with other SEATO units in 'showing the flag' exercises over various Thai towns.

Although the deployment of a fairly substantial SEATO force had been the result of a false alarm the Thai Government was very anxious to have us remain. Laos was still considered to be the powder keg that might set off a serious communist thrust into Thailand (Vietnam was not as yet thought of as a likely problem in the region); and the Australian, New Zealand and UK and US Governments were delighted to leave their forces in situ given the new climate of diplomatic warmth that was emanating from the Thais.

We deployed the six aircraft from Don Muang, plus a further four from Tengah, to Chiang Mai a fortnight later than we had expected, and settled down to make the most of it. To give all the pilots an opportunity to sample Thailand, and leave no one over-long and underemployed at Tengah, we established the principle of rotating people between there and Chiang Mai at three-weekly intervals.

Our camp, on what was formerly a paddy field on the fringe of Chaing Mai airport, comprised a motley collection of tents and marquees. These were reasonably adequate for our purposes but they leaked in the daily downpours of the south-west monsoon, were stinking hot in the midday sun, airless at night and, in no time became the adopted homes of myriads of mosquitoes, scorpions, and the occasional snake. The aircraft stood in the open on the concrete parking apron next to the airfield's modest two-storey terminal building, becoming so hot in the sun that the ground crew had to be careful to avoid blisters while working on them. Air traffic control was provided by a radio-equipped Land Rover parked next to the mid-point of the runway, supplemented after a few days experience by a 'Ground Control' vehicle charged with chasing off passing water buffaloes that tended to wander onto the runway from time to time.

For the first couple of months we fed off 'compo' rations, gradually developing an exchange scheme with our nearest allies, the F-100 Wing at Takhli; we could never quite understand why they were prepared to barter butter for our margarine, and coffee, tinned cream, and tinned chicken for our corned beef and tinned Irish stew, but I suppose change was what mattered. Later, once an Anthrax scare had subsided, and authority to buy locally was conceded by HQ FEAF, our diet became rather more acceptable, greatly improved by the addition of fresh fruit and vegetables bought from merchants in the town of Chiang Mai.

The flying was superb. We roamed widely over Thailand, over paddy fields, over flattish areas of grassland and sparse woodland, over jungle, over uplands and down deep gorges. We sought out targets, and had our best 'shots' film them so that we had some means of checking the range at which the rest of the pilots were pressing triggers or rocket-firing buttons in their mock attacks. One structure that we took to be 'the' bridge over the River Kwai got a lot of attention from us, not just because of its historic associations but also because it was at a testing distance from Chiang Mai. There were no flying restrictions, nothing to prevent the lowest 'on the deck' stuff, no regulations preventing intercepts on, and combat with, any military aircraft encountered. Everyone entered into the spirit of getting the maximum value from the Thai experience. We fixed a programme of air combat encounters with the F-100 squadrons; we defended our base against repeated attacks by USMC Skyhawks; we attacked the other bases, sometimes with toilet rolls loaded in our air-brakes that, when released, shredded into a confetti storm. The rivalry was continuous and mainly good-natured though it became a little strained with the Australians as they didn't have the range to reach us to retaliate for our repeated attacks on their base at Ubon. And there was humour: once, for example, when I closed on a USAF C119 intending to film an attack from the rear and then shoot past it to show the crew that they had been 'hacked', the ramp door at the rear of the transport opened as I moved into 'firing' range to reveal a crew-member standing in the opening menacing me with a pistol.

We were provided in our third week at Chiang Mai with a Cossar mobile surveillance radar to help with airfield defence. It might once have been an effective bit of kit but the best it could do for us midst the surrounding hills was to provide about 20 nm warning of any incoming low-level aircraft. On a visit to Chiang Mai the Senior Air Staff Officer from 224 Group, suggested that we ought to consider the Lane System as a solution to defending ourselves from air attack, and we were asked why we had not already drawn up a matrix. He was a New Zealander who had probably had the merits of the United Kingdom system recommended to him without a full environmental briefing and an explanation of the system's application. Had we been subject to air attack our only means of defending ourselves would have been to mount Combat Air Patrols overhead or not far from the airfield, ready to take on anything that appeared, as it could have done from almost any direction. This was, in fact, the very thing we were doing most mornings in anticipation of a USAF or USMC 'attack'. The Boss craftily left me to try to explain to the SASO, as diplomatically as I could, that the Lane System was not quite the thing for Chiang Mai.

The weeks went by, slipping into months, with fun in the air by day, and tedious evenings sweating in the Mess marquee, swatting away at the myriad of mosquitoes and other insects that sought to share it with us. The airmen displayed much more nocturnal ambition – or courage – than the officers. After a few beers in the NAAFI tent many of the younger element would set off to Chiang Mai town in the fleet of small open scooter-powered taxis that assembled each evening at the airfield to meet the demand, returning in the early hours of the morning having enjoyed the place's readily available professional services (within one month of our setting up camp the RAF police detachment had identified 173 functioning mini-brothels in Chiang Mai).

Towards the end of the fourth month we decided to organise an 'Open Day', an idea triggered by the fact that we had a daily audience of about two hundred people watching our every activity from the edge of the airfield. HQ FEAF liked the idea of a flying and static aircraft display and agreed to send for it a version of every aircraft that Singapore had. We organised a battalion of Thai soldiers from the local garrison to help us with security, crossed our fingers, laid on a two-hour flying programme and allowed people to have a close look around the parked aircraft throughout the day, like any air show back home. At least, it was like any air show back home in concept, but not quite in execution. Something like a hundred thousand people turned up, some coming from as far away as the Shan Hills in Burma, walking for several days to get to us. In terms of the numbers who came it was an incredible success, but a hellish nightmare, as we had to keep chasing gentle and incredibly curious people off the runway during the flying display to allow each take-off and landing. And for most of the day we had a battle keeping others out of the parked aircraft. How we got through the day without an accident was little short of miraculous. And, mentioning miracles, it was remarkable that we got through five months of operating without loss from an airfield with one 2,500 yard runway, no taxiway that might have served for emergency landings, no barrier or other means of arresting an aircraft in an emergency, water buffaloes likely to wander across it at the wrong moment, and with no suitable diversion airfield within 160 nm.

The Thai adventure came to an end in November. We flew the aircraft back to Tengah on the 15th, most of the pilots feeling a measure of regret at leaving such a splendidly unrestricted flying environment behind. However, few of us, officers, NCOs and airmen, were sorry to be giving up the environment of sweaty, bug-ridden tents, the primitive ablutions, and the less than appealing product of the camp-kitchen. And most were unquestionably glad to get back to wives and families and the clean comfort of their own beds at night. Sadly, there was a price to pay for the Chiang Mai experience: a number of our airmen had contracted rather bad 'doses' of what are now known as Anti Social Diseases, and one or two of the more callow had foolishly entered into forlorn and doomed marriages with Thai prostitutes.

But we didn't stay long back at base. On 10 December the squadron was ordered to get four aircraft as rapidly as possible to Labuan, an island a few miles off the coast of Brunei. A revolution of sorts had broken out in the Sultanate of Brunei led by people whose objective was to form Brunei, Sabah and Sarawak into a unitary state separate from the proposed Federation of Malaysia. The revolt was proving somewhat more serious than had first been anticipated. Two companies of Gurkhas, trained for deployment against rioters, were the first British troops despatched from Singapore. On landing at Brunei airport they met a level of resistance that suggested the need for a stronger force. No. 20 Squadron was to provide support for the extra British troops that were now being sent to sort things out.

Our aircraft were readied and armed for departure by midday and we set off, led by Dickie Calvert, hoping that we might get into Labuan between the thunderstorms that were forecast to be thick and frequent. The Inter-Tropical Convergence Zone, an extremely disturbed air mass that shifts north and south with the changing monsoon periods, tends to lie at that time of the year along the coast of Borneo and produce seriously torrential downpours. The flat windscreen on the Hunter was rendered opaque by heavy rain and, while it was possible to have a stab at landing by skidding the aircraft sideways on the approach and looking out of the curved side panels, it was not advisable to try this unless there was a pretty compelling reason to do so. When we made radio contact with Labuan, at just under 200 nm range, we were not surprised to find that the airfield was being rained upon heavily. We could have gone on at height for the twenty minutes or so that it would have taken to reach overhead Labuan, hoping that the storm might have slackened off in that time, and still have had just about enough fuel to get back to Tengah if it had not. Or we could have risked descending to see for ourselves whether a landing was possible and, if it was not, we could have tried a diversion to Kuching, some 340 nm away. As Kuching was subject to the same ITCZ nastiness as Labuan it was not at all difficult for the Boss to discard that option and decide to turn back for Singapore.

We set off again early the following morning, aiming to get in before the cumulo-nimbus had brewed up for the day. This time we found a totally different weather state: the ITCZ had wafted a little northward overnight and Labuan was dramatically bright and sunny. As soon as we landed, and in the expectation that we would

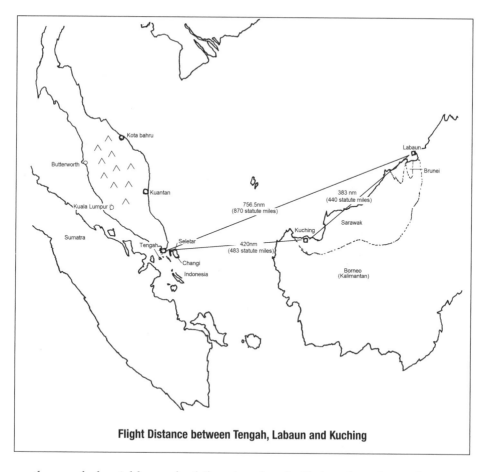

Flight Distance between Tengah, Labaun and Kuching

be needed quickly, we had the aircraft refuelled and made ready to go. The airfield, a joint RAF staging-post and civil airport, was already getting crowded with Hastings and Beverley transport aircraft flowing in from Singapore with troops and supplies, among them our ground crew and the rest of the pilots of my flight. As our aircraft guns were armed we requested and were given a corner of the rather crowded parking apron where we could point them away from all the other activity – unfortunately a good quarter of a mile from any of the buildings. As neither running nor cockpit alert was desirable in the tropical heat, we rather hoped that we would be given decent warning of any sorties that might be required of us.

Our first mission was mounted the following morning. A number of hostages had been taken from the Shell Oil Refinery at Seria and were being held in a local police station, about half a mile from the coast. We were tasked to take our four Hunters to the area, fly about at low-level making as much noise as possible, and end with one pilot firing his guns over the police station, climbing as he did so to make the high-explosive shells carry to and fall into the sea. The Boss decided that he would be the one to do the firing – much to the disappointment of the other three members of the formation. The Hunter's four 30-mm cannon probably sounded quite threatening as he pulled up in front of the building, firing as he passed over its roof – closely followed by the three non-firers each determined to take the roof-tiles off with their aircraft's jet-wakes. The shower of heavy brass shell-cases that would have cascaded down in the building's vicinity would have helped create some doubt in the minds of the hostages' captors as to what might be happening. It was not the most war-like of actions but, as we later discovered, it proved to be effective as the hostages were released immediately after our 'attack'.

That afternoon we were ordered to cover a Royal Marines company that had gone up-river to Limbang in a couple of hastily requisitioned make-do landing craft. They had assaulted at first-light, taken a number of casualties including five killed, scattered the surviving members of the opposition into the jungle, and rescued some hostages (including the local Resident and his wife). When we arrived they were searching the town and surrounding jungle and there wasn't a great deal we could do to help other than to make threatening noises overhead. Later that afternoon we were dispatched to support the Green Jackets at Miri, also making a landing from requisitioned boats. We made a lot of noise, diving and aiming at figures we saw firing at the landing parties – but we were refused permission to open fire ourselves. We realised of course that the embargo on using our guns, while frustrating, was probably correct: the *Daily Express* was happy enough to splash our bloodless hostage 'rescue' over its front page the day after the event, but the British press in general might well have been highly critical of 30-mm high-explosive shells pounding some local insurgents in a far-off land. That said, there is too frequently a whiff of wimpishness in political circles about the application of air power when timely and robust action might well serve the situation better.

We continued flying over various parts of Brunei for another three days in support of what was happening on the ground. Then, as the week progressed, and order was gradually restored, we were sent to 'show the flag' over the various towns of Sabah and Sarawak, and over any villages we could find in the dense hilly jungle and swampy coastlines in between. Finally, on Christmas day, with the rebellion well and truly suppressed we were released to fly back to Singapore – where I found a forlorn, formerly frozen, but now well rotted turkey waiting for me in a midday temperature of over 33°C on the table in the Mess on which the Christmas orders had been set out a few days before.

1963 started with a welcome return to the routine of squadron life at Tengah, and with it the opportunity to slow down a bit and enjoy what Singapore had to offer. And it had plenty. My primary pleasure was sailing from the RAF Tengah yacht club where I had bought, and kept, a Snipe dinghy. For others there was a myriad of active pursuits from golf to tennis to swimming – or inactive ones such as simply sunning by the pool at the Officers' club at Changi, or at the rather more exclusive Tanglin Club in Singapore itself. There were boat trips to be had to one of the islands just offshore to the south of Singapore, or drives up-country for picnics on one of the deserted beaches on the east coast of Malaya. Glorious food could be had from a wide variety of eating places, from unpretentious market stalls to sophisticated restaurants; and the odd gin sling could be enjoyed in historically glamorous spots such as the long bar at Raffles. There was, in fact, everything in Singapore to please, pamper and entertain, and a generous overseas allowance to help fund the good life.

However, not everyone was as happy as might have been expected in this splendid environment. The problem was the climate. The combination of high temperatures and very high humidity that persisted throughout the year was unquestionably enervating. Some respite from both could be obtained if one could find the time to escape to a hotel in the Cameron Highlands or Fraser's Hills, both popular resorts in the mountainous area north of Kuala Lumpur. However, such respite was rare and invariably fleeting. At the turn of the year, when the north-east monsoon lowered the temperature about a degree centigrade from the normal daily average of 29 degrees, the local population would don pullovers and cardigans if going out in the evening. Those used to a more northerly climate and to genuinely changing seasons could detect no real difference. The humidity was a constant discomfort; the act of towelling oneself dry after a cold shower, for example, could cause sweat to break out and, trying to tie a formal bow tie, as we foolish Brits too often did in the evening, would cause dress shirts to become totally saturated before the knot was achieved. Few of us had air-conditioning in our houses and the ceiling fans were, in some people's opinions, little more than a minimal aid to survival.

I actually enjoyed the climate and I flourished in Singapore, not least because my skin had never been so comfortably moist and unflaky. But many succumbed to it in one way or another. Some lost all ability to be in the slightest degree energetic. Some became susceptible to every passing infection, and it seemed almost as if the climatic conditions winkled out inherent physical and mental weaknesses that might never have surfaced at home. I had never known before, nor have I known since, fighter pilots reluctant to get ready to fly; normally they crowd around the operations desk importuning to be put on the flying programme but, in Singapore as we got further into our second year they were very difficult to shift from our (air-conditioned) crew-room. Chiang Mai had been quite different, in spite of the primitive conditions in which we lived and worked there – possibly not so much because of minor differences in climate but rather because we were all then still in our first year in the tropics. I have often wondered since just how much part climate-induced torpor played in exacerbating the other factors that led to the feeble capitulation of the British to the Japanese in Malaya and Singapore in 1942.

Dickie Calvert was as comfortable as I was in the climatic conditions of Singapore but he found it difficult to cope with the outbursts of acerbity and recalcitrance that those conditions could – and too often did – bring out in some people. In an environment where firmness and decisive leadership were badly needed he tended to back off from confrontation and too often failed to slap down individual assaults on his authority as squadron commander. In Labuan, for example, when a couple of local residents complained about the noise that a few of the 20 Squadron pilots were making in the bar of the airport hotel, and Dickie asked them to tone it down or leave, he was told by one of his officers to 'fuck off'. Dickie's response was simply to leave himself.

Those of us who could see the strain that command was increasingly subjecting the Boss to were concerned and supportive. Others were not and, as a result, I sometimes went further than perhaps I should in leaning on members of both flights in the interests of maintaining discipline and an effectively functioning squadron. This didn't make me popular with some and, hardly surprisingly, not at all with my fellow flight commander. Moose – and a few others – took the view that Dickie was the author of his own misfortunes, didn't deserve sympathetic support, and that what I was doing was simply self-interested sycophancy.

We received four new pilots in February to add to the two first-tourists who had joined us just before the Chiang Mai detachment. The newcomers, arriving fresh from operational training, and from temperate climes, were an invaluable addition, bringing a dollop of energy and enthusiasm to the original bunch that had brought the aircraft out. Because the Air Ministry had wanted 20 Squadron to be instantly operational in Singapore the original complement of pilots had had at least one previous tour on fighters. Had we been required to engage in operations this level of experience would have been great, but for the everyday routine of any squadron it is a not ideal. The more experienced members should have the stimulus that derives from taking youngsters under their wings, imparting their knowledge to them, and nurturing them to operational status. Until we began to get our first-tourists we had too many chiefs and too few Indians.

In March we went up to Butterworth again, this time to spend a fortnight in air-to-air gunnery and air-to-ground rocket-firing. All went well, and once more we enjoyed our time with our peers on the Sabre squadrons. However, one of our first-tourists fell foul of Butterworth's Wing Commander Administration in the Mess bar one evening and, having been banned from the base, had to be sent back to Singapore. He was held to have been 'behaving badly in the bar'. As he had merely been part of a jolly – and noisy – group of

Australians and British we were left wondering at the Wing Commander's reaction. It was in fact not the first time that we had had an example of an older Aussie apparently carrying some chip on his shoulder about the British.

In June we went again to Thailand on an exercise in many respects similar to the one that had taken us to Korat in April the year before; this time, however, each of the participating outfits were dispersed to the airfields that they had occupied during the previous year's response to Thailand's appeal to SEATO for help. We flew up to Chiang Mai as a twelve-ship formation in three battle fours, spread widely across the sky – for once clear of cloud at 40,000 feet. I can't say that many of us were thrilled to be back in the familiar camping environment and compo ration cuisine[1] of Chiang Mai airfield, but being back again in the free-range flying environment of Thailand very considerably made up for the discomforts on the ground.

At the end of this year's exercise, rather than fold our tents and fade away as we all did at the end of the last one, the participating SEATO partners were required to mount a firepower demonstration for the King of Siam. We protested to HQ 224 Group when we learned that our part in this was to be restricted to four aircraft firing cannon at ground targets. As the targets were, for safety reasons, about three quarters of a mile from the spectators our display was clearly going to be somewhat less than spectacular – especially as others would be dropping bombs and, the Thai Air Force, napalm. We felt that a ripple of three-inch rockets with high-explosive heads from each Hunter would be more likely to bring us credibility in the arena. On the day, our relative feebleness was compounded for the watching British dignitaries when the British Army participants drove their personnel carriers onto the arena in front of the crowd and became irretrievably bogged down in mud.

The aftermath of this was a misdirected blast of anger from HQ FEAF and a demand that the Station Commander at Tengah act to 'sort out 20 Squadron's weapons delivery'. Seething slightly, we persuaded Tom Pierce that, before anything else, he should go up to Asahan range and see for himself what we could do, and what we had wanted to do at Bangkok. He agreed and I was assigned to lead four Hunters, each armed with eight rockets, to try and restore faith in our capability. We flew up as usual at low level just off the coast, pretty sure that we could do so.

Twenty minutes into the trip, however, my cockpit cooling system stopped coping with the moisture in the air at that height and, as a result, began to blow water over the gunsight in considerable volume. We all carried absorbent cloths to deal with the cockpit canopy misting that could occur on a rapid descent from high level, so I got that out and began wiping furiously. I was still wiping as we approached the range, and still wiping as I pulled up and winged over to dive on the target. The target was the usual ten-foot square of hessian pegged out on the ground. I wiped, selected weapons live, wiped, corrected my aim, wiped, and fired. Pulling out immediately the rockets went and, climbing steeply, I could see over my shoulder black smoke rising from where the target had been. Each of the other three pilots fired in turn at the smoke and, as we sped away, we were pretty sure that we had managed a gratifying level of accuracy – and delivered a two-fingered salute to our detractors at Command.

The rest of the year sped by on the familiar training routine with nothing to disturb our existence beyond a visit by 'The Trappers' (a team from the CFS charged with an annual visit to squadrons to check that they were flying to the laid down standards of airmanship), and a visit by a USAF F-100 squadron based in the Philippines. However, it also included the beginning of 'Confrontation' by the Indonesians.

Confrontation could be defined simply as the petulant physical reaction of the Indonesian Government to the proposed merger of Malaya with Brunei, Sabah, and Sarawak. The British Government's announcement that this would take place, and that the new entity, 'Malaysia', would come into existence on 16 September 1963, coincident with Malayan independence, appeared to be taken by the Indonesian Government as an affront. The British embassy in Jakarta and a number of embassy staff houses were burnt down as an opening shot, and on 25 September President Sukarno announced that he would 'gobble Malaysia raw'. These actions were followed almost immediately by small-scale penetrations by Indonesian forces across the border between Kalimantan (Indonesian Borneo) and Sarawak and Sabah.

No. 20 Squadron very quickly became involved through requests from HQ FEAF to fly sorties from Singapore to Labuan whenever an Army patrol in the border area reported sighting an Indonesian aircraft, usually a Hercules re-supplying their forces on the ground. These trips were totally futile as we were not initially kept on standby for them. Even if we had been, the time required for us to cover the 700 nm between Tengah and Labuan, refuel and get airborne again, would have given any reported aircraft ample scope to do its business and be long gone before we got there. After I had left the squadron, and 'Confrontation' had begun to hot up along the border, a more sensible approach led to the positioning of Hunters on armed standby at Labuan and Kuching. Meanwhile, the perceived risk throughout the period of Confrontation of Indonesian air raids on Singapore put the Javelins of No. 60 Squadron permanently on air defence alert at Tengah.[2]

As my tour in the Far East approached its end I couldn't help wondering what might be coming next. I knew that it would be totally presumptuous to expect anything like command of a squadron – even though I had passed the promotion examination for the rank of Squadron Leader while I was on 19 Squadron – as the fastest movers did not 'go up' in less than five to six years, and I had only reached four as a flight lieutenant. But one can dream, and it was what I would have loved. What I got, however, seemed to be such a backward move that I was left wondering where I had gone wrong. I had clocked up a total of 1,620 hours on the Hunter and was completely at home in it, had enjoyed myself thoroughly on 20 Squadron, loved Singapore, and relished my role as flight commander. However, I was now being posted back to Chivenor to do again what I had done there considerably less experienced. Esmé suggested I think of this as a rest cure after the excitements of the Far East, but I could not see the logic in it and could not take it quite so philosophically.

My tour on No. 20 Squadron ended on 21 November 1963. We travelled back to Britain as a family in a RAF Comet, stopping for refuelling at Gan in the Maldives, Aden and El Adem. As we sat in a bus on our way to breakfast in the Red Sea Hotel during our stop in Aden I was struck by the extraordinary barrenness of the Aden landscape in contrast to the lush tropical greenness that I had taken so much for granted over the past two and a bit years in the Far East. There was something repelling about Aden with its dirty sand, coloured by nothing more than the green of broken beer-bottles and other detritus. At least Chivenor was a pleasant spot – and I would still be flying. Hell, I thought, I could have been posted to Aden on a ground tour.

Notes

1 When researching for this book I read No. 20 Squadron's Form 540. I found that I had recorded for June 1963, writing as acting squadron commander, that: '…it is the opinion of this squadron, after two years' experience, that compo rations are unsuitable for pilots flying intensively in high performance aircraft in tropical conditions'. I can't have liked them!

2 No. 60 Squadron was reinforced for the task from the UK by No. 64 Squadron, another Javelin outfit. In the event, no raids occurred, although there were frequent provocative Indonesian flights to within a few nm of Singapore. The end of conflict came when growing political discontent within Indonesia created a climate that made negotiations possible. Confrontation was formally declared over on 4 August 1966.

CHAPTER TEN

Why Am I Here?

One good thing about coming back from an overseas tour is that one could normally expect to have a decent slice of leave. I had six very welcome weeks. This gave Esmé and me ample time to go over to Belfast, enjoy a spell with each set of parents, look up old friends, buy a car, acclimatise, and do some desperate phoning of estate agents in the area around Chivenor to try to find some suitable accommodation. It was pure luck, or rather a moment of low demand, that had got me a Married Quarter at the tail end of my previous Chivenor tour. However, this time, although I was one rank higher, had several more years' service, and had had a second child, all essential elements in the mix that gave one qualifying points for Quarters, there were none to be had. There were no Hirings available either but the Married Families Officer helpfully put me in touch with the owner of a small hotel, closed for the winter, and I was able to rent this until the end of March.

When I reported for duty at Chivenor, on 22 January, the feeling of *déjà vu* was less than I had expected for there had been quite a few changes in the four and a half years since I had left on my way to No. 19 Squadron. The Vampires had gone, and had been replaced entirely by Hunter T7s. Mark 6s, each carrying two drop tanks, had replaced the Mark 4s. And, as the Lightning had now replaced the Hunter in the air defence role, the emphasis at the OCU had switched to ground attack; and there was a section dedicated to fighter reconnaissance training, something that I had taken to very readily on the DFCLS course, and rather thought I would like to do by way of a change. Chivenor had also become responsible for running short courses to train an agreed number of Army officers each year as Forward Air Controllers.

I was rather pleased to be assigned to 234(R) Squadron as it had the FR section. However, this line of business was well sewn up by a small coterie of ex-RAF Germany pilots and, probably quite reasonably, only those who had served on a FR squadron could join the club. I was to be, once again, a tactical instructor, but this time I was also to be one of three weaponry instructors on the squadron. There was some discussion about sending me on a PAI course to prepare me for this but I demurred. The long defunct PAI course had been resurrected and a new Interceptor Weapons Instructor course created to cater for the Lightning force. I could see no point whatever in repeating what I had had at West Raynham but, as nobody currently on 234 (R) Squadron had done the DFCLS course it took a fair amount of arguing to get the point across. By the time I had finished, I think that my flight commander, Pete Heighton, was convinced that I was simply being refractory. He was right, up to a point.

However, by the end of my first week back at the place, and in spite of my misgivings at having apparently taken a career-step backwards, I knew that I was going to enjoy myself, and especially so in the role of weapons' instructor. A new and more complicated cine exercise had been introduced that was difficult to master and a challenge to teach. Air-to-air firing was still in the syllabus and had been joined by a fair amount of air-to-ground gun and rocket firing. On the purely tactical side the emphasis was very definitely on low-level work. Within the first week, too, I realised just how much more dual instruction had been introduced to the course, and how much the quality of the training had accordingly benefited.

As a follow on to the earlier sale of Hunters to India the British Government had agreed to provide OCU training for Indian Air Force pilots and, coincident with my arrival, a new course of seven Indians was just beginning. This scheme had not been in existence for very long and it surprised me, given that we had begun delivering Hunters to the Indian Air Force before my sortie to Cawnpore in 1958, and I had met a sizeable bunch of Indian Hunter pilots at Palam in 1961. We very nearly got off to a bad start with this latest course when one of the OCU instructors, running the operations desk in the squadron, and with it the flying programme, addressed the course leader and another Indian student as 'you Westernised Oriental Gentlemen'. Although a fair amount of badinage has been common currency between aircrew members in crew-rooms across the ages, and anyone getting upset by it could expect nothing more than the old military retort of 'if you can't take a joke you shouldn't have joined', this was in a different category of tactlessness. It was crass, stupid and insulting, even if, as was the case here, it was not meant to be. The course leader was very put out by what he considered to have been a serious bit of post-Raj racism and telephoned the High Commission in London to complain. Luckily whomever he spoke to must have realised that this was likely to have been nothing more than an isolated bit of idiocy and told him to accept it as such, and the crisis subsided.

I had something of a weapons' training success with one of the Indian pilots, Pilot Officer D' Silva, that gave me considerable pleasure and, rather undeservedly, established my reputation as a weapons' instructor. D' Silva had not found the cine exercises easy, had achieved the same low average standard in air-to-air gunnery as I had done on my OCU course in the Vampire F5, had not distinguished himself at air-to-ground gun-firing, and had lost his confidence completely over rocket-firing. It was decided that he should have a further RP dual sortie and I was assigned to do it. I gave him a very thorough briefing beforehand and, as we were walking out to the T7 I suggested to a fellow weapons' instructor, who would be on the range concurrently with another student, that we ought to have a bet on which of our students would get the best score.

We bet a fiver and I told D' Silva that I was not prepared to lose. We took off as a pair with the other T7 and headed for the air-to-ground range at Pendine Sands in Carmarthen Bay. Once there, and settled into the pattern, I talked us around a couple of non-firing or 'dry' attacks pointing out the features on the ground that should be flown over to set up a consistent attack circuit and a precise 30-degree angle of dive. It was then just a matter of holding the bottom diamond of the gunsight on the target (selecting 'RP' fixed the diameter of the diamond circle, and the bottom diamond at the 'six o'clock' position) and recognising the look of the target at the correct range for firing. Putting the 'pipper' on the target for gun-firing was a lot easier than manoeuvring the bottom diamond, and a good attack depended on rolling into the dive with the pipper at the right distance above the target so that the bottom diamond came onto it as the wings came level. One then pushed on the stick to hold the diamond on the target as speed built up in the dive. This sounds awkward, and it was. I got D'Silva to follow me through on the controls on the third pass and left him to do it himself on the fourth. Two more non-firing passes and it was time to 'go live' with the four rockets we were carrying. I turned in to fire the first RP, talking away encouragingly as I did, and hoping that I would get near enough to the target both to impress my student that I knew what I was talking about, and to convince him that RP firing was easy. The range controller called 'Direct Hit' and, as a five or even a ten-yard miss distance was then considered very good, I was both surprised and delighted. Given the flight characteristics of the rocket (practice RPs had rough concrete heads) a direct hit had to be a fluke. 'There,' I said, 'see how easy it is.' I went around again, fired, and, amazingly, got another direct hit. This is my lucky day I thought, but said: 'There you are, my friend, I told you it was easy. Now you get the same.' And, damn it, if he didn't. Twice. A direct hit by a student was very rare; two in a row was unheard of. His delight was a joy to behold and his subsequent confidence unrestrained.

Taking Army officers up to show them how ground targets and surrounding features looked from the cockpit was a periodic and not unpleasant diversion from the main syllabus tasks. The first FAC's course that I was involved in was held during the last fortnight in March and followed a pattern that was now well established: a week of lectures followed by a split week when half the course flew while the other half went out into the local countryside and practised controlling. The basic problem was to wean them off the methods that the Army had taught them to describe ground features and to show them that there is a dramatic difference in the visual significance of an object when it is viewed from a few thousand feet above as opposed to from a prone position under a bush. The old army favourite, the 'bushy topped tree' that stands out boldly for the man on the ground was, when seen from above, merely a small flat patch, at best a different colour from its surroundings. The theory was that the penny would drop when the budding FACs saw things from aloft. I suspect, however, that only one of the several enthusiastic young officers that I took up hoisted anything aboard at all from the practical demonstrations of FAC-controlled attacks that they were given. Bumping along in the turbulence of low level, pulling up at 2 to 3 g, rolling over, pushing and pulling to get the aiming mark on the target, pushing negative g to keep it there, and pulling out of the dive at 6 g is really not the best way to ensure that the uninitiated remain at their most observant.

Meanwhile, I had been badgering the Married Families Officer about Hirings as my rented hotel was going to be given a pre-season face-lift at the beginning of April. In the nick of time he came up trumps and we moved into a rather charming thatched-roof cottage in Braunton, a village about three miles from the Station. This was both more comfortable than the hotel, and more convenient. However, because of the rigid enforcement of catchment area rules it meant a change of school for Caroline after three months, her third since she began school eighteen months before.

In April I was asked if I would like to work up a solo aerobatic sequence for the coming season of air shows and airfield open days. I was more than happy to do this and set about dusting off my previous routine and getting in a bit of practice between other sorties. Near the end of the month I was given the opportunity to concentrate to the exclusion of everything else on working up in a T7 – or rather down, as before, from the standard aerobatic practice minimum height of 7,000 feet – via a few sorties at 3,000 feet.

During some of my practice sessions I experienced a somewhat disquieting sensation: the application of negative g made me feel rather dizzy, in an odd oscillatory way. On others I could subject myself to all sorts of aerobatic manoeuvres, and to the maximum permissible g limits of the Hunter, without feeling the slightest adverse effects. On the occasions that dizziness struck, and it could do so almost as soon as I had begun my practice sequence, I had to break off and hold the aircraft steady until the world had stopped oscillating and I had stopped feeling slightly sick. On practices away from base and off the coast where, this time, I normally did my stuff, and with only summer visitors on the beach watching me, I could break off the aerobatics without it mattering. But I was haunted by the fear of an attack of this odd form of acceleration-induced vertigo occurring during a display. It was certainly not something that I wanted to experience while running along a display line upside down at a low level. Nor was it something I wanted to admit to the Station doctor, at least until I discovered whether or not it was going to persist. I just put it down to some odd after-effect of my spell in the tropics and hoped that it would pass.

In due course, and after a dual aerobatic sortie above 7,000 feet with the squadron commander, Nigel Walpole, I was authorised to do my five-minute sequence at 1,500 feet over Chivenor for official approval by the Air Officer Commanding 11 Group. A week later, after another session at 1,500 feet over the airfield watched by the Wing Commander Flying, Mike Hobson, I was authorised to come down to 500 feet. This was a more controlled approach than I had experienced on my last tour at the place – a first indication, perhaps, that higher authority had tightened the rules in the intervening years.

My first display was on 13 June at Eelde, a civil airfield in the north of Holland near the town of Groningen. I flew out to the Dutch Air Force base at Leuwarden in a T7 the day before, carrying the squadron's junior engineering officer as passenger and (highly qualified) ground crew, and spent the night there. The following day, apart from a slight problem in finding Eelde in a thick summer haze, all went well – and by that I mean I felt not the slightest hint of vertigo and my five-minute sequence was reasonably professional. My second display was at Filton, Bristol, on 20 June and again I felt perfectly fit and well.

June is also the month during which Her Majesty the Queen's official birthday is celebrated and, on that day, the Birthday Honours List is promulgated. The half-yearly promotion list follows on 1 July. There was a rather silly little ritual within the RAF concerning the contents of both: no advance notification of Honours was given, and only very seldom was anyone below the level of Group Captain told in advance that they were to be promoted. At one minute after midnight on both days – and similarly for the New Year's Honours and Promotion Lists on 1 January – both would be available on the Stations, and would often be read out at parties in the Messes (in those days the media, too, scrupulously avoided jumping the gun).

No one seemed to mind this method of disseminating the news but it always seemed to me that a little advance warning could have been given, if only to allow those concerned to get their new medal ribbons or rank tabs on their uniforms in a timely fashion. And it was sad to see the odd person, convinced that promotion was in the bag, prematurely lining up the champagne on the bar. As some hopefuls were inevitably going to be disappointed the ritual of the late night promotion-list readings was widely referred to by the wags within the Service as the 'feast of the passed-over'. Given my apparent backward lurch in career terms I was not expecting anything from the Birthday Honours List but got a Queen's Commendation for Valuable Services in the Air. As this would have been recommended from Singapore for my tour on 20 Squadron I began to feel somewhat better about the future – but more puzzled than ever about my current posting.

The award, coming when it did, was welcome for another reason too. I was presented with it by the Station Commander, Don Farrar, one week later in a small ceremony in the Mess bar. He had been Wing Commander Flying at Odiham during my first few months on 247 Squadron and, although nothing was ever said, I had the distinct impression then that he had shared the poor view of me that my OCU report and my initial weeks on the squadron had created. Then, a month into this second tour at Chivenor I had given him reinforced cause to believe he had been right. I was Duty Officer, a twenty-four hour task that normally kept the incumbent on the ground for its duration. On this occasion, however, I was put on the flying programme late in the afternoon by the Boss, and he stood in for me and took charge of the Duty Officer's Book while I was airborne. When I got down, debriefed and changed, he and the book had disappeared. It was remiss of me not to have attempted to track him down and get the book back before I left the squadron offices at the end of the flying day. However, I did not, and at two in the morning I suddenly desperately needed it. The airman on duty in the station communications' centre had telephoned me in the Duty Officer's room to say that he had received a signal with just a code word on it – 'Quicktrain'. He didn't know what it meant and, without the Duty Officer's book, neither did I. It took me thirty minutes to track Nigel down, get him awake, and get the book, and just another few seconds to discover to my horror that Quicktrain was the code word that set a NATO practice alert going. The UK air defence system had been integrated into the NATO system during my spell in the Far East and some new measures had been introduced of which I was unaware. I didn't know, until I read it in the middle of the night, that from receipt of the code word 'Quicktrain' fighter stations – and the OCU was classified as one of them – had six hours in which to prepare and arm up 50% of their aircraft, and a further six hours in which to produce another 25%. Sounds simple, but with unserviceabilities, normal servicing schedules, and spares on order but not yet delivered, it was no mean trick to produce 75% in twelve hours.

I had the Station alarm sounded, set in motion the 'cascade' system that was designed to call in Station personnel living in the surrounding countryside, sent a fire engine to make a clamour around the Station Married Quarters, all the time painfully aware that I had lost Chivenor thirty minutes of preparation time. I rather expected Don Farrar would not be happy about that, and so it proved. I was summoned to the Station Commander's office later that day to explain the delay. Having listened to my explanation the only words he said were: 'If this had been wartime I would have court-martialled you. Now, get out.' Perhaps it was just as well that Chivenor managed to meet both preparatory states with a couple of hours to spare.

My next aerobatic display was at the end of August at Little Rissington, the home of the Central Flying School. I had felt distinctly unwell for several days beforehand, with streaming nose, flu-like symptoms, and recurring vertigo on almost every practice. I took off from Chivenor the day before the show, not feeling too good, but determined not to cry off with so little time to go. I spent the night at Little Rissington, didn't sleep, and felt terrible the following day but, imprudently determined as ever, I took off to do the display. I had to contend with a strong crosswind, positioned dismally for the looping manoeuvres and generally delivered a pretty poor show. Back at Chivenor and into bed I was diagnosed as having pneumonia. So much for flying with a 'cold'.

Later in August, having recovered from both the pneumonia and my embarrassment at having produced a crappy display at the holy of holies I flew a low-level dual sortie with one of the students, Mike Steer,[1] a hefty rugby player with a ham-like grip on the controls. We got airborne and set off on a pre-planned cross-country. His navigation was dramatically accurate and he was hitting all the pinpoints with ease. I bent over to look more closely at my map to see if I could make things slightly more testing for him. As I did so he snatched the stick back, loading us with a sudden 8 g, having suddenly spotted a power line rather close ahead. My head, weighted by my 'bone-dome' almost smacked into my knees, and my neck gave an alarming crack. For weeks afterwards I could hardly look to left or right but, again anxious to avoid doctors and probable time off flying, I did nothing about it. As I write, some forty-three years later my neck is still stiff, and occasionally sore enough to make me wish that I had taken time out to have it seen to.

My last show of the season was at Rennes St Jacques in Brittany at the beginning of October. I flew out in a Mark 6 – for my first display in that aircraft – on a Friday afternoon for a Sunday display. Someone from HQ 11 Group had done a reconnaissance trip (in a Devon, a piston-engined aircraft) and declared the runway to be fit for a Hunter to land on and operate from – and so it was. However, what he did not report was that the runway had a dramatic gradient for about half its length. When I arrived, with thunderstorms flashing and banging around the airfield, and the surface wet, I was directed to land towards the down slope – which I couldn't see from the air in the prevailing conditions. As I went over the brow of the slope and saw how little runway there was beyond it I knew that I would be very lucky to stop within the distance remaining. As I approached the end of the tarmac I was still doing about 40 knots. Directly ahead and about fifty yards away was a small brick-built structure, probably something to do with an instrument approach aid. I put on a boot-full of rudder and brake as I went onto the grass beyond the runway's edge and managed to steer clear of the brick obstacle. Happily the grass was reasonably firm so I simply put on some power and kept going fast enough to avoid becoming bogged in the ruts I was creating. I steered in a wide circle around the brick structure and turned back towards the runway and then onto the adjacent taxiway. To my surprise and relief my tyres had suffered no damage at all from this bit of cross-country taxiing – nor did they from the unswept carpet of stones that I noticed on the taxiway. The following morning I did a practice over the airfield and this time insisted on an uphill landing – which was unquestionably the way to go.

On the day of the air show the participating pilots were entertained to a formal lunch in Rennes by its organisers. The only course served was boiled mussels, which I detest at the best of times, supplemented by bread. I felt that I had to eat something before flying so I filled up on the bread and got through the mussels with the help of a couple of glasses of wine. I had become a lot wiser and quite prudish about the dangers of drinking and flying since my imprudent evening at Orange in 1959 and, if asked, I would have ventured the opinion that drinking before performing low-level aerobatics was suicidally foolish. I would not have countenanced anyone else drinking before flying – when I found Derek Gill having a pint one lunchtime at Tengah I gave him a heavy dressing down and suspended him from flying for the rest of the day despite his protestations that this was what they had always done on 92 Squadron before a formation aerobatic practice. However, on this occasion I felt that circumstances justified a little hypocrisy. And, whether there was any causal relationship or not, my display, which confidently included on that day a run along the runway upside down at very low level, was the best I had ever performed. I got both a gratifying round of applause from the crowd as I taxied in past them and, later, a presentation cup for the performance. I must confess I wondered for a moment or two if a couple of glasses of red table wine might possibly do more good than harm before a show, but didn't pursue the thought. I was just glad that my last show of the season had gone well. Best to quit when you're ahead. And alive.

About a week later I was informed that I would be going to the RAF Staff College at Andover in January 1964 and, as an essential preliminary, I was to join the next month-long Command and Staff School course at RAF Ternhill starting almost immediately. All was now suddenly clear, but the fact that I had been left to wonder for almost a year made me feel that there was something definitely wrong with the system. And to make matters more irritating, I found out while playing squash three months later with the officer who had been responsible for posting me to Chivenor that he had considered posting me to the staff of DFCLS on my return from Singapore – an experience that I would have been delighted by – but had thought it hardly worth while for just a year.

I had time for just one flight before setting off for Ternhill, and two after the course there ended, and that, apart from a few hours that I managed to beg during, and subsequent to, Andover, was the end of my Hunter flying. I finished with 1,800 hours on the aircraft, which probably represented – I have not counted them – more than 2,400 take-offs and landings. It was a superb aeroplane to fly, manoeuvrable as any fighter during the 1950s, and an excellent air-to-ground platform well into the 1960s.

I drove up to Ternhill each Sunday evening and back down each Friday evening for the duration of the Command and Staff School course. The journey took five and a half hours each way (no M5 then!) and the thought struck me as I did it for the second time that if I could find eleven hours each week to sit in a car during this course, I could find eleven hours later to do something useful. As I had got the only two Service examinations that involved a fair amount of study-time out of the way, I felt that it might be worth having a look at what I could do in the academic world while continuing to function effectively in the Service one. I contacted London University (then the only institution in the United Kingdom that set external degree examinations) and found that, once accepted for, and registered, to take a degree it was simply necessary to turn up to sit the examinations at the prescribed intervals. The snag was that there were very few degrees that could be tackled successfully with just a bundle of books in a kit bag, a requirement that I felt my itinerant life would dictate. Law seemed to be the best bet and I went for it – not realising then that law is such a dynamic and rapidly changing thing that I would need more than a bundle of text-books to keep up to date with it. And, more foolishly, ignoring the likely demands of the coming Staff College course and whatever lay beyond it.

Having begun my second tour at Chivenor, puzzled about being sent there, I left having very thoroughly enjoyed it – and, of course, more than pleased by the outcome. At the dinner night that I attended before leaving I think the Station Commander found it difficult to include me in the valedictory pleasantries that were customary on such occasions. He had previously made a passing remark about people who only served the Station for a few months before swanning off elsewhere – a sort of implied lack of loyalty. He was fulsome in praise of two officers who were leaving with acting promotion to fill squadron leader appointments and mentioned that he expected that they would be 'substantiated' in the near future. He clearly thought it improbable that I would be among those to be promoted that New Year and, for that matter, although I was pretty sure that normally only squadron leaders were selected for the Staff College course, I wasn't prepared to count any chickens. His congratulations at midnight on 31 December, after he had read out my name from the promotion list signal, seemed just a little insincere.

Notes

1 Later Air Chief Marshal Sir Michael.

CHAPTER ELEVEN

On the Ground

I had four days to get gold rank-tapes on my Mess Kit – as there was to be a formal dinner night on the third day of the course – and get up to Andover, look for accommodation, and move Esmé and the girls in. I found a small thatched-roofed cottage about a mile from the College and had it quite readily accepted as a Hiring. So far so good. The next task was to get Caroline into a local school – her fourth at the age of six and a half.

The RAF currently operated two Staff Colleges. The other was at Bracknell, in Berkshire. Andover was the original and longer established one but, because Bracknell took no foreign students, and could accordingly delve more deeply into security classified material, it was held by many young officers to be the more desirable of the two to attend. This view took no account of the variety and interest that the 50% mix of foreign students at Andover contributed to all aspects of college life. And it ignored the fact that most of the classified material disclosed was either ephemeral or was quickly in the newspapers, or both.

Military Staff Colleges everywhere attempt to open and broaden minds by a variety of well-tried means. Usually these include: encouraging students to study a wide range of topics in reasonable depth, discuss them, and stand up and speak about them before an audience (usually of hyper-critical fellow students); arranging visits for them to Service establishments, industry, and government departments; and giving them problems to solve, both military and political, requiring well-argued written solutions. And, to show both foreign and domestic students at Andover what Britain had to be proud of, there was a series of visits to places and things of historical, industrial and constitutional significance.

Asking questions of visiting lecturers was encouraged, and there was a feeling that if one failed to ask questions one would be marked down as a dull student. Sitting directly behind me for the first term – we all had chairs allocated to us in the lecture theatre – was a chap who was very much into amateur dramatics, a natural thespian behind the footlights. When he stood up to ask a question, however, my chair shook as he gripped the backrest in a paroxysm of fear. There then followed a pause before he managed to stutter out his query. We were all nervous in the first weeks but we were forced out of that and into confidence on our feet as time passed – even the thespian.

Most times the question and answer session provided a lively supplement to a lecture. But sometimes answers could leave one less than impressed by the speaker. For example, when I asked the then head of the Army Air Corps why the Army felt that it needed to acquire and operate helicopters as opposed to relying on the RAF, as specialists in the air, to operate them in an army support role, his response was: 'We need to have them because you chaps couldn't cope with living roughly in the field as our chaps happily do when required.' Perhaps he thought I was being deliberately provocative and was answering me in the same coin. However, I felt that the question deserved a serious answer and was about to point out that we could rough it with the best of them and, in support of that I was going to tell him that I had recently been on an outfit that had camped very successfully for several months in primitive conditions on a (mostly) dried up paddy field. However, I sat down without doing so, having noticed the Commandant fixing me with one of his beady do-not-attempt-to-follow-that-up looks.

Syllabus days were set aside for working on and writing up the solutions to the more complex problems that were set for us, but occasionally it was necessary to wrap the proverbial wet towel around one's head and continue into the late evening. Because by now I had gone ahead with my really badly timed decision to embark on studying for a law degree, and London had accepted me, I was committed to finding the extra eleven hours that I had convinced myself would be available 'in my spare time'. I had to work late in the evenings a little more than most. But, in reality, eleven hours was not so difficult to squeeze out of a Staff College week. If I'd had any idea then how very much more time I would need to devote to the final stretches of study for the degree I would have thrown the venture away immediately. As it was, while I didn't have as much time as some to patronise the local golf courses, I missed nothing of the social life of the College and had time to get to know several of the delightful country pubs that abounded in the area – more often than not dragged away from my books to one of them by a particular mate on the course, Paddy Hine.

Among our tasks in the final third of the year was a requirement to write an article to be considered in competition with articles by the other forty odd Andover (and hundred Bracknell) students for inclusion in the yearbook published jointly by the two colleges. I decided to write about Indonesia, in part because of my passing experience of Confrontation and all the briefings we had had on Indonesia as a result, and in part because there was a very comprehensive cross-indexed book, newspaper and magazine archive at Andover, created by a very dedicated librarian over the years, that contained some very pertinent stuff on this topic. At the time the conventional wisdom was that Indonesia was on the verge of a communist take-over. A bit of research into the Indonesian psyche convinced me that, while this was possible, it was very unlikely to be successful, and I wrote my article to support this view. It was a real relief to get the thing finished and handed in, and I was happy to forget about it when I had done so. Then, a month after the deadline for submission, and well into the run-down period towards the end of the course, there was indeed an attempt by the PKI, the Indonesian communist party, to take power. It failed dismally. My thesis had been validated – and at the same time made as stale as last week's newspapers. However, greatly to my dismay I was summoned to the Deputy Commandant's office, told that my article had been selected for publication, and directed to write a postscript to emphasise both the strength of the previously prevailing view and my advance prediction of the opposite. This was a bit of hasty extra work that I had not expected, and which I would have been greatly delighted to avoid if only my effort had been allowed to sink into obscurity there and then.

Just before the course ended I was sent to HQ Transport Command to be interviewed by the then C-in-C, Air Marshal Sir Kenneth ('Bing') Cross, as a possible Personal Staff Officer. There were two others besides myself up for the interview, both from Bracknell, and I rather hoped that Bing might prefer one of them as he had a reputation for being rather crusty. As it turned out he wanted none of us, preferring someone from within his HQ staff, and was probably seeing us simply to keep the Air Secretary happy. The downside was that the postings waiting for the two from the Staff Colleges that the latter expected Bing to reject were to staff appointments in Aden! In fact, all three of us went there. Esmé and the girls stayed put at Andover, unable to join me until the availability of accommodation in Aden ticked the magic box in the Ministry of Defence[1] and a movement order was generated.

I enjoyed Staff College and found it a lot more usefully mind-stretching than I had found university to be. But then, I had started off reluctantly reading for a degree in a subject that held little interest for me and from which I could see no future enjoyment flowing. Changing horses, even well beyond mid-stream, had been one of my better decisions.

Aden was a bit of a shock. That miserable bit of rock, sand, ugly architecture, complex of small townships and warring factions, was in a very sad state when I got there in January 1966. Terrorist attacks were a daily – and nightly – occurrence. Before Christmas Eve 1964, when malignity and mayhem had been set running by a grenade thrown into a children's party killing the teenage daughter of the Principal Medical Officer, Middle East Command, life for the Service community had apparently not been at all bad. All that had changed dramatically. The children's party atrocity had been rapidly followed by the murder of Adeni Special Branch Officers. And things had not got better. A nightly curfew had been imposed on Service personnel and their families, and gatherings of more than six people in Service homes were forbidden. Aden had become a very small place indeed for them all.

Accommodation in the Headquarters Mess at Steamer Point was bursting at the seams in January 1966 and, in spite of the risk, some officers were being accommodated in the only two decent hotels in that part of Aden, the Crescent and the Rock. These were situated in the formerly flourishing commercial area of Steamer Point, Tawahi, a duty-free shopping centre known to generations of shipborne passengers transiting the Indian Ocean, and more latterly to the passengers of cruise liners.[2] I spent my first three months in the Rock along with a bunch of ten other officers, all of us suffering on a daily basis from what I presume to have been the effects of unclean kitchens. On the bright side, during that period the Rock's catering brought me down two stone to a comfortable eleven and a half.

At the end of the three months I was allocated a Hiring in one of the many blocks built by local entrepreneurs specifically to cater for Service families along, and next to, a mile-long stretch of main road known to its occupants as the Mallah Straight. This was a ground floor flat in a far from salubrious building opposite the gates of the Aden Supply Depot (over whose high walls passing Arabs surreptitiously flung hand grenades almost as a daily routine). Apart from the noise of exploding grenades, and the nightly disturbance from mortar shells aimed at the Depot, and falling a few yards away from the wire-covered glassless windows of our bedrooms, my one abiding memory of that flat was the day, three months after we had settled in, when the lavatory in the one bathroom gushed with all the enthusiasm of an over-active geyser every time the occupants of the flats above flushed theirs. As the mid-day temperature was hitting 35°C at the time the resultant horror was hard to take.

The mess was cleared the following day by a gang of locals whose Muslim susceptibilities must have been sorely tested by the task. But more important to Esmé, the girls and me, the flat was declared unfit to be a Hiring and we were rehoused a few weeks later in the top floor flat of a six-storey building. This had a splendidly large balcony with a view across the harbour. It was a real joy to have breakfast on the balcony in the relative cool of the morning looking at the panorama of minor maritime activities, or to sit on it in the evening gazing up at the stars and the very visible satellites passing above us in the clear cloudless sky. The other side of the building faced Shamsan, the 1,800-foot high mountain rising abruptly out of and dominating most of Aden. Our neighbours on that side suffered occasionally from machine-gun fire mounted from among the closely packed makeshift dwellings clustering along Shamsan's lower slopes about half a mile away – and survived by learning to stay below the level of their window sills after dark.

My appointment in Aden was to the Secretariat of the C-in-C, Middle East Command, a small busy office whose function, in short, was to oil the wheels of joint-Service co-operation within the Command. The head of the Secretariat was an officer of commander RN, lieutenant colonel, or wing commander rank and there were three single-Service secretaries at my level. Oiling the wheels brought us all sorts of tasks, often matters on which the other staffs felt they had too little time to waste, but nevertheless which impacted on all of them. And sometimes we had to follow up things that the C-in-C had stumbled upon during one of his disarmingly informal visits across the Command. One of my regular responsibilities was to attend the one-star Joint Administrative Committee's meetings, record the minutes, and produce a draft of them for the Chairman to amend as he later saw fit.

Another of my responsibilities was to produce a draft signal each week on the operations that had being going on across the Command during the previous seven days. This would then be discussed, massaged, and amended at a meeting of the C-in-C's Committee and sent off to reach London in time for the weekly meeting of the Chiefs of Staff.

Assembling the material for the draft signal required me to run rapidly around the Command HQ in advance of the meeting and knock together what I had been given into a reasonable précis. I always got an abundance of items from the Army staff as the soldiers were having a bloody time both with dissidents up-country and with the terrorists within Aden itself; the Navy had a very small presence in Aden and were unconcerned by the fact that they rarely had anything to give me; and, although the RAF's Aden-based Hunters, Shackletons and tactical transport elements were constantly and riskily engaged in giving support to the Army, most of what they were doing was repetitive and had become rather stale as far as newsworthiness was concerned. My RAF seniors inevitably, and justifiably, felt a little sore about how infrequently their Service was mentioned and when, one morning, Group Captain Operations passed me an item about four Hunters carrying out a firepower demonstration on the doorstep of a dissident tribal leader, he urged me to see that it was not omitted. Firepower demonstrations – the term, as used in the Middle East, meant the practice of first warning recalcitrant elements to remove themselves from their property and then pounding it from the air – were a time-honoured RAF tactic that had been used, for example, effectively and bloodlessly to keep order in Iraq for most of the years between the first and second world wars. Knowing how much the C-in-C, Admiral Sir Michael Le Fanu, appreciated a joke I was quite relaxed when my typist suggested that we might replace 'firepower' with the words that at the time were much used by the 'hippy' crowd, 'flower-power'. I felt sure that they would disappear during the editing session within the C-in-C's Committee. Unfortunately, although the AOC, Air Vice-Marshal Andrew Humphrey, vigorously argued that they were obviously a typist's error and should be corrected, Sir Michael refused saying that the joke would brighten up the Chief of the Defence Staff's day.

Sir Michael was C-in-C throughout my time in Aden. Known within the Navy both as the 'Chinese Admiral', Lee Fan U, and as 'Ginger' because of his hitherto brightly coloured mop, he was a delightful, gifted and mischievously humorous man for whom it was a pleasure to work. When, hard on the heels of the dispatch of the 'flower-power' signal it was suggested to me, doubtless jokingly, that I should consider myself fortunate that my own Service was not writing my annual report, I was doubly pleased that I was working for him. Jokingly or not, the fact that I was reported upon upward via the Head of Secretariat, at that time a lieutenant colonel, to the Chief of Staff, then Brigadier Roly Gibbs (later Chief of the General Staff), and thence to the Admiral, was comforting.

I had hoped when I first arrived in Aden that I could get myself airborne with one or other of the Hunter squadrons based at RAF Khormaksar, Nos 8 and 43 and (later) 208. I knew many of the pilots on them as most had either passed through Chivenor when I had been there or had been on a squadron with me. Peter Taylor from my time on 19 Squadron was one of the Hunter flight commanders at Khormaksar throughout my tour, and he took me up once in a T7. However, I simply couldn't escape from the Secretariat long enough during the working day to get to the airfield, fly, and get back in time to deal with the matters piling up at the end of it. And, on two of the three rare occasions when I did have the time, security alerts had stopped all movements between the HQ complex at Steamer

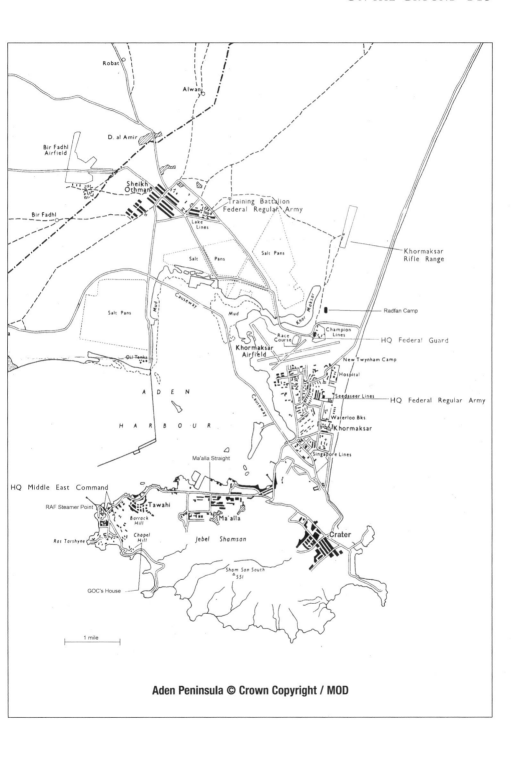

Aden Peninsula © Crown Copyright / MOD

Point and Khormaksar. There was nothing for it but to be happy to be a full time staff officer.

Actually, my life in the Secretariat was not at all unpleasant, and included a number of authorised escapes from behind the desk, mostly hitching a lift with the C-in-C on visits up-country and, once, to Kenya, Malawi, Swaziland and Lesotho. And there were occasionally interesting joint-service matters being pursued in the Command operations room, the responsibility for which belonged to the top management but to which I was privy as the duty scribe from the Secretariat. One such involved the use of the (then) new Landing Shop Logistic, HMS *Fearless*, while it visited Aden; the idea was to use the ship and its landing-craft to support a surprise landing at Hauf, a village some distance eastward along the coast, where it was thought a number of dissidents were based. Surrounded in the operations room by senior figures busy with the intricacies of the operation upon which their forces were embarking I wondered if anyone had remembered that, at that particular time of year, the waves along the coast were often quite mighty rollers. They had, but felt that they would not baulk the landing craft carried by the LSL. In the event they were not entirely baulked, but in the interests of safety in an operation of minimal priority my own Service had to be asked to help to carry the embarked troops ashore by helicopter. That week I was left in no doubt about what I was to include in my draft for the C-in-C's Committee.

The terrorist situation was getting progressively worse as 1966 moved onwards towards 1967 and there were signs of the beginning of a deliberate targeting of the British Security hierarchy. The first manifestation of this was an explosion during a drinks party in the flat of a man rather disingenuously listed as a 'foreign office official', Tony Ingledow. An anti-personnel mine had been hidden behind a bookcase, which by good fortune his wife had later moved to clear more space for her guests, thereby causing the mine to fall on its side; as a result, instead of jumping up to head height before exploding, as it was designed to do, most of the force of the blast went through the nearby French windows. Nevertheless, its effect was still nasty: it killed the wife of the MI5 representative in Aden, the wife of a major in the Intelligence Corps, and wounded ten others. How bad things were getting can be measured by the fact that in the first quarter of 1967 there were over 300 security incidents and, in the second, over 1,000.

The British Government had granted Aden a constitution and a Council of Ministers in 1962 and, by 1963, Aden had become part of the Federation of South Arabia, an entity that it was hoped would be fully functioning and capable of governing after British withdrawal. By 1965, sixteen of the twenty treaty chiefdoms in the Aden Protectorate had joined the Federation, and plans were well advanced for creating a Federal Army comprising some nine battalions of infantry plus supporting artillery. In early 1966 the British Foreign Minister, George Brown, had announced to Parliament that British withdrawal would be 'not later than 1968', and it was hoped that this announcement would reduce the indiscriminate killing in Aden, particularly as the date for British departure approached. However, this bit of wishful thinking in Westminster was subverted by the determination of the two main terrorist groups, the Front for the Liberation of South Yemen (FLOSY) and the National Liberation Front (NLF), to compete for ultimate control, and to do so by intensifying terrorist activities. And, of course, it did much to undermine the confidence of those in the area who had been persuaded to go along with the idea of a Federation.

Meanwhile, the elements decided to add to everyone's problems. Almost in the style of a biblical omen the weather did something on 1 April that one could well believe it had not done in that part of the world since Noah built his ark: rain fell very heavily in Aden for about twelve hours non-stop.[3] In the morning the Mallah area was swilling in a two feet deep mixture of water, mud and the accumulated goat droppings of the ages. The mud and the droppings had flowed down from the shanty settlements on Shamsan, and, as no provision had ever been made for any form of drainage, none of it had anywhere readily to go. The balcony of our flat had filled to a depth of over six inches overnight, rather like a bathtub, and I had to drain it in the morning by opening the French windows and letting the water flow through the flat and down the lift shaft.

The flood in the Mallah area slowly dried up under the sun's influence but left everywhere a rock-hard brown mess of permanent nastiness about a foot deep. It says much for the grit of the many families housed along the Straight that they got on with their lives in spite of the unsavoury smell emanating from this new surface – and this coming on top of curfews lasting for days, lack of maintenance (any foreign tradesman capable of fixing a lift or an air conditioner had long since left Aden), and worry about personal safety.

However, all this was nearly over. A planned evacuation of Service families began in late April, with the occupants of the Mallah Straight area going first. My family went in early May, taken to Khormaksar by coach heavily escorted by the Army, speeding up whenever it passed one of the many knots of Arabs who were standing about shouting. To compound the feeling of gloom and finality of that day, terrorists fired a couple of rocket projectiles into the naval fuel tanks situated on the narrow coastal strip backed by cliffs beside the road linking the airfield with Mallah and Steamer Point. Flames, billowing black smoke, and a flow of heavy oil across the road trapped those of us who had gone to see our families off until finally a landing-craft was organised to take us up the harbour.

With the completion of the evacuation of women and children, and a thinning out of Headquarters personnel, those of us who remained were moved within the wire at RAF Steamer Point. I was allocated a room on the ground floor of a lovely beach-side Married Quarter – how absolutely marvellous it would have been to have had the points needed to get it when I had a family there. In fact, such houses were few, and generally one needed to be at least two ranks higher than mine to stand a chance of obtaining one.

Among the extra tasks that I attracted during the wind-down of the HQ was to see that the Secretariat's archive of top-secret files was dealt with strictly in accordance with the rules. This involved me in classifying all files either for retention and despatch to London, or for destruction. Destruction required shredding and burning the covers and their contents, both activities to be witnessed and recorded by an officer. When I found that one top-secret file had been opened purely to contain the sensitive saga of Married Quarter allocation in Aden, I could hardly believe the absurdity of it. The problem had been created by the difficulty in getting the single Services and supporting civilian staffs to agree on an equitable system for this. The Army pointed to the fact that RAF officers tended to get promoted at an earlier age than their Army rank equivalents and thus a system based on rank would be unfair. The Navy felt that because its personnel had normally so little opportunity to live with their families anyone in a shore-based job should have special consideration for Married Quarters. The civilian attitude was simple: unless they were to be allocated acceptable family accommodation they would not go to Aden. My satirical corporal typist suggested, as he handed me yet another file for perusal, that the main reason we were leaving Aden might be because we could not agree a MQ allocation scheme; it was a joke, but it had some pertinency.

The evacuation of families had been timely for, on 1 June, FLOSY and the NLF organised a general strike. This was accompanied by considerable violence and bloodshed. Then the Six Day War, which began on 5 June, inflamed the Middle East, and its peripheral effects were felt in Aden. While it was on, every Adeni seemed to have a transistor radio permanently attached to his ear, and they all heard, among other things, King Hussein's foolish broadcast falsely charging the Royal Navy with flying sorties in support of the Israelis from a British aircraft carrier that had recently gone north from Aden via the Suez Canal. This broadcast contributed to the total and permanent withdrawal of local labour from Aden Port and this, plus the closure of the Suez Canal, caused a severe headache for those on the staff tasked with organising the removal of military stores from Aden in advance of our final departure.

But more serious problems were building. On 20 June 300 trainees belonging to the second battalion of the Federal National Guard, based in Champion Lines, barricaded the gate, seized weapons and ammunition and positioned a machine-gunner in the minaret of the camp mosque. He began to spray RAF Khormakar and Radfan British Army camp, killing several people. In the middle of this a lorry carrying nineteen men back from rifle-firing practice was machine-gunned from the minaret as it passed; three were killed immediately and the rest bailed out only to be pinned down for three hours during which time seven more were killed and six wounded.

Rumours of likely British retaliation spread wildly and, by midday, the bulk of the men within the Aden Armed Police Barracks in Crater had mutinied, had broken into the armoury, equipped themselves with its contents, and were ready to fight. Contact had been lost with part of a platoon of the Royal Northumberland Fusiliers (the unit currently on security duty in Aden) that had been sent to remove a barricade near the Armed Police Barracks. Their company commander went to see if he could find out what had happened, taking with him a Major from the newly arrived Argyll and Sutherland Highlanders, the unit shortly due to relieve the Fusiliers; they came under intense cross-fire and eight of the nine officers and soldiers in the party were killed. Concurrently some terrorists took up position in the old Turkish fort commanding the Main Pass road into Crater and added to the Army's problems by firing at anything that attempted to move along it.

These various speedily developing events caught the military off-guard and a great deal of confusion followed, made worse by lack of clear and understandable reports reaching the Command HQ. A meeting of the members of the Commander-in-Chief's Committee was hastily called to discuss what was known of the situation and decide what ought to be done about it. Admiral Le Fanu was in London and it fell to Andrew Humphrey, who was in charge in his absence, to chair the meeting. The GOC, Major-General Phillip Tower, who had been in post for little over a month, counselled caution and advised against any precipitate action. His views prevailed and the Committee nervously decided that it would be best, for the time being, to keep all units out of Crater and to try instead to contain the trouble within it by cordoning off the main routes out of it.[4] They did, however, sanction one timely and essential action: they allowed a Saladin light tank to fire its cannon at the Turkish fort and dislodge its occupants.

A state of total anarchy and lawlessness developed and persisted in Crater for almost a fortnight. Then, on 3 July, when it had become patently obvious that something had to be done to restore order, even if this meant risking a mutiny among the entire South Arabian armed forces, the GOC (urged and encouraged to action by the C-in-C) ordered a move into Crater. This was carried out by the Argylls, who by now had replaced the Fusiliers. Almost entirely due to the robust and determined tactics of the Argylls' commanding officer, Lieutenant Colonel Mitchell, the action succeeded dramatically well and by nightfall on 5 July the re-occupation was complete. It was fascinating to be on the fringe of decision-making on the top deck of the HQ at this time – the Secretariat provided a very privileged observation post – watching the discharge of responsibility without having to assume any oneself, at risk from nothing other than the occasional mortar shell lobbed in the HQ's direction.

Once he and his men were established in Crater, Mitchell was determined to show the local populace that the Argylls were in charge. He was sensibly suspicious of all, and particularly so of the Aden Armed Police. On his orders, his men set about conducting extremely rigorous patrols, stop-and-search operations, house-searches and interrogations, and these suppressed terrorist activities within Crater for most of the next fortnight. However, the hope in Westminster, even at this late stage, was that we would be able to hand over to an established South Arabian Government, and the British Government's policy therefore remained one of treading softly and winning 'hearts and minds'. The fact that winning hearts and minds was a military nonsense in the circumstances was ignored, as was the fact that the chorus of complaints, now being raised and broadcast widely about the Argylls' actions, was deliberately designed to attract international condemnation and weaken resolution in London, in the High Commission, and in the Command HQ in Aden. On 18 July the GOC summoned Mitchell to meet him and, after telling him that he must 'throttle back a bit', made it clear that his hitherto successful methods of control in Crater were to be dropped.

Back in Crater Mitchell issued a Battalion Order to explain the new situation to his men. Unfortunately he expressed himself in a manner that could readily be construed as implying criticism of this limitation on his regiment's actions and, in essence, of official policy. And, although he made the point that as a soldier under orders he had to be '100% loyal to his superiors', he introduced a touch of ambiguity dangerous to himself by ending up with the injunction: '...so let us be even more alert – with fingers on the trigger for the good kill of terrorists which may soon present itself'.

Philip Tower interpreted the Battalion order badly and there can be little doubt that he would have had Mitchell removed from command of his battalion had it not been for the nasty situation on the ground. In the circumstances it was decided that Mitchell would have to stay in command and that the C-in-C, acting in support of his GOC, would interview Mitchell and informally express to him the unacceptability of his 'disloyalty'. I suspect, though I have no proof of it, that Ginger's heart was not in this action. Nevertheless, it was done, not in the HQ, but in the GOC's house. Mitchell was not invited to speak.

Lieutenant Colonel Mitchell was a gifted soldier, popular with his men. He was presented with an almost insoluble problem and tackled it firmly. It was suggested at the time that his head had been turned by the media attention he and his men were receiving, and maybe it was. And, as a serving soldier, he must have known the risks inherent in even hinting publicly at dissatisfaction with the policies of his superiors. However, he deserved praise for what he achieved and it was in my view distastefully small-minded of those superiors to recommend him merely for a Mention in Despatches when he left Aden; even I got a Mention, for simply manning a desk! He had done enough to merit a more significant gallantry award.

I finally got the wretched task of the disposal of Top Secret files done, bar one file, just as the remaining members of the HQ staff were bailing out of Steamer Point in a planned move to Khormaksar. I couldn't find the missing file, which had a recorded number but no title. I had been to just about every office in the HQ that I could think might conceivably have had a Secretariat file but drew a blank – until, at the last moment, I thought of bearding the Foreign Office people in their den in the crypt-like basement of the building. There had clearly been a clean out in this previously busy little empire as the normally locked entrance was open and there was only one person in the place when I went in. He was sitting in an almost bare office looking at, of all things a holiday brochure. 'Do come in, old chap,' he said, 'what can I do for you?' I explained my problem and he shuffled to his feet, and without another word, led me into what I imagine a strong room in a major bank might look like. It was empty other than for one top-secret file – I spotted the familiar scarlet hue immediately – lying on a top shelf. 'Help yourself,' he said and retreated back to his chair. Unfortunately for me the file cover was empty, the contents gone. 'Don't fuss old chap,' he said when I remonstrated, 'the contents were far too sensitive to keep and we destroyed them.' I recorded the destruction of the 'file' and hoped that the papers that it had contained would never turn up where they should not.

By September it was clear to everyone that the South Arabian Government had no future. In October the Federal Army threw its weight behind the NLF, and that hastened the end. The Federation collapsed and the British Government rather shamefully bowed out, our final withdrawal negotiated with an unsavoury bunch of Marxist terrorists. Distasteful as that was, however, the negotiations allowed the remaining British forces to withdraw without our having to call for assistance from the fleet that was lurking just over the horizon to cover the possibility that we might have to fight our way out over the beach.[5]

The planned run-down in the HQ staff brought my job to an end in late October and I was on my way home. I just had time to try to ensure that my bits and pieces, and my Aden-appropriate Fiat 500, stood some chance of being loaded onto a Ministry of Transport chartered ship as indulgence cargo – on deck – before climbing onto a Britannia for the flight to the United Kingdom. As we took off and climbed, and I watched the monotonous stretches of sand and rock fall away below us and recede, I felt a great sense of relief to be leaving behind all the nastiness and risk that had been part of our lives in Aden. And yet, in spite of my misgivings about the place when I first saw it on my way back from Singapore, and the nature of our existence during my time there, there were some things I had enjoyed about it and, in a perverse sort of way, I was glad to have been there at that particular time. I had had a splendid opportunity to cut my teeth on staff-work in a role that I had found to be a lot more satisfying than I had expected. However, I was now going back to take up an appointment as a flight commander on a Lightning Squadron at RAF Leuchars in Scotland, and I had no mixed feelings about that: I was delighted by the prospect of getting back in the air.

Notes

1 The Air Ministry had become the Air Force Department of the Ministry of Defence when that enterprise in 'jointery' was formed in April 1964.

2 Steamer Point lost its appeal as a shopping area as 1966 wore on and the risk from terrorist incidents there grew. An example of the sort of thing that was happening was provided by a member of the staff of the High Commission, Susan de Heveningham Boekeland. Walking to her office from the Crescent Hotel one morning she noticed an Arab coming out of the Steamer Point Tourist Office and saw that he was starting to pull the pin from a grenade. Rather more robust than most strollers – and armed – she shot at him and the grenade exploded, killing him.

3 In fact, the last recorded downpour in Aden had occurred in 1943.

4 The township was so named as it was actually within the confines of an extinct volcanic crater. It was relatively easy to isolate.

5 The fleet included the carriers *Eagle, Hermes* and *Bulwark* (with an embarked Commando). Its size suggests that the possibility of a fighting withdrawal had been taken seriously in Whitehall.

CHAPTER TWELVE

A Real Man's Aeroplane

Esmé and the girls had set up home in Belfast after leaving Aden and I went to join them for another post-overseas spell of leave. Belfast at the time was a relative haven of tranquillity and it was a pleasure once again to be able to wander about without worrying about people trying to shoot or hurl hand grenades as one passed by; a bit ironic to think how desperately all that changed less than two years later.

At the end of my leave I set off for RAF Manby in Norfolk to join a Jet Refresher Course, a thirty-hour burst of all the usual training exercises conducted on what had by now become the RAF's basic trainer, the Jet Provost. The Refresher Flying Scheme had been introduced in the late 1950s when it was decided that pilots in staff jobs should no longer be required to try to keep in flying practice. Hitherto, keeping in practice had been the essential condition for retaining flying pay, itself a useful slice of the aircrew wage package. Providing the facilities to enable people in ground jobs to keep flying was expensive, and too many staff officers, unable or unwilling to get airborne sufficiently frequently to be safe in the jet era, had been having silly accidents and now and again producing the odd fatality. It was a blow to those who liked to escape from their office-desks to enjoy a burst above the clouds but, in the post-war era of cuts and modernisation, the flying facilities had to go.

I am sure that many pilots enjoyed the shortened version of the basic flying course that they got at Manby. For those whose career paths had taken them onto aircraft designed for straight and level work there would certainly have been novelty and fun in getting their hands on a fully aerobatic machine and tossing it about the sky. However, after thirty hours on the Jet Provost, pleasurable as they were, I had had enough to persuade me that I was ready to move on. I was impatient for the next stage, and felt – as an experienced, and possibly just a little conceited, ex-Hunter pilot – that I should be able to tackle the Lightning without any more time spent on refresher flying. Luckily for my desire to move on to the Lightning, I had not also been scheduled to do a Hunter refresher course, the normal next stage in the 'rehabilitation' process for people destined for the fighter and ground-attack forces.

The Lightning course was a five month-long affair, conducted at No. 226 Operational Conversion Unit, RAF Coltishall, a few miles outside Norwich. I started it in late February 1968. On the first morning the CFI, Wing Commander George Black, welcomed us and, doubtless anxious to impress upon us the complexity of the aircraft and the need to apply ourselves assiduously to the task of learning to fly it effectively, began by saying:'The Lightning is a real man's aeroplane; it's not for boys.'I thought this a bit over-dramatic but, as I was aware that George had been flying Lightnings almost from the moment they came into service,[1] I accepted that he knew what he was talking about.

We started the course with an intensive series of exercises in the simulator – a dramatically more sophisticated machine than even the latest Hunter simulator had been and therefore much more capable of teaching – and of overloading – the occupant. Then we moved to the flight line to get airborne in the Lightning T4. On my first trip my instructor, Flight Lieutenant Al Morgan, got me to do the cockpit checks, start up and taxi out. He then did the take-off. He lifted us off the ground at about 180 knots, held us level a few feet up, raised the undercarriage smartly as speed was rapidly building and, before we reached the end of the runway, snatched the T4 into a near vertical climb. This was the Lightning's party piece, shown at Farnborough when the aircraft first entered service. It was very impressive for the spectator on the ground and doubly so for the newcomer in the cockpit. I knew then that I was going to like the aircraft.

After five dual sorties in the T4, averaging forty minutes each, and twelve sessions in the simulator, the course members went solo in the single-seat Mark 1A, and twenty-four general handling 'Conversion Exercises' later, started the radar phase of the course. The Mark 1A was a delight to fly. Its two Avon engines, each producing 14,400 lbs of static thrust in reheat, a total not far off its al-up weight, gave it impressive acceleration, climb, speed, and height capabilities – all dramatically greater than those of the Hunter, itself no mean performer. For an experienced pilot, learning to handle the aircraft posed few difficulties, but there is no doubt that it was a fairly sensational bit of machinery for youngsters coming straight off the training courses. They had to be the pick of the training crop, and were.[2]

Getting used to handling the aircraft's radar, or to give it its full title, the airborne intercept radar (AI), was the real problem for the OCU students – and, according to Coltishall's records, not least for ex-Hunter pilots. For anyone coming new to AI it was first necessary to develop some dexterity in manipulating the dinky little joystick by which the radar was controlled in the Lightning. This was mounted on the left-hand console, just aft of the throttles, and carried on it what seemed like a myriad of functional controls. The radar scanner, or aerial, swept automatically to 40 degrees either side of the centre-line, but the pilot had to move it manually to search in elevation; he could do this, using the joystick, to 30 degrees above the radar sight-line and 10 degrees below it. When he had found his target in elevation, and had adjusted the scanner with some precision to 'highlight' it, he was ready to select 'acquisition mode'; in this, scanner sweep was reduced to 5 degrees either side of the target thus enhancing the likelihood of a 'lock'. When 'lock mode' was selected the scanner centred on the target and held it in azimuth and elevation during any subsequent manoeuvres of the fighter and target relative to each other. Lock mode also enhanced the scanner's ability to move in elevation to –30 degrees.

The real problem, however, both for newcomers to the role and for those interceptor pilots who had learned to scan the sky with the 'Mark 1 eyeball', was to interpret what the radar-scope[3] was telling them and manoeuvre accordingly. A rubber 'boot' was fitted to the scope to enable the pilot to peer at the images on the screen in conditions of bright sunlight, rather as an old-time photographer might shield the back of his camera with a black cloth. It was impossible to peer in the rubber boot and simultaneously see anything else in or outside the cockpit and it was also necessary, therefore, to learn to alternate rapidly between the scope and the outside world and absorb fully the information available from both.

The OCU syllabus introduced the students progressively to canned 'intercepts' with targets crossing the intercepting aircraft's heading at 90, 120, 150 degrees, and on a reciprocal of 180 degrees. The student had to assess the target's heading from the behaviour of the blip on the scope and to manoeuvre to get himself into position for an 'attack' on it. At this stage of the course the intercepts were all subsonic ones, flown at Mach 0.9 at 36,000 feet. At this speed and height a comfortable 45 degrees of bank produced a radius of turn of 4 nm. If the student could organise his intercept to have the target crossing his nose on a 90-degree intercept at 4 nm he would achieve the OCU's concept of the perfect subsonic PI, and with it, maximum brownie points.

To assess the target's heading it was necessary to know what to look for in terms of a blip's position on the scope on initial pick-up, and what its movement suggested. This had to be learned and practised and wasn't immediately easy. And, there was a need to know what azimuth angles to go for at what ranges while manoeuvring if one was to achieve the ideal curve onto the target. These too had to be learned and committed to memory.

The longer the range of initial AI pick-up the easier it was to get the assessment right and still have time to manoeuvre correctly. For a perfect intercept on a 180, for example, the student needed to have time to turn to put the target blip at 40 degrees of azimuth by 12 nm range.[4] A Canberra-sized target could be seen on the Lightning's radar at up to 25 nm but it was seldom possible to see a fighter-sized target at more than 18 nm, which left very little time for interpretation and the necessary manoeuvring. Away from the academic approach of the OCU there were many adherents to the view that an entirely satisfactory intercept on a target of unknown heading could be made simply by 'smashing it to the edge', that is, turning to put the radar blip on the edge of the scope and then keeping it there until, at less than 40 degrees of turn to go, the image began to move into centre of the screen. Whatever approach was adopted, however, on closure with the target the pilot had to pull the 'steering dot', generated by the radar computer, into the centre of the scope to allow the missile heads to 'acquire'.

Halfway through June, and with a total of forty hours on average on the T4 and Mark 1A, the course members moved on to the T5, the aircraft that was the twin-seat version of the Lightning Mark 3. There was also a new set of instructors to meet and get to know. The one I was allocated to, Flight Lieutenant 'Oscar' Wild, greeted me on our first meeting with what he probably meant as a joke, asking: 'Are you going to try to be one of the few squadron leaders we let through this course?' The thought of failure had not seriously crossed my mind but, as I was well aware that an embarrassingly high proportion of designated flight commanders had not made the grade on the Lightning course, I was not totally sold on either his sense of humour or his tact. I also hoped that his comment was not made as the result of something that had been written on my report from the T4 section of the course. I had been squeezing in about twenty-eight hours' work each week on my law books on top of the work needed to get all the radar facts and figures into my head and I knew that I was coming perilously close to overloading myself, and was not always as sharp as I should have been. Whatever the reason, Oscar's comments were unsettling. However, I simply grinned as he made them, and said nothing.

The trouble was, I was well and truly caught between the demands of the course and determination not to waste the time and effort I had already expended on the law degree. And I didn't help myself, as far as my apparent commitment to the course was concerned, when I asked for a week off in June in the middle of our introduction to the T5 phase to go to London to sit my Final Part I Examination. Certainly, George Black was not impressed and suggested that I ought to sort out my priorities. His responsibility as CFI was to ensure that the OCU passed out properly trained students and he clearly didn't feel that my absence at that point was compatible with that mandate. However, he didn't refuse my request and I sat the examination. It was a considerable relief to get it out of the way, get back to Coltishall, be free of the crippling work-schedule that I had set myself, and be able to tackle the remainder of the course more readily, productively and enjoyably.

There were marked differences in the cockpit layout and instrumentation between the T4 and the T5, and some slight handling differences, but a week in the Mark 3 simulator and two familiarisation dual sorties were enough to take us into radar exercises on the new aircraft. There were differences too in the radar, brought about by the needs of the Red Top missile, which was now superseding the Firestreak, the standard fit on the earlier marks of Lightning.

It is an advantage if a missile can be fired pointing ahead of the target, particularly against fast ones. In simple terms this reduces the amount of manoeuvring required of it after launch. The Firestreak's homing head had to 'see' the hot metal in a target's jet pipe in order to acquire, and thus effectively had to be fired from pretty nearly astern of its target. The Red Top had a more sensitive homing head and could be 'slaved' to the radar sight-line by up to 30 degrees (in essence, launched pointing ahead of the target by up to this amount). Additionally, as the Red Top's homing head was sufficiently sensitive to acquire on the reheat plume from an engine, it could not only be fired from decent angles off the rear but also head-on against anything flying at supersonic speeds.

The head-on attack against a supersonic target was exciting but, with the radar computer doing the work, relatively simple. Some Mark 1As had been fitted with a radar reflector, the 'Luneberg' lens, in place of the radar scanner. This gave a target response more like that of a large aircraft and thus enabled the Lightnings so fitted to simulate supersonic bomber-size targets. The intercepting pilot could lock-on early enough for the computer to do its stuff, getting him on a collision course in azimuth, but holding him initially level to allow him to accelerate to as high a speed as possible. At about 15 nm from the target the steering dot would give a command to generate lead on the target in elevation. At missile launch range a 'breakaway cross' was displayed and the pilot immediately initiated a hard roll and pull downwards to avoid hitting the target – a desirable miss at a closing speed around 2,000 knots.

My penultimate flight on the OCU was a final evaluation with George Black as my examiner. The target thrown at me was a '150' passing behind – a bastard of a set-up. I made the interception, not neatly, but adequately and was about to head for home when the pilot who had been flying the target Lightning, Al Blackley, asked me to do a target run for him. Calculating that we would have just about enough fuel to allow this I complied, but his interception was more drawn out than I had anticipated and we started home at a lower fuel state than I should have allowed us to reach. However, as I knew exactly where we were, there was less than half cloud-cover, and the visibility below cloud was excellent I was not unduly concerned. I brought Al into battle formation, let down visually, ran into the airfield for a break and landed. During the debrief he complained that he had been unhappy with the amount of fuel he had for the descent and landing. George took me to task for not starting back to base with enough fuel to enable us to follow the standard Lightning practice of flying to a designated dive circle, and being directed down under radar to a point at a distance from the airfield suitable for either a GCA to landing or a radar-directed approach for a break in good weather.'That was punk,' said George, 'you might have got away with that sort of thing on the Hunter but there's no place for it in the Lightning.' Although I felt like protesting the validity of what I did in the prevailing weather conditions, I had to accept that he was entirely right to uphold the laid down procedures, and to emphasise the merit of erring on the side of prudence as far as fuel states were concerned.

That not very encouraging assessment of my performance notwithstanding, I passed the course, delighted and relieved to have done so. I had my last flight at Coltishall three days after my ride with George and, having said my farewells and packed my bags, I headed eagerly north for RAF Leuchars and No. 11 Squadron. I was looking forward to getting to grips with the single-seater interceptor role in an aeroplane that was both a delight to fly and a considerable advance over the Hunter in the role. The Lightning's radar was a real plus; the TACAN it carried was a splendid bit of kit that gave both range and bearing from a ground beacon, and thus a ready 'fix' on position; its twin engines offered a level of redundancy that was well worth having over the cold North Sea; and its supersonic speed capability and its high service ceiling[5] gave it a level of performance that was most certainly going to delight anyone who had flown in the air defence role in the pre-Lightning years. It could perhaps have been designed to carry a larger weapon load, and have a higher g limit and hence a decent combat manoeuvring capability.[6] However, at this stage I simply wanted to fly the aircraft, not argue for perfection.

Notes

1 The Lightning was introduced into RAF service in June 1960 as the F Mark 1. No. 74 Squadron was the first and only outfit to be equipped with them. The Mark 1A (essentially a Mark 1 with an air-to-air refuelling capability) followed in November 1960, the first ones going to No. 56 Squadron. The dual-seat version of the Mark 1A, the T4, followed in 1962. A Mark 2 version was developed but few were procured. The Mark 1As were replaced by the Mark 3, No. 74 Squadron getting the first of these in April 1964.

2 Before the development of a British supersonic fighter there was a lot of speculation about the difficulties that might be involved in flying it, and the qualities that its pilots might be required to possess. Not everyone made the right guess. Sir Ben Lockspeiser, Controller of Research and Development, announcing the cancellation of the supersonic research project, M.52, in 1952 said: '…We have not the heart to ask pilots to fly the high-speed models, so we will make them radio-controlled…'

3 The scope was a tiny cathode-ray tube, four inches square. Its face was etched vertically to depict azimuth angles at 10-degree intervals from its centre out to 40 degrees either side. Horizontally etched lines depicted range at 10 nm intervals out to 40 nm. A 'steering dot' was generated on the scope when 'lock' mode was selected.

4 Having achieved 40 degrees of azimuth at 12 nm the intercepting pilot then aimed for 22 degrees at 9 nm, 8 degrees at 6.25, and on the nose at 4 nm.

5 The Lightning was capable of exceeding, but was restricted to, Mach 2. The T5's Release to Service ceiling was 60,000 feet; the Mark 6's was 65,000 feet. Brian Carroll, one of my fellow course members at Coltishall, reported taking a Royal Saudi Arabian Air Force Lightning (the Mark 53) to Mach 2.18 and to 85,750 feet while serving in Saudi in 1979.

6 The Mark 6 was limited to a maximum of 6 g – provided that its speed was below Mach 1.8 and there was less than 1,000 lbs of fuel in the ventral tank. With 1,000 to 3,000 lbs in the ventral tank the maximum was 5.5 g. With more than 3,500 lbs in the ventral tank the maximum was 5 g. Above Mach 1.8 the maximum was 4 g.

CHAPTER THIRTEEN

Balls! Keep Fighting

I drove up to Leuchars in my ex-Aden Fiat – its bodywork already rusting badly from its trip around the Cape of Good Hope as deck cargo. I knew nothing about my destination and wondered what to expect. After Newcastle the skies were leaden and, as I drove into Scotland, they took on a distinctly dark and drear look. My first impression of eastern Scotland was of coldness and greyness. And this was July! No. 11 Squadron's Boss, Wing Commander David Blucke[1] was a little cool too in his welcome, so I had to assume that Coltishall had probably not exactly lauded me.

I had my first sortie on the squadron on 11 July – an initial check by the squadron QFI, John Sims – and was sent off immediately afterwards for my first ride in the Lightning Mark 6. This was essentially a Mark 3 with a 600-gallon ventral tank replacing the latter's 250-gallon tank, an arrester hook, a slightly modified wing (the cambered wing), provision for carrying two 270-gallon over-wing jettisonable fuel tanks (for use in the ferry role) and a useful addition to its TACAN to enable aircraft so fitted to determine their range from each other.

As the squadron was holding the northern Quick Reaction Alert, or QRA as it was invariably referred to, which tied up two armed aircraft in a specially constructed alert shed at the end of the runway, and another as back-up, I didn't get a great number of trips in July. Just nine hours on the Mark 6 – but enough to whet my appetite for the AWF role and, once I was reassured that the sun did occasionally shine over Scotland, for the location. Leuchars is on the coast, near St Andrews, in the middle of some delightful countryside and close enough to Dundee and, for that matter, to Edinburgh for the convenience of anyone with quasi-metropolitan tastes. The Station had, as I came to know later, a special atmosphere of its own, rather as Chivenor had; this was accorded by some to the fact that for most English personnel it was far enough from home to be almost an overseas posting, but that didn't entirely explain the affection that people posted there developed for it. As my time on 11 Squadron lengthened I found a great number of things to like about Leuchars in particular and Scotland in general. But one thing Esmé and I never did get used to while I was on 11 Squadron was the chill of the northern climate – but this was possibly because the Married Quarter we were allocated was the coldest house we have ever lived in.

As I settled into the routine of training on the squadron I was intrigued to note how far the fighter world had come since my days on the Hunter in the air defence role. We had believed in our tactics and our ability to stop Soviet bombers if they had come, but we had been, in truth, woefully lacking in numbers and in the technical capabilities needed to have made success a sure bet. Now, although fighter numbers were down to sixty Lightnings and twelve Phantoms stretched along the east coast from Leuchars in the north to Wattisham in the south, capabilities had been greatly enhanced.

The role had changed too. The emphasis had shifted from pure air defence, held to be of prime importance for the protection of the V-force in its heyday. It was now given as 'the prevention of reconnaissance, the investigation of unidentified aircraft movements, the deterrence and prevention of attempts to jam our radar system, and the supply of reinforcements for overseas bases and operations'.

For anyone who had flown PIs in the Hunter days, the AI could almost be taken to have made fighter controllers redundant – except, perhaps, for pointing fighters in the right direction at long range. But that would have been a facile judgement and we were well aware that there was more to the world of fighter controlling than simply setting up interceptions. The United Kingdom Air Defence Ground Environment, as the package comprising radars, underground bunkers, communications networks, and controllers was collectively labelled, had a wide range of responsibilities and values. The United Kingdom had become one of NATO's four air defence regions in 1960 and as such the UKADGE shared information with NADGE (the NATO Ground Environment) and maintained a picture of aircraft movements from Murmansk southwards. It also liaised with civil air traffic systems, provided safety surveillance for activities such as air combat practices and air-to-air refuelling exercises, and generally kept a helpfully watchful eye on fighters allocated to a UKADGE radio frequency. Because we valued the controllers we were more than happy to give them, in their dark caverns, plenty of practice in setting up interceptions, and they were happy in turn to leave us to finish them off using AI.

From Leuchars we worked mostly with Buchan to the north of us, sometimes with Boulmer to the south, and occasionally with the reporting-post radars at Benbecula in the Outer Hebrides and at Saxa Vord on the northern tip of the Shetlands. And it was not just the old Hunter Mach 0.9 stuff at 40,000 feet. We practised against targets at all heights from 250 feet up to 50,000 feet plus, and at a variety of speeds up to and over Mach 1.5 – the speed that it was thought the most sophisticated Soviet supersonic bomber then in service could do (the TU-22 A or, in the NATO designation, the Blinder).

Getting to grips with the entire spectrum of activities and practices in the single-seat AWF role was going to take a little time. The OCU course had allocated only four trips in the dark, one dual and three solos, and now, on the squadron, virtually half the laid down training syllabus had to be done at night. There was a whole raft of new things with which to try to develop an easy familiarity. One of these, for example, was the technique for getting close enough to a target obscured by darkness – or by cloud – to see it and identify it, the 'visident' in air defence parlance. This required closure initially to close line astern of the target using the AI, first establishing the target's height by using the scanner elevation reading to attain level flight behind it, and its speed by holding steady with it on the radar at about 1,000 yards until this had been assessed with some precision. Provided the target was not at low level, when a different technique had to be used, the next step was to drop a hundred feet below it and to close on it at a gentle overtaking speed. The radar would break lock at about 300 yards, but the slow steady closure that had been set up would get the interceptor close enough to find the target in all but the thickest cloud, or 'skylight' it against the stars on a dark but cloudless night. As pilots became comfortable with the technique, and had been assessed as competent at it, visidents were flown against practice targets at night with their lights switched off. A successful visident required a considerable degree of concentration, split between flying smoothly on instruments and peering in the radar-scope boot. A manoeuvring target complicated the process enormously as I discovered on one occasion as I closed on a mischievously crewed Russian Badger bomber in cloud.

At the beginning of August I was introduced to another advantage of the Lightning: its ability to take on fuel in the air.[2] One of the more experienced members of the squadron, Dave Eggleton, took me up in the T5 to introduce me to the tricks of this trade. Tanking was a splendid leap forward in the fighter business, making airborne readiness a realistic tactic where circumstances suggested it, and making the role of oversees reinforcement an entirely practicable proposition. The trick was to close on the tanker, as one would on any aircraft that one intended to formate on, holding steady by using it as the reference point, and giving just a fraction of attention to the refuelling basket. The latter, about three feet in diameter at its open end, was designed to guide the receiving aircraft's probe – on the Lightning, a length of pipe extending from under the port wing to a few feet short of the aircraft's nose – into the refuelling nozzle. Once contact was made it was necessary to move forward just enough to put a little pressure on the hose and ensure that the socket in the basket held the probe in a leak-proof lock. At the same time the refuelling pod automatically wound in any slack in the heavy hose to keep it from developing a refuelling probe-damaging ripple. This did not damp out all undulations, however, and even in smooth air the refuelling hose, and hence the basket, were seldom steady. If the pilot gave up concentrating on the tanker as the point of steadying reference, and tried to follow the movements of the basket while closing on it, he was lost. And if he was using a wing-pod hose, and allowed his aircraft to rise just a little above the level at which the basket was trailing he was likely to be seized by the turbulence coming off the tanker's wing and hurled outward. To break from the basket he simply reduced power and slid gently backwards. At least that was the idea but it didn't always work that way. David Blucke and his number two, Brian Fuller, found this out on one tanking sortie: after filling up they both started to slide back but the Boss's probe-tip refused to disconnect and broke off, and Brian came away with the basket and about six feet of heavy hose still attached to his probe.

The tanker towline was normally flown on Lightning practice sorties around 30,000 feet, with height variations to avoid cloud. There was a whole raft of procedures, worked out by No. 1 Group, the parent body of the tanker force, with the good intention of keeping things simple and safe for the people they were serving. These ranged from a routine for ensuring a successful *rendezvous* to rules and techniques for joining a tanker and conducting business in radio silence. We accepted and followed No. 1 Group's procedures but sometimes felt a touch of frustration when a particular tanker crew stuck unnecessarily rigidly to them, especially when a little flexibility and trust in our capabilities would have speeded things up. As far as the Lightning force was concerned, finding and closing on the tanker was very straightforward given that our AI could illuminate a Victor at 40 nm.

On my first solo-tanking trip my confidence that tanking was easy took a beating. I closed rapidly on the tanker using my radar. I curved in behind it, slowed almost to its speed, moved forward at walking pace to the basket, and then committed the cardinal error of trying to steer into it by fixing my gaze on it. I found out the hard way what Dave Eggleton had told me: the basket, undulating gently in the wash off the tanker's wing, was an impossible thing to formate on. The harder I tried to stab it with my probe the more I got out of phase with its movements. Things just got worse – and I got a little desperate – with every failed attempt to engage and finally, short of fuel, I had to give up and head ignominiously back to base. As I entered the squadron operations room to sign in after the sortie I got, as I expected and deserved, a few smirks and a chorus of gibes about spending less than an hour in the air on a tanking trip.

In October I led six aircraft to Gutersloh for a fortnight to hold the RAF Germany 'Battle Flight' while the Lightning Mk 2As of the two squadrons based there were undergoing some essential modifications. At Leuchars, with long-range warning of intruders approaching UK airspace available from Norwegian, Icelandic and Danish radars, and closer in from Benbecula and Saxa Vord, we could almost have been home in bed and still got airborne in good time. As it was we held a ten minutes' alert state – a belt and braces measure just in case something popped up closer than expected. We could strip off to some degree and sleep reasonably successfully at night in the accommodation provided next to the two armed aircraft in the 'Q' shed, and still get airborne within that time. In Germany, a five-minute state was held and this meant remaining fully kitted and dozing off only if one was pretty sure that one was going to be instantly clear-headed should a call come to scramble. The disadvantage of allowing oneself to fall asleep at Gutersloh was well illustrated the first night I held 'Q' there. I was torn out of a doze by the telephone jangling at the other side of the room to find the other pilot on standby with me sitting by it and staring at it as if he had never heard or seen a telephone before; dazed with sleep he was totally unable of answering it straight away.

Gutersloh was a whole new experience in a number of ways: being taken along the border 'buffer zone' by the radar people and being told that one was being shadowed by a Soviet fighter just across the divide; carrying out supersonic PIs overland seemingly without protest from the populace below; having a drink in the tower room in the Mess at Gutersloh that had often been patronised by Goering in bygone days when he felt the need to come and crack a joke or two with his *Luftwaffe* crews. And, silly as it may sound, it was good to be able to fly in standard flying overalls rather than the immersion suits that were the norm for our sorties from Leuchars for so much of the year.

The immersion suit had not changed since I first used it on 19 Squadron and, potential lifesaver as it was, it was unquestionably uncomfortable. The neck and wrists seals had to be irritatingly tight if they were to do their job properly, and the rubber boots, in which sweat always seemed to collect, were an essential part of the whole. That said, few people grumbled about it – or about the practices with dinghies and other bits of survival equipment that were conducted routinely and frequently on the squadrons. However, an experienced pilot who had come to us from 74 Squadron, now based in Singapore, sadly paid the price for taking neither the suit nor the requirements of survival in cold seas sufficiently seriously. I remember him gazing out of the window in a bored fashion during a session of 'dry' dinghy-drill in the crew-room just a couple of days before he had to eject, at night, because his aircraft was on fire. He lost his dinghy-pack on the way down because he had not attached it to his Mae West; he had not tightened the waist strap of the Mae West itself and, as a result, it rode up as he entered the water and did not keep his head clear as it should; he wasted time until his hands numbed, unnecessarily trying to get the survival beacon battery out of its housing in the Mae West rather than the beacon itself; and, because he had cut the rubber boots off his immersion suit trousers (so that he could wear his leather flying-boots instead) he had created a path for the icy water into the suit.[3] He had gone down just off the coast and was being looked for very quickly both by rescue helicopters and by the local lifeboat. The sea was calm and visibility was good but, as his survival beacon had not been activated, he could not be homed onto and it was several hours before he was found. He had succumbed to hypothermia, lost consciousness and drowned long beforehand – and so totally unnecessarily.

Throughout November and December the squadron concentrated on air-to-air refuelling by day and by night, in preparation for a deployment to Singapore planned for January. There was an extra-heavy engineering task too, imposed primarily by the need to reorganise servicing schedules to get ten aircraft ready for the deployment. And there was also the task of fitting and testing the over-wing fuel tanks. Things were not helped by a Special Technical Instruction issued by Strike Command requiring engines to be changed on most of the aircraft and replaced by modified ones. All that notwithstanding, the normal spread of PIs was flown. And a NATO call-out that had us out of our beds at 0300 hours was taken in our stride, me flying an air-test at 0600 hours as part of the intense scramble to get six aircraft serviceable and armed in the required time. Call-outs had become more commonplace since my unhappy introduction to them at Chivenor, encouraged by a NATO-led determination to promote a high state of readiness, and a home-grown determination to do well in the operational readiness testing by NATO teams that was now an annual event, known colloquially as 'Tacevals'. Ambitious squadron and Station commanders had of course quickly come to recognise the value of a good Taceval result as an essential element in the competition for advancement.

The trip to Singapore was to test the Lightning force's ability to reinforce the Far East with minimum stops *en route*. In November the previous year the squadron had flown a two-aircraft endurance trial to find out if there were any problems in keeping the Lightning in the air to its original Release to Service limitation of eight hours. Dave Eggleton and Pete Collins had circled the United Kingdom, tanking periodically, for eight and a quarter hours. The amount of oxygen and engine oil consumed on this, and on other eight-hour flights subsequently carried out, showed that the aircraft could be cleared to cope with the two nine-hour hops to Singapore that the planners wanted for an operational deployment. As 11 Squadron would not be rushing out to counter any aggression, it was decided that we should do the trip to Tengah in three hops, via Muharraq on Bahrain island and Gan in the Maldives. Unfortunately, few countries were happy about refuelling operations overhead and we were thus going to be forced to follow a pretty tortuous route to begin with: Leuchars to Nice (with no refuelling over France), down the length of Italy just off the east coast, Malta, Cyprus, the CENTO route to Tehran, and then directly to Bahrain. The planning required for a Lightning squadron deployment to Singapore, and its cost, were well illustrated by the figures that emerged from the Air Refuelling Planning Cell at No. 1 Group: we would need a total of 228 refuelling contacts and the pre-deployment of about 400 – mainly Victor – air and ground crew.

Our parent body, No. 11 Group, wanted to make the trip 'as testing as possible' and to this end the first two pairs of Lightnings were scheduled for a take-off at night at forty-minute intervals. I led the second pair at 0140 hours from a crisply cold Leuchars into a beautifully clear star-filled night. My cockpit was a clutter of maps, booklets of flight and airfield data, a packet of absurdly neat bite-sized sandwiches designed to be popped into the mouth during brief removals of the oxygen mask, a pint-sized Tupperware container of orange juice plus straw and, most important of all, even if we didn't know how the hell we were going to use them, given that we were well trussed up in our immersion suits for the first leg, a 'Piddle-Pack'.

My number two, George Reynolds, and I rendezvoused with our first Victor tanker over Cambridge. This topped us up straight away and then transferred fuel to a second tanker designated to accompany us as far as Malta. We were, in fact, accompanied by tankers the whole way to Singapore, flying in formation with them, closely or loosely depending on cloud conditions, from time to time exchanging one tanker for another at pre-planned rendezvous points. The 1 Group policy of requiring deploying fighters to fly under the protective wing of a shepherding tanker brought the Lightnings the benefit of the Victor's long-range radio communication facilities and its superior navigation gear, but there were penalties. No. 1 Group's chosen speed for the accompanied transit, Mach 0.8, was on the slow side for the Lightning, particularly with over-wing tanks fitted, and the consequent slight loss of effectiveness of flying controls and engine response at the heights and weights experienced on the trip made flying in close formation for any length of time – and my number two and I were in dense turbulent cloud for two hours on the Gan to Tengah leg – very tedious indeed.

Additionally, on that leg our tanker took us up to 47,000 feet seeking sufficiently smooth conditions to enable us to get our probes into the baskets, using bursts of reheat to hold our wallowing beasts in contact when we finally got there. In similar circumstances, my fellow flight commander, Wally Hill, had the good sense to ask his tanker captain if he could go faster and found that the latter was happy to push the speed up to a very much more Lightning-friendly Mach 0.87. There were sections of the trip where we were quite definitely pushing our luck: on the leg to Gan, and again after Gan, there were two stretches where we were beyond any possible diversion unless we were completely fuelled up and, as a consequence, and to guard against failing to get a fill, we had to remain with the probe in the basket, essentially burning fuel directly from the Victor's tanks.

Arriving in the circuit at Gan, and eager to get on the ground

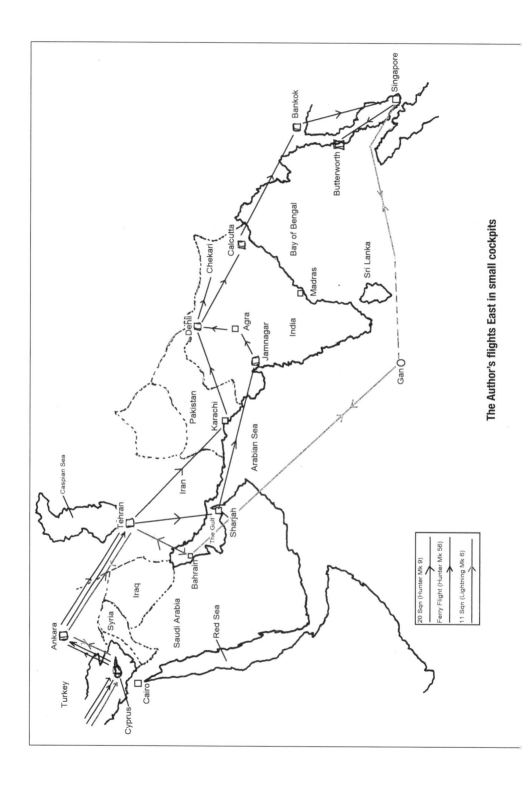

The Author's flights East in small cockpits

Legend:
- 20 Sqn (Hunter Mk 9)
- Ferry Flight (Hunter Mk 56)
- 11 Sqn (Lightning Mk 6)

Map labels: Turkey, Ankara, Cyprus, Cairo, Caspian Sea, Syria, Iraq, Red Sea, Saudi Arabia, Tehran, Iran, Bahrain, The Gulf, Sharjah, Pakistan, Karachi, Jamnagar, Arabian Sea, Agra, Delhi, Chekari, Calcutta, India, Madras, Sri Lanka, Gan, Bay of Bengal, Bankok, Butterworth, Singapore after nearly five hours in the cockpit on the leg from Bahrain, I was somewhat disturbed to find the starboard undercarriage failing to respond when I selected 'down'. Normally a reassuring 'clunk' could be heard as the wheels locked down, quite apart from the indication given by the undercarriage lights in the cockpit, but I heard only one main wheel lock and I knew without having to look that I would have one main wheel green light and one red. The advice in Pilot's Notes was that a landing should not be attempted in the Lightning unless both main wheels were locked down as it was suspected that the aircraft would cartwheel if one were not. While my number two landed I flew low and slow over the air traffic control tower for a check. This brought the information that the starboard wheel was out of its housing in the wing by several inches but that was all. I tried a further couple of selections up and down but without improving the situation. I could not see any logic in attempting to blow the undercarriage down using the emergency air bottle (charged at 1,000 psi) as there was nothing apparently wrong with the normal hydraulic system (charged at 3,000 psi), but I tried it anyway. The final, and I felt quite useless, piece of advice that I got from the laconic Lightning pilot pre-positioned in the tower at Gan to advise on emergencies was: 'Eject over the lagoon, there are fewer sharks there.' At this point I decided to ignore the 250-knot speed limit for flying with the undercarriage down, accelerated to 500 knots and, with a boot-full of rudder, skidded the aircraft away from the recalcitrant wheel. To my great relief this did the trick: the force of the airflow caught it and blasted it down – without apparently damaging it or the other two, or dislodging an over-wing fuel tank. I landed a little tentatively but the wheels and brakes worked as advertised and I came to a safe stop on the runway. The ground crew met me with a tractor, towing arm and undercarriage leg-clamps – and a cold beer. The beer tasted absolutely magnificent. I was more than happy to have avoided a swim in the lagoon.

As a postscript to this mini-drama I might add that my aircraft was ground-tested at Gan and, as is so often the case in the flying business, no fault was found. Mounted on a test-rig, as it was almost immediately, the undercarriage raised and lowered repeatedly without the slightest hesitation. I took the engineers' reassurances on trust and with no (serious) reservations climbed into it the following day and took off for Singapore. Although pilots are well aware that faults that occur in the air can disappear once back on the ground, few are happy without the discovery of the cause and the rectification of any problem that has occurred. And no one likes the implication that he imagined a problem. We had one case on 11 Squadron where a pilot reported a control restriction. No fault was found during the subsequent ground-test and the aircraft was declared fit for flight. However, two flights later the same fault re-occurred. This time the engines were removed to facilitate a thorough check of the control runs and the source of the problem was revealed: a broom-handle had been left in the fuselage, possibly during manufacture of the aircraft, and something had eventually caused it to move into a position where it was interfering with the freedom of control movement.

It was an interesting experience to be back at Tengah in a different aircraft. In the Hunter we stood a fair chance of blundering inadvertently into viciously turbulent and electrically violent thunderstorms if we were flying in any sort of cloud. In the Lightning the hard centres of such clouds showed on the AI and could be avoided. We could also get above a lot more of it more readily. When we engaged in a couple of air defence exercises against the Australians attacking from Butterworth, now equipped with Mirages, the AI gave us mastery over the cloudy conditions that had left us blind in the Hunter. We intercepted all the targets with ease, and it was interesting to see how readily the AI held lock on furiously diving Mirages to the advertised 30 degrees of downward scanner elevation

Leuchars' Station Commander, John Nicholls, came out to visit the detachment and, on his first night, we took him down town to sample the nightlife. No monkey on roller-skates this time but a bunch of light-fingered sarong-wearing girls surrounded us as we went to get into our cars to return to Tengah, clamouring and importuning. I suddenly realised that a fairly substantial sum of money that I had had in my hip pocket had gone, and I very determinedly scanned the sea of faces surrounding us in the hope of recognising the girl who had distracted my attention momentarily by caressing my crotch. Meanwhile, Boss Blucke was desperately trying to persuade us to get into the cars but I, for one, was not going to leave until I had made an attempt to recover my cash. I thought I recognised the likely thief and grabbed her. John Nicholls came to my aid shouting 'Hold her and I'll get the police.' That set up a wail of entreaties from the other girls: 'No, no, no police!' I shook the one I was holding and saw money emerging at her feet from beneath her sarong. I shook harder and continued shaking until I felt that about the right amount had reached the ground. I picked it up and we beat a rapid retreat, much to David Blucke's relief, back to Tengah and a few drinks in the air-conditioned Mess bar – the air-conditioning, incidentally, was a great improvement on the ceiling fans that had whirled rather ineffectually in the bar when I was last there.

The return journey to the United Kingdom, after a month at Tengah, went smoothly as far as the Lightnings were concerned; nothing very serious malfunctioned for once. Just one little thing marred the smoothness: the Victor that George Reynolds and I were flying in company with as we crossed the French coast at Nice suddenly began diving steeply. I thought something catastrophic must have happened and started following it down, asking on the radio what the trouble was, conscious as I did that if there was a serious problem there was little I could do to help. The Victor levelled after losing about 10,000 feet and a rather shaky voice answered my call telling me that they had suffered 'a major electrical failure' and that they were diverting into Orange. As we had filled our tanks just before the incident occurred, there seemed no good reason to go with them, so I told the Victor captain that we would continue as planned to the next rendezvous off the Norfolk coast, and asked him to radio the air-refuelling cell at HQ 1 Group at Bawtry and tell them what we were doing. I then told the controlling French radar station the same thing and asked them also to pass the message to Bawtry.

The weather was good and I had flown the length of France before in an aircraft less well equipped with navigation aids than the Lightning, so I thought nothing of waving farewell to the 'mother-ship' and wishing its crew well. Unfortunately, I had not reckoned with the mind-set at Bawtry, where I think it must have been believed that Lightning pilots should not be allowed out on their own over foreign parts. Perhaps I am being churlish, and

Bawtry was genuinely concerned, but the unscheduled despatch of two Victors to meet us, which they did over Paris with hoses already deployed and fuel ready to flow, was both a bit of an over-reaction and also the cause of a diplomatic row. The French invariably insisted on having any request for military over-flights submitted well in advance and always very severely restricted the areas where air refuelling could be done. It was most certainly not permitted over Paris. Even the act of trailing a hose was unacceptable. I don't know what the reaction was at HQ 1 Group but I had to justify later to my superiors at 11 Group what I considered to have been a perfectly reasonable decision. The important point in all of this, however, was the realisation that should such an electrical failure have occurred in the critical stretches over the Indian Ocean we could have been in a little trouble.

Four days after returning to Leuchars the squadron took up the Northern QRA commitment once more; life had returned to normal. The QRA task came around regularly, with 11 Squadron alternating with 23 and the Phantoms of 43 for a fortnight at a time throughout the year. With just seven pilots on each of two flights plus the Boss,[4] one flight on a day shift and one on a night shift, running a full flying programme could occasionally be a bit tricky. With two pilots in the QRA shed, one possibly in the tower if the weather was dodgy by day and certainly there, weather dodgy or not, during night-flying, it was necessary to do a bit of juggling. Add in absences for leave or sickness and the problem of running a flying programme could become acute. Luckily both 23 Squadron and ourselves were housed within sprinting distance of the QRA shed and so we often used one of the two QRA pilots to mind the shop; and there was often a continuous rotation between the tower, the operations' desk, and the shed in order to get the programme covered and most people airborne during the working period.

There were of course compensations for long hours spent in the shed: Russian long-range maritime aircraft out of the Murmansk area (Bears in the NATO designation) were a pretty constant presence in the Norwegian Sea, patrolling down into the Atlantic, joined on occasion by other types, such as Badger bombers coming cheekily down into the North Sea. Official policy was to show them that we had the ability to intercept them anywhere in the UKADR, which meant the ability to go north almost to the Faroes and north-east to the boundary of the Norwegian ADR. And of course to make the point that we could do it we had to respond to everything that came our way even if we suspected that the Bears were just on their standard weekend jolly to Cuba and back.

The sort of thing we did on a pretty regular basis is exemplified by my experience on Easter Monday morning. I was scrambled just after dawn to intercept two tracks that had been passed from Norwegian radar as they came around the North Cape. As I climbed into the cockpit one of the ground crew was pressing the switch to open the shed doors. As they slid open I could see that the airfield was shrouded in the Haar that had been forecast the night before – the thick North Sea mist that often affected the east coast of Scotland and northern England each spring and autumn. I started, taxied out of the shed, lined up, and accelerated down the runway using the runway lights as they emerged from the mist to steer by and, some 250 nm north of Leuchars, intercepted two Bears. We were required to fly close to and underneath our targets on all such sorties to photograph anything that looked new or different, and this I duly did. Just occasionally we got a cheery wave, or a rude sign, from a member of the crew of an intercepted aircraft, and sometimes at night a bright light might be deliberately shone in the interceptor pilot's eyes but, on this occasion, I was completely ignored.

On the way back the radar people told me that Leuchars was still 'Red', that is, the weather had remained below landing limits. The Haar had not thinned but was lifting into low stratus and it was thought that it might lift enough to allow a landing by mid-afternoon. I diverted to Lossiemouth, which was at that time operated by the Royal Navy, and was slowly, laboriously, and cheerfully refuelled by the jack-tar duty crew there. By 1300 hours there was some hopeful news from Leuchars: the Haar had lifted into low stratus at 200 feet, which was only 100 feet below the laid down minimum that my instrument rating allowed for a GCA in the Lightning. And there was a possibility that the cloud-base might lift further while there was still some warmth from the sun. At this point, however, the question of whether to take off immediately or wait for further improvement in the Leuchars' weather became totally academic: I was scrambled out of Lossiemouth to intercept two targets about to pass between the Faroes and the Shetlands heading north-east. By the time I had caught up with them and had had the required look at them, I was some 400 nm north-west of Leuchars. Whatever the weather was doing back there I was going to have to land as soon as I could to refuel, and that meant Lossiemouth again. Given the slowness of my earlier refuelling session, and the certainty that the stratus would begin to sink as the afternoon cooled, I was going to have to be very lucky if I was to avoid spending the night there. The prospect of living for another night in my immersion suit was not appealing.

In fact I got away from Lossiemouth at 1500 hours. I had spoken to Leuchars and learned that the cloud-base – which had lifted a little – was already down again to 200 feet. However, as the layer of cloud was less than 500 feet thick, and conditions were absolutely smooth with hardly any surface wind and no turbulence, I felt it worth trying a couple of GCAs to see if I could get in. I would have ample fuel to do this and get back to Lossiemouth if necessary. And, as I would be approaching the Leuchars runway from the sea, over a flat beach, I was not unhappy about the cloud-base.

As I neared the airfield on the first GCA I saw the runway approach lights at a little over 150 feet but they were too far off to the left to enable me to make a late correction and land. So I overshot and went round the GCA circuit once more. This time I set up the ILS (Instrument Landing System) and linked it in to the autopilot using the information from the GCA controller as a cross-check and, as 150 feet approached, was delighted to see the runway lights shining through the cloud straight ahead. I think from the shaky sound of the GCA controller's voice on both approaches he had not been a happy conspirator in getting me home below the limits.[5]

A couple of days later the AOC of No. 1 Group, Air Vice-Marshal Ruthven Wade came to talk to us about tanking in general and about our experiences on Exercise *Piscator* (the code name given to our trip to Singapore) in particular.[6] He had also asked for a flight in the T5 to see for himself what the air-to-air refuelling operation was like from the recipients' point of view, and to try his hand at a bit of basket-prodding. As he had not flown in the Lightning before it would have been normal procedure to put him in the right-hand seat. (The aircraft was designed to be operated from the left-hand seat, and not every switch, knob or gauge was repeated on the right; the starting sequence, for example, had to be initiated from the left-hand seat.) However, I felt that if he was to stand any chance of getting the probe in the basket he had better sit on the left, not because the probe was on the left-hand side, but because the throttles for the occupant of the right-hand seat were on the starboard console, a complete reversal of the standard cockpit layout. The pilot in the right-hand seat had to fly left-handed, and this magnified the normal problems of tanking: under pressure to get the probe in it was too easy to find oneself trying to throttle back with the stick and manoeuvre with the throttle.

Remembering my own failure on my first tanking sortie I gave the AOC a very thorough briefing and was pretty confident that I could talk him into the basket once we had settled in position on the tanker. However, I could not, and no amount of demonstrating a steady formation position seemed likely to get him past the situation that I had first experienced. As fuel got low I realised that I was going to have to get the probe in from the right-hand side or go home and I hoped that I wasn't going to fail to do this after all my talking. Sometimes things do go right, however, and it went in first shot. That gave us some more time to get AVM Wade a bull's-eye, which to his great delight, he did.

May, June, July and August passed with nothing out of the ordinary. Just the normal round of training flights, interspaced by one-off activities such as flying some Army officers visiting from the Staff College at Camberley, flight commander's checks on my lot, a couple of fly-pasts, three readiness call-outs; and a visit from the Trappers. The 'normal' naturally covered the very wide range of things that the Lightning could do in the interceptor role – high, low, fast interceptions and visidents, sometimes against targets jamming communications and radar and sometimes against the more sophisticated form of Electronic Counter Measures carried by the more modern bombers, such as 'gate-stealing' where the fighter's radar 'lock' is craftily moved off the real target sufficiently to render the missile head unable to acquire. The training task for the Lightning squadrons was very precisely spelled out and was tailored to the twenty hours' flying time per calendar month funded for each of the pilots on strength. Where this figure of twenty hours came from is probably lost in the mists of time but everything else flowed from it: servicing schedules, the provision of spares, the purchase of fuel, and so on. We had the same hours' allocation per pilot on 247 Squadron but until we got drop tanks we couldn't achieve it. Even allowing for the Lightning's propensity to catch fire – twenty-six aircraft were lost to this cause during the years that the Marks 3, 6 and T5 were in service – and the consequent downtime spent on trying to cure the fire problem, plus a parsimonious decision to hold too few spares at the point of need, it was not impossible to achieve the required total. It did, however, require the willing co-operation of the ground crew and a lot of juggling and hard work.

As time passed and I became more and more at home in the Lightning, I derived increasing pleasure and delight from flying it. It was a thoroughbred. However, it was also a working military machine, and one could not pretend that it was perfect in this respect. For a start, considering how small the United Kingdom-based fighter force was at the time, the Lightning's two-missile load was far short of what it should have been (the Phantom could carry four radar-guided Sparrow missiles and four Sidewinder heat-seeking ones and had the option of carrying a 20-mm Gatling gun in an under-fuselage mounted pod). Secondly, the Lightning's radar was not at all good against low-level targets. Over land it was impossible to distinguish a low-flying target in the clutter produced by ground returns; over the sea, provided the pilot worked like the proverbial one-armed paper-hanger to manipulate scanner and gain, he could expect to 'see' a bomber-sized target flying at, say, 500 feet above the sea, at about 7 nm – and, with a heavy sea state, at less than that. Normal low-level procedure was for the fighter to fly at 3,000 feet looking down, hoping to get a radar lock, and from that to get the missile head to acquire (we permanently carried one practice missile, complete with all the necessary electronics, and a balancing dummy on the other mounting). Visidents at low level were particularly difficult and could only be accomplished by easing down until just above the target's level and then easing out to one side of it, looking for it as one drew abeam. On a dark night it was all too easy to drop too low while concentrating on the AI (and there is probably not a Lightning pilot who has not given himself a fright on taking his head out of the rubber boot, glancing at the altimeter, and seeing it reading very close to zero).

The third weakness was the lowish g specifications that the RAF had accepted for the aircraft. These would have been sufficient had the Lightning only had to contend with hostile bombers but, in Germany, or in the context of the new overseas' reinforcement commitment, where it might have had to meet fighters in combat, they were insufficient.[7] All that said, it was a superbly satisfying aircraft to climb into, lift off the ground in a surge of power, and zoom upwards in a near vertical climb, gloriously 'slipping the surly bonds of earth'.

We could, and did, practise air combat in the Lightning in spite of the g limitations and its consequently wide turning circle, though we seldom had enough aircraft available to do much more than fly one aircraft against another, an exercise referred to in the fighter business as '1 V 1'. Occasionally we got the opportunity to practise against a Hunter or a pair of 43 Squadron Phantoms. We could not out-turn a Hunter in a level turn, and the ability of the Phantom to call a kill with the Sparrow missile out of range of our weapons was frustrating. However, our power gave us the ability to out-accelerate and out-climb a Hunter type fighter, zoom up and pull down hard using gravity to tighten the turn – a tactic that was also the only way that we could get anywhere near, say, a hard-turning Vulcan at height. The object, in all of the combat exercises, was to record a missile 'kill' and this required the interception to have the right parameters for the missile to acquire and for it to be 'fired' within its range brackets. A second radar-scope, in combination with a camera to film what the scope showed, was situated in the spine towards the Lightning's tail and thus it was possible accurately to assess the success or otherwise of a claimed 'kill'. We could also sometimes see during a combat that the opponent's airborne claim was unjustified. Flying one day against Terry Butcher, a member of my flight, I was so convinced that he had made an erroneous claim that I yelled out: 'Balls! Keep fighting!' For some reason he thought this exhortation worth introducing to the flight and it became a bit of a catchphrase used from then on in a wide variety of situations – but especially if someone got behind another in air combat.

In September I took my flight to Rygge, in Norway, on one of the NATO exchanges that had long been a generally welcome part of squadron life. We spent eight days sampling the way the Royal Norwegian Air Force approached fighter training and testing NATO's success at ensuring that we could operate in each other's environment. On the first night our hosts very hospitably entertained us to dinner in their Mess. The main course comprised nothing but crab. The Base Commander, in welcoming us, proudly stated that the unit had sent an aircraft to Bodø in northern Norway earlier that afternoon for the sole purpose of bringing back fresh crab for us. Unfortunately I dislike crab and so was somewhat apprehensive about how I was going to show my appreciation of our hosts' generosity. At the table each British officer was flanked by a Norwegian officer charged with showing us how to tear open the crabs and avoid the poisonous lungs. I was just mopping my brow having forced down two when the door from the kitchens burst open and Mess orderlies emerged bearing more platters piled high with the beasts. 'Good!' declared the Base Commander. 'Give them to the British. They do not often have the chance for this pleasure.' The following morning I spent the entire local flying-briefing wondering if I could get through it before having to dash out. I have since had to add crab to my list of disliked foods along with pork pies.

For the rest of the detachment only two things stick in my memory. The first is the displeasure that showed on the faces of the Norwegians who were in the Mess bar with us on our penultimate evening when we were joined by two *Luftwaffe* pilots, stopping overnight on a NATO 'land-away'; clearly the memories of wartime occupation had yet to fade completely in Norway. The second thing was an illustration of how an assumption might have produced an accident. I had led two other aircraft, one piloted by Brian Fuller, and one by our French exchange pilot Michel Pochoy, on a PI sortie plus a practice diversion to Stavanger. While we were airborne the weather deteriorated at Rygge (it was the Haar season there; the very word is Norwegian) and, reluctant to leave either of the others to carry out an instrument approach alone I called them both into close formation, one on either side of my aircraft. The standard procedure in the RAF is for the number two to come into formation on the starboard side with the number three automatically slotting in on the port side. Before descending I briefed them to call if either failed to get a brake 'chute on landing, or had trouble with their brakes, explaining that I would move ahead of the other one, and to one side, to let the faster-moving aircraft pass. We broke cloud at 300 feet and landed, happily without any problem. During the subsequent de-brief, however, I discovered that the number three, Michel, had moved in on the starboard side (as the French Air Force had no similar standard formation numbering), and Brian, without demur, had moved in on the port. Had one of them called a braking problem I would have moved the wrong way. Of course, I should have specified which side I wanted each on and not assumed they would follow the standard practice. A small thing, perhaps, but then flying accidents so often result from the smallest or simplest of things coinciding at the wrong moment.

Back at Leuchars, and moving into the shorter days of winter, we were able to start the night-flying periods earlier – in high summer it didn't get dark in Scotland much before midnight and genuine night-flying was difficult to come by unless one was prepared to fly into the small hours and risk alienating the local populace. In winter we could have a productive session of night-flying and get to the Mess in good time for the traditional, and much loved, 'night-flying supper' of eggs, bacon, fried bread, beans and a pint or two of best bitter. This was a not-to-be-missed way of winding down after two or three, or sometimes four, adrenaline-producing trips in the dark. We all felt the need for the wind-down, perhaps because there was something not entirely natural about emulating bats, or possibly because landing a Lightning at about 200 miles per hour in the dark was more of a closely controlled crash than a nicely judged touchdown. But, for some pilots the wind-down was not enough to wipe out the stress they were obviously feeling about operating in the dark: one member of my flight asked to speak with me privately as he was about to walk out to get airborne one night and confessed that he simply could not do it; he could not face going up at night again. Another, a very experienced Lightning pilot, got to the take-off point, found he could not bring himself to open the throttles, and taxied back in almost on the point of breaking down. And, for one young first-tourist on 11 Squadron, it was not just the dark that was the problem: he had what seemed to be a panic attack during a daylight flight, calling out to Wally Hill, the leader of the pair, as they were about to complete a sortie at height that he could not distinguish up from down. He was totally mentally disorientated and it was only when Wally came into close formation with him, and he had that reassuring point of reference, that it proved possible to lead him down and back for a landing; subsequently his state of panic developed to the point where he couldn't bring himself even to climb into a passenger plane. While I am certain that all who fly feel some apprehension before take-off – it is the essential ingredient for self-preservation – I cannot recall the same level of stress in the Hunter world. Perhaps the Lightning really was a 'man's aeroplane'; luckily there were plenty of men willing to fly it.

Time passed, with 'ordinary' squadron activities interspaced with spells of QRA – and lots of dark time. As we got into December, and the time approached for us to record on our annual report forms, the 'thirteen-sixty-nines',[8] the hours we had flown during the year, and state our preferences for our next posting, I felt that I ought to take some advice about the latter. In truth, I wanted to ask for command of a squadron but as that request was likely to be seen as premature, and possibly presumptuous, I might simply be wasting an opportunity to ask for something that would be interesting as well as obtainable. We had a new Boss, Jeremy Jones, who had taken over from David Blucke in November. He had done a tour in the Air Secretary's Department and therefore should, I felt, be able to give me a useful steer and, because he was so new in the job, be able to do so without thinking that I was asking for a personal assessment or importuning for a recommendation.

'How long have you been a squadron leader?' Jeremy asked. When I told him that my seniority was within a month of five years he said 'It's a bit early for you to hope for a squadron but I would ask anyway. You would be amazed how few people actually do that.' When I expressed surprise at this, saying that I would have expected that commanding a squadron would have been at the top of every middle-ranking officer's wish list, he said 'No, people will take it if it comes along, but generally they are nervous about asking for something that might prove to be dangerously testing.' I thought that just a little odd, but thanked him for his advice and asked for a squadron.

In January I was sent to the Air HQs at Episkopi, Cyprus, via Brize Norton and a VC-10 trip, to act as advisor for the return flight through Cyprus of No. 5 Squadron on its way back from a Singapore deployment. I was briefed beforehand at HQ 11 Group and, in passing, thought it slightly odd of the Senior Air Staff Officer to tell me that it would be in my interests to see that the squadron got back safely. As it happened the flow through Cyprus went smoothly, apart from my having to put a bit of pressure on one member of the squadron to persuade him that unserviceable AI was not an obstacle to getting airborne to get his aircraft home.

In March I took my flight to RAF Valley in Anglesey to the Missile Practice Camp there. Valley's prime role was as an Advanced Flying School, constantly buzzing with training aircraft, but in one corner of the airfield there was a collection of huts, a small hangar, and a concrete hardstanding large enough to accommodate a squadron of fighter-sized aircraft. Some sand dunes on the seaward side of the hardstanding provided the necessary safe backdrop for the live missiles with which the firing aircraft were armed. There was a small staff of instructors, and some armourers to supplement those that squadrons brought with them. The MPC worked in conjunction with the Royal Aircraft Establishment airfield at Aberporth, which was equipped with the radar and computer equipment needed to control activities on the Aberporth Range, including the radio-control of pilotless target drones against which the missiles were fired. The range extended over a wide area of the Irish Sea beyond Cardigan Bay. The drones were based at Llanbedr, further up the coast from Aberporth. As with all weapon firing programmes a number of things had to coincide for a successful missile firing: there had to be serviceable drones and acceptable surface winds at Llanbedr for their launch, serviceable radars and computers at Aberporth, the range reasonably clear of shipping, and flyable weather and a fully functioning airfield at Valley.

Frustratingly, in twelve days we got no further than practice runs on the range, as the necessary coincidences did not occur. A more successful approach to missile firing, and one that tied squadron aircraft up less than the set-piece deployments to MPC, was the odd deliberate scramble of one of the QRA aircraft to the range. This was possible when everything was right for a firing, there was a free time-slot, and the selected pilot had already qualified on the range but had not yet fired his allocated one missile per tour. Had there not been a requirement for prior qualification we might have saved the cost of running the MPC.

Halfway through April Leuchars' Station Commander, by now Neville Howlett, called at the squadron. He took me aside, and told me that he had just had a call from 11 Group to say that I was to be posted to command No. 5 Squadron at RAF Binbrook at the beginning of June as an acting wing commander. I could not have had a more pleasing bit of news, particularly as 5 Squadron was one of the three Lightning Mark 6 squadrons in the United Kingdom. I had not read any particular meaning into SASO's comment in January but now I realised that he might have been dropping a hint without going so far as breaching the RAF's preference for confidentiality in these matters.

The rest of my time on 11 Squadron went rapidly and ended with a fair number of parties and the usual farewell formal dinner night. However, the thing that touched me most in this pre-departure round was the presentation to me by my flight of a cigarette lighter engraved 'Keep Fighting'. 'I was going to have "Balls" engraved on it too,' explained Terry Butcher, 'but I chickened out as you might have thought it inappropriate.' I most certainly would not have done.

Notes

1 The command of Lightning squadrons began to be upgraded from squadron leader to wing commander in July 1965.

2 The RAF had ordered an air-to-air refuelling system in 1944 for a force of Lancasters preparing to deploy to the Far East (cancelled when Japan surrendered). It was cumbersome (a grappling-hook was fired by the tanker at a line trailed by the receiving aircraft and, contact hopefully made, a hose would be hauled across between the two aircraft). The RAF was very slow to recognise new developments in air-to-air equipment. Sir Alan Cobham had produced a hose and drogue (or basket) system in the late 1940s, which the Americans bought and used extensively during the Korean War. The RAF, awakening late to its merits, decided in 1954 to give the new V-force an air-to-air refuelling capability. In 1956 a Valiant squadron (No. 214, commanded by Wing Commander Michael Beetham) worked closely with Cobham on the RAF trials of the system and the Valiant, with one under-belly hose, became the RAF's first tanker. After the Valiant was grounded by fatigue failure in 1964 the Victor K2 took over the role. In addition to the belly hose

(which had been developed on the Valiant to allow the large V-bombers to refuel) the Victor was fitted with a refuelling pod under each wing thus allowing two fighter-sized aircraft to refuel simultaneously.

3 Ironically, not long after this incident, the rubber boots were replaced by waterproof fabric socks vulcanised to the bottom of the immersion-suit thus allowing leather flying-boots to be worn.

4 Before the Sandys cuts fighter squadrons had been larger. The 16 aircraft we had on Number 247 squadron was the norm, and our pilot strength averaged 21.

5 The GCA display consists of two airfield radar-produced pictures. Each shows the position of an aircraft on the approach path, one giving horizontal displacement of the aircraft and one vertical displacement above or below the glide-slope. The GCA controller keeps up a patter telling the pilot where he is in relation to the horizontal and vertical ideal. The pilot adjusts accordingly. With experience and practice it is possible to fly a GCA approach very accurately. The other system, the ILS, transmits approach path information automatically and this activates the installation in the aircraft. In the Lightning two needles on the main compass/navigation display showed horizontal and vertical displacement; the pilot had to fly to centre these in a small ring. It was possible to select 'Automatic ILS' in the Lightning, something rarely found in a fighter-sized aircraft; this facility enabled the autopilot to fly the approach while precisely maintaining the speed set by the pilot at the beginning of the procedure Oddly, the minimum approach height for an ILS in the Lightning was 100 feet higher than that for a GCA.

6 Invariably referred to by our ground crews as 'Piss-taker'.

7 The 1957 Defence White paper (Mr Sandys again) imposed restrictions on the design of the Lightning decreeing, among other things, that the aircraft would have no use outside the UK.

8 The Form 1369.

CHAPTER FOURTEEN

Squadron Commander

Binbrook, perched on the Lincolnshire Wolds, was known for its miserable winter weather and its semi-isolation. However, when I got there on 1 June 1970 the sun was shining, I was full of anticipatory pleasure at having my own squadron, and Binbrook could have been in Siberia for all I would have cared. Siberia? Well maybe that's taking anticipatory delight too far, but I was very much looking forward to running my own show.

Besides 5 Squadron's Lightnings, Binbrook was home to a Canberra squadron, No. 85. This was an odd mix as the two aircraft were so totally different in terms of the technical support they required from the Station, in their operating requirements, their age, their roles and their capabilities. At Leuchars, the existence of another Lightning squadron, and a Phantom squadron, had provided compatible outfits that allowed all to establish a competitive, and friendly, rivalry – and, in the case of 23 Squadron, get and give some mutual support. I asked the Station Commander, Group Captain Mel Shepherd, during my arrival interview, how the two outfits got along together. 'Just fine,' he said, before asking me to shorten the flagpole that stood outside 5 Squadron's crew-room as it was three feet taller than the one outside 85 Squadron.

When one takes charge of something it is an unquestionable advantage to find that it is ailing, or at least has not been a success story. It is then relatively easy to show an improvement. Eight months earlier 5 Squadron had been very ailing and the squadron commander had been removed prematurely. George Black, coming to the end of his tour at Coltishall, had been put in as an emergency stopgap to pull the squadron up to scratch. Now, on the point of George's departure, and following a successful squadron deployment to Singapore and a win in the 1970 AFCENT Air Defence Competition, things were on the up and up and morale was high. I was taking over from a very successful and popular predecessor.

The unfortunate who had got the boot had himself been preceded by a squadron commander who had gone all out to squeeze as many hours from the aircraft as he could each month – a policy that will always be popular with the hour-hogs among the pilots but irritates the ground crews and screws up the aircraft-servicing schedule. It doesn't take a great deal of wit to work out that the most sensible *modus operandi* is simply to aim to complete the syllabus of training flights as specified by Group, and get the annual hours' total. This should be the proverbial blinding glimpse of the obvious, and most saw it. However, with bad weather, unserviceable aircraft, pilot sickness, and the unexpected occasionally getting in the way it was not always easy to achieve either. I was determined to have a good try, and I felt that it would be wise to start by making this clear to all the squadron personnel, officers, NCOs and airmen.

So, on my first day at Binbrook I had everyone assemble in the hangar, climbed on a chair, and set about explaining how I intended to run the squadron. I told them that I would not seek a single hour over the required 3,600 per calendar year, but I would want to get a few more than 300 each month so that we could approach December – the end of the training year – and the Christmas break with a few hours to spare. I would play fair with them, I said, and stand up for them should outside influences press too hard on them. However, and I emphasised this, they should understand that I would not accept anything less than 3,600 hours, and they would stay in the hangar and on the flight line until I got what we needed each month. As I spoke, I looked about the group clustering around, trying to assess reactions. All eyes were on me; all faces totally blank. I got no response at all, and I wondered if I was wasting my time. I hoped I was not.

That night, shortly after midnight, I was awakened by the telephone ringing beside my bed. It was a 5 Squadron airman, sounding very drunk. He wanted me to intercede with the RAF police who had hauled his mate off to the guardroom for fighting in the NAAFI club. 'Sorry to be ringing you Sir,' he slurred, 'but you said in the hangar that you would stand up for us.' God, I thought, somebody listened – but what message did I get across today? 'Standing up for you,' I explained, trying to avoid an edge of exasperation creeping into my voice as I spoke 'does not mean that I am going to get up in the middle of the night to bail people out whenever they get into a scrap. Now, bugger off to bed and I'll look into this in the morning.' Happily I had no more nocturnal disturbances from the airmen; but there remained a risk from some of the pilots – and particularly from the squadron's two practising miscreants, Ali McKay and Chris Coville (who tried hard, but couldn't quite hide the talent that eventually took him to the rank of Air Chief-Marshal), looking for someone to serve them bacon and eggs in the post-Mess-party hours.

The thing that I found I was really going to have to concentrate on straight away, if I was to come anywhere near meeting the syllabus requirements, was night-flying. Half of the training year had gone by – and with it the long dark spells of the early months of the year – but less than a quarter of the required night hours had been achieved. George Black had rightly concentrated on the short-term needs of the situation he had found: raising morale, getting the engineering right, and pulling out the stops to win the AFCENT competition. Now, however, it was time to try and get back on to the normal training schedule. As Binbrook was not a Master Diversion Airfield it was not manned for twenty-four-hour a day operations, and so pushing hard at night-flying in the summer months meant asking for a lot of extra hours of work from all manner of support staff. This involved sweet-talking Wing Commander Engineering for technical support, Wing Commander Administration for the provision of medical and catering cover, and Wing Commander Operations[1] for ATC staff and the Station fire crews. Years afterwards, when I had an opportunity to see some of the monthly reports written by Bill Maish, the man in charge of operations wing throughout my time as squadron commander, I found that he frequently mentioned in them the efforts that he had to make to maintain the peace between 5 Squadron executives and those who thought the squadron was demanding too much from them. He said nothing to me directly during my time in charge. If he had, I would have bought him a beer, and pressed on.

As always on squadrons, normal syllabus work was going to be interrupted, sometimes disrupted, but more often made more pleasurable, by a variety of additional items. At the beginning of July, for example, we flew a nine-ship formation to mark the award of the Freedom of Grimsby given earlier to the Station; engaged in a ship protection exercise which involved flying CAP, supported by tankers, some 250 nm north-east of Binbrook; and sent six pilots and four Mark 6s on a NATO exchange to Beauvechain in Belgium. I flew Mel Shepherd over to Beauvechain in the T5 to pay the detachment a visit, which gave me an opportunity to see how things were going there, and Mel an opportunity to try his hand at handling the Lightning – and decide to stick to Canberras. At the end of the month I had another brief continental holiday when I took a Mark 6 to Bruggen over a weekend, accompanied in another by one of the two flight commanders that I had inherited, Jerry Seavers. I had not seen Jerry since I left 20 Squadron where I had known him as a young, cocksure, second tourist, one of the prima donnas from 92 Squadron's aerobatic team – and a naturally gifted pilot. I was now interested to discover if he had matured into a responsible executive, and was very pleased to find that he had. The other flight commander, Barry Holmes, was a steady, dependable, Cranwell Sword of Honour winner, with an engagingly quiet sense of humour. I was lucky to have them both.

July, and part of August, were characterised by a large number of major component changes and a seemingly endless round of modifications, all part of a determined attempt to reduce the number of Lightnings being lost as a result of fires in the air. In fact, the series of initiatives that this – the Fire Integrity Programme – continued to produce throughout my time on 5 Squadron put a tremendous burden of work on the hangar crews, sometimes almost more than one felt they should have to tolerate. This was particularly true on two occasions, both on Friday evenings after work had stopped and everyone had gone home, when an order came from Strike Command to take the engines out, do a bit of intricate work on fuel pipes, and get the aircraft serviceable by Monday morning. I joined them in the hangar in sympathy, but also to crack the whip had that been needed. There was a lot of grumbling, but the work was done.

On 8 September, at 1930 hours, a NATO Tactical Evaluation Team suddenly appeared on the Station and declared us to be at 'readiness for war'. As usual there was a rush of activity to get the maximum number of Lightnings serviceable, and live missiles out of the 'bomb-dump' and onto the aircraft. The preparatory phase achieved – we got six aircraft armed and ready within two hours – the 'war' phase started. As darkness fell our USAF exchange pilot, Captain Bill Schaffner, was brought to cockpit alert. An experienced pilot, he had been with us since March but still needed to complete a few sorties before being formally declared 'Operational' by the squadron. I assessed him to be competent to take part in the flying phase of the Taceval, and authorised him to do so. After an hour in the cockpit he was scrambled but, before he reached the take-off point, the scramble was cancelled. Returning to dispersal he ordered the ground crew to 'top up the fuel' but, once again scrambled, he started the engines and began to move before the turn-round servicing required by the rules had been completed. He climbed to 10,000 feet and, on being handed over to the MRS at Patrington, was told to accelerate to Mach 0.95 to intercept and shadow a low-flying target then at 28 nm range from him. What he was not told was that the target was doing a mere 160 knots. He called 'contact' when he had picked it up on AI and went on to say that he had 'to manoeuvre to lose speed'. Very shortly after, he hit the sea about 200 yards behind the target, a Shackleton, whose crew saw his lights go out. With a shaky start, a need to lose a lot of speed as he hurtled towards a low and slow target, Bill Schaffner fell foul of the dangers of low-level work in the dark.

I was strapping into a Lightning to come to readiness when Mel Shepherd came up its ladder and called me out of it to go and break the news to Bill's wife, Linda. I grabbed Esmé and we went to do what we could in the circumstances. As the hours passed without the searching helicopters or lifeboat finding anything it became more and more obvious that he had not survived. Linda, however, was convinced that he was alive and would eventually be rescued. Esmé and I sat with her through that night and the following day, and every time a vehicle moved on the road outside her Married Quarter she jumped up, thinking that Bill was on his way home. The USAF made arrangements to fly her back to the States a few days later but she wanted to stay, totally convinced that he would turn up. It took a lot of sympathetic persuasion by her friends on the squadron, together with the people sent up from the USAF base at Alconbury, to get her to see that she had to go. When two months later the wreckage of Bill's aircraft was located and raised, and the cockpit was found to be empty, her distress was compounded by renewed hope that he had indeed survived the crash.

It proved possible to deduce a sad sequence of events from the wreckage. Bill had survived the initial impact with the sea, as was shown by the fact that he had attempted to eject. Tragically, by one of those coincidental and terrible misfortunes that can literally make the difference between life and death, his ejection seat did not fire. By design the seat will not go unless the hood has first jettisoned. This should occur as the ejection seat handle is pulled to it full extent, and this had been done. However, the canopy gun had not fired because, as the accident investigators discovered, the firing head had been incorrectly seated.

Bill was clearly determined to survive for he had then opened the hood electrically and released his seat straps. He had also released his dinghy-pack connections, doubtless to help him get free of the seat. The Board of Inquiry concluded that before successfully freeing himself he had probably been pulled too far down by the sinking aircraft, may have become unconscious, and may never have reached the surface. Linda's uncertainty and distress cannot have been helped by articles later published in both the Grimsby *Evening Telegraph* and the Hull *Daily Mail,* mentioning the empty cockpit, connecting this with alleged sightings of 'bright lights' and UFOs, and reporting local loony claims that Bill had been abducted by aliens.

September passed into October and on the 9th, because we had hit a patch of excellent serviceability, and because I felt that it would be good to show the ground crew the fruits of their efforts in the air, we flew eleven aircraft in a figure five configuration. It was quite a difficult formation to get right as numbers two and three had to fly a fairly wide line abreast on the leader. We put up a twelfth aircraft to tell us how we were doing and to get us into a neat figure '5' before we flew over the airfield. A bit of swank, I know, but it was great for squadron morale. The following day we took over the Southern QRA. And it was back to pretty standard stuff.

One other event in October, which we were delighted by, was the fitting of the first twin 30-mm Aden gun pack to one of our Mark 6s. A modification programme had been under way since the beginning of 1969 to prepare the aircraft on the Mark 6 squadrons for the packs and now they were being delivered. The two guns together with 240 rounds of ammunition were mounted in a redesigned front compartment of the aircraft's 600-gallon ventral fuel tank for the loss of just 170 gallons. John Ward, the squadron IWI, went off to check out the guns by firing into the sea. While the new gun pack may not have been the complete weapons' enhancement that many would have wished, the provision of guns recognised, at last, that missiles alone might not be enough for either a sophisticated ECM environment or for a fighter V fighter dust-up abroad.

Meanwhile, back to missiles. We went to Valley on 15 November with six Red Tops to fire. It was a bad time as the weather was very poor and Aberporth's radar was unserviceable for the first fortnight. While we waited for range slots to be allocated to us I decided to press on with normal syllabus flying – a bit of a gamble as it was imperative that we kept enough aircraft serviceable and ready to fire should the call come. We even persuaded Valley to keep the airfield open on a couple of evenings so that we could get a few night hours. One night the weather was particularly dodgy with the severe thunder storms around and about. I sent Jerry Seavers to the ATC tower to keep an eye on the storms and we achieved what we set out to do, albeit at the cost of losing some goodwill from a rather shaken IWI, fresh from descending through one of the thunder clouds.

Towards the end of the detachment all fell into place: we were allocated two slots on the range and were able to fire five missiles, and so went home happy. The sixth missile was fired off a QRA scramble a few days after we got back to Binbrook.

By mid-December, a couple of weeks before the end of the training year, we had achieved the 3,600-hour annual task, and completed the syllabus requirements. I was thus able, and glad to be able, to fulfil my promise to let the squadron quietly stand-easy in the run up to, and over, the Christmas period.

11 Squadron Officers in February 1970. Standing, left to right: Graham Clarke, Mike Lawrance, Terry Butcher, John Calnan (SEngO), the author, Jeremy Jones, Alan Taylor, Derek Nicholls, George Reynolds, Brian Fuller and Tony Doidge. Kneeling: Tom Parkinson (JEngO), Ian Martindale, Steve Gyles, Terry Bushnell, Pete Debney and Ian Frost.

New squadron commander with his squadron executives; Barry Holmes, Jerry Seavers, and Bob Jones.

The squadron signature "Big Five".

The 1971 AFCENT competition team (in immersion suits): Bill Tyndall, Ken Jones, Ali McKay, Ross Payne, John Ward and John May.

Mrs Elizabeth Dacre presenting the Dacre trophy.

5 Squadron pair taking off from Akrotiri for an air-to-air firing sortie.

Champagne after the author's final flight on 5 Squadron. It was flat. Also in the picture, from left to right are: Captain Mike Lanning USAF, Tim Guvain, Tim Nelson, Mal Gleave, John May, Laurie Anderson and Jock Byrne.

(Left) The new Station Commander, Leuchars, trying out his desk.

(Below) The "Ark" Hanger. Note the Station's white-painted buildings, all in need of being toned-down – and the proximity of Leuchars' village just beyond them.

The C-in-C, Strike Command, ACM Sir Andrew Humphrey with, members of 43 Squadron in November 1973. The squadron's CO, Jeremy Cohu (next to the C-in-C) was in the process of handing over to his successor (opposite), Keith Beck.

Visit by the Second Sea Lord, Sir Derek Empson, 25th February 1974. I think Mike Layard is wondering if he needs to whisk Sir Derek away for a piddle.

The auther landing on HMS *Ark Royal* in a Phantom of the PTF, June 1974.

AOC's Inspection, June 1974. AVM Bob Freer inspecting the PTF.

The author after landing on *Ark Royal*, with the Flight Deck Officer Lt Cdr Pete Sheppard and the COs of the PTF, Andy Walker, and 892 Squadron, Bill Peppe.

Visit of the head of the French Air Force, General Maurice Bret, October 1974, seen here in one of Leuchars' "Embry Follys".

43 Squadron Phantom intercepting a Bear. (Crown Copyright/MOD) (Stewart Scott)

Harriers of the Gutersloh Wing in hides at Sennelagar. (Paul Jackson)

Jaguars showing their long-range tank fit.

The author after his first Jaguar flight, with Wing Commander Peter Johnston the CO of Number 17 Squadron.

The author about to fly in the Berlin Control Zone.

(Above) Looking at the Berlin Wall from the back of the Reichstag with the Brandenburg Gate to our right. With the author is Esmé, the Station Commander, Gatow, Dave Loveridge, the author's ADC, Ian Jenkins, and two members of the Reichstag.

(Left) The author with Esmé and Julia at the Klienike Brücke.

The author with Major General V. Myescheryakov, COS of the Soviet Air Forces in East Germany.

The author with Brigadier-general Golytsin and the members of SOXMIS at Bunde.

Carrying out an AOC's Inspection at Gatow.

The C-in-C of the Army Air Force of the Chinese Peoples' Republic visiting Bracknell.

The author laying a wreath at the tomb of Muhammad Ali Jinnah, Karachi.

The author being shown over the Peshawar museum.

The face at the window. Tail-end gunner in a Badger.

Commandants and guests at the joint staff college dinner in the Painted Hall at Greenwich, 1985. The CDS, Field Marshal Sir Edwin Bramwell was the guest of honour. The two senior airmen are (on the left) the CAS, Sir Keith Williamson, and (on the right) C-in-C Srike Command, Sir Peter Harding.

January saw us starting to prepare for the 1971 AFCENT Competition. I had been left in no doubt by Strike Command that we must attempt to win it again but, also, that we must not expect the considerable level of support that had been provided for the 1970 event, the first year that Strike Command had decided to compete. The rules too had been changed since the previous year and had been made more stringent – for example, in 1970, interceptions had to be completed within 300 seconds, but this time every second to completion was going to be counted. The tactics that had enabled the squadron to win in 1970 were clearly going to have to be changed quite drastically. I made John Ward responsible for tactics and training, and Jerry Seavers overall Project Manager. I charged Barry Holmes with the rather difficult task of ensuring that pilots not in the running for selection for the competing team, mainly the newcomers on the squadron, would not miss out on flying while the lion's share of effort went into training for the competition.

John Ward went over to Patrington and sorted out with the controlling team there – and particularly with the advice and assistance of Flight Sergeant Lofty Weatherill, who had been heavily involved in the previous competition, and was an instinctively good Fighter Controller – how we were to tackle the airborne side of the event. This was divided into four phases: day low-level; day subsonic; night subsonic; and day supersonic. Each competing squadron would be required to fly two pairs on each phase. Our low-level interception phase was to be sited over the lumpy Yorkshire Moors and would have to be tackled by scrambling to set up a CAP across the 10-nm wide corridor that the target could appear in; the essential visual sighting would be very dependent on where the fighters were on the CAP when the target came through, and on the level of visibility 'on the day', but we were confident that our ability to accelerate the Lightning in a matter of seconds from a low-level loiter speed of 300 knots to the permitted maximum (short of going supersonic) of 600 knots would more than compensate for late pick-ups. Film of missile acquisition and 'launch' had to be delivered to the competition judges after the sortie. To help with the low-level work-up Bill Maish acquired, and had sited in the Moors, a mobile radar (of much the same capability as the one we had at Chiang Mai but, nevertheless, just what was needed).

On the high-level phases the AFCENT people at Patrington would give the nominated fighter-controller the go-ahead to scramble a pair when its designated target entered a box of fixed width but whose length depended on whether the target was subsonic or supersonic. The scrambled pair then had to be controlled so that they were kept at least 5 nm apart from one another throughout the intercept. The first fighter had to be vectored onto the target, ideally at the moment it crossed a 'start-line' depicted on the controller's radar screen, fly past it and call out its identification letters; then and only then could the second fighter be directed in for the 'kill'. As with the low-level phase, film of the attack and 'kill' was essential. Penalty points were accumulated for every second that elapsed from the target crossing the start-line until the kill was made. The difficulty in achieving the minimum time was compounded by the fact that the target was allowed to change heading within the box once it was within 90 nm of the start-line; the change was not excessive but for the controller on the ground, aiming to position the first visually-identifying fighter along the start-line for a perfect 90-degree intercept the moment the target crossed it, any change of heading could make all the difference between the 90-degree being impossibly tight or so slack that precious time would be thrown away on a stern-chase. And, the later the change of heading was made the greater the problem for the controller.

Our opponents were expected to be USAF Phantoms, Mirages, F104s and RAF Germany's Lightning Mark 2As. But, early on in the work-up period, the Mirages, F104s and Lightning Mark 2As withdrew. We had not been too concerned about the first two types, as we knew that the Lightning's radar was more capable than that of either, and we would have welcomed a like-for-like contest with the Mark 2As. However, we were concerned about the capability of the Phantom's AI and the aircraft's ability to 'launch' its Sparrow missiles from a frontal attack on subsonic as well as on supersonic intercepts, and from a greater range on any type of intercept than we could hope to 'launch' our Red Tops. We reckoned that we would have to seek to complete the subsonic interceptions in less than 125 seconds if we were to beat the USAF Phantoms. And we would have to use the Red Top's head-on capability for the supersonic phase – something of a gamble as the relatively short firing range of the missile meant that the 'kill' aircraft would have to be committed to the attack profile before the 'visidenter' had completed his task; any delay by the latter would make it impossible to maintain the required five-mile separation between the two Lightnings.

Our preparations on the ground included the assiduous identification of the best AI radar sets, and ensuring that all of these, and the aircraft that were going to carry them, would be in peak condition for the competition itself, scheduled for mid-April. We did not give up all normal flying training while we practised the AFCENT stuff during February and March as I remained determined to avoid the hard chase after short-falls in the syllabus exercises and in night-flying that had characterised the second half of the previous year – and I didn't want to make Barry Holmes' task impossible. But the competition had to have as much effort as it required and by mid-March we moved out to the Operational Readiness Platforms situated at the ends of the runway.

The competition rules required the nominated aircraft to get airborne within four minutes of a scramble being ordered. A second pair was allowed to start engines as substitutes should either of the first fail to get airborne. Penalty points were given for any failure to scramble and these on top of other things could lose the competition. Pilots were required to be out of their aircraft, and not touching them prior to the scramble. Jerry Seavers organised a horn to sound the order to go, backed up by the waving of a large flag in case anyone was slow off the mark. We practised leaping into the cockpit, dropping into the seat and plugging in the connector for oxygen, communications and anti-g suit with the left hand while getting the Number 1 engine started with the right, pushing the Number 2 start button as soon as the AVPIN burn for the Number 1 was complete, plugging in the leg-restraints and completing strapping in while checking that the engines were lighting correctly and all warning lights were going out. The ground crew member up the ladder would then remove the top ejection-seat safety pins, stow them, shin down, and remove the ladder. Closing the canopy was the signal for the chocks to be removed, and we were off. The pilots finally chosen to comprise the team for the competition itself had worked up to the point where no scramble took any of them more than two minutes from the order to go to the wheels lifting off the ground; and, when we got to the competition itself, the AFCENT people were so surprised by the speed achieved that, after the first scramble, one member insisted on climbing the ladder after the pilot to check that he was actually strapping in fully before moving.

At the beginning of the work-up period we were not achieving anything like the target of 125 seconds that we had set ourselves. By the end of February, despite a series of disruptions to the programme caused by fuel leaks and the Fire Integrity Programme, we were getting around 200 seconds for the subsonics and just a little less for the supersonic profile. Then, in mid-March, the people at Patrington were able to watch the USAF Phantom squadron based in Holland undergoing its competition runs off the Dutch coast, and reported that the Americans were achieving times as low as 90 seconds. Things didn't look good and a practice dispersal exercise called by STC on the 18th while we, and some of the Patrington controllers, were sitting with wet towels around our heads trying to think how we might improve matters, was not a morale booster. By the end of March, when the Commander-in-Chief Strike Command, Air Chief Marshal Sir Andrew Humphrey, paid us a visit, we had improved to just under 150 seconds. He asked me if we were going to win and I told him that we were going to try, adding the warning that 'the USAF Phantoms have achieved much better times than I think we can hope for'. His immediate response suggested that candour was not what he wanted. 'Just make sure you win,' he snorted.

By 19 April, when the AFCENT team turned up to test us, we were still short of our target of 125 seconds but everything else was going well and the 'firers' were consistently meeting the scope steering demands, getting good 'acquisitions', and 'firing' at the right ranges. Over the course of the next four days, while we were put through the phases of the competition itself, the ground crews worked magnificently, the aircraft suffered no unserviceabilities, and the pilots turned in performances that were magical – Ali McKay, for example, controlled by Lofty Wetherill, achieving an incredible sixty-three-second day-subsonic visident. And our concerns about the capabilities of the Phantoms were proved to have been unnecessary, for their times were not as good as Patrington had seen achieved in practice (as low as 95 seconds by one pair on the day subsonic event, but stretching to 300 seconds on the day supersonic one). Both of our pairs came first and second on the day subsonic (118 and 144 seconds) and the day supersonic (120 and 127 seconds) events, and first and third on the night subsonic (136 and 163 seconds) one. All competing pairs were judged equal on the low-level event. Our times, together with our performance in successfully meeting all the other requirements, clinched the competition for us and, for the second year running, the Lightning came out on top.

May started well with a very straightforward MPC. We got the range slots and we got the weather and fired off the allocated five missiles in two weeks. By mid-May four of our Mark 6s had been fitted with the twin 30-mm gun-pack and the modified sight that was part of the deal. However, we were still having problems with fuel leaks on two of the aircraft and a third, due to come to us after major servicing, was held up owing to its failure to satisfy a series of air-tests at the Maintenance Unit doing the work. We finally got it on 25 May and gave it an acceptance check. On the 26th Ali McKay took off in it for a night sortie but about a minute and a half after take-off he got an indication of fire in the Number 1 engine followed by fire-warnings for both reheat areas. He declared an emergency and headed for the coast, climbing to a good ejection height of 10,000 feet. His number two, Merv Fowler, reported a brilliant white flame from the rear end of the aircraft and, with controls starting to malfunction, Ali baled out. He did everything correctly on the way down and, despite the night being particularly dark, was picked up within minutes of climbing into his dinghy by a rescue chopper from Leconfield. The bad news was that he suffered compression fractures of the spine and was flat on his back for several weeks and off flying for several months. When this happened I was down in London sitting my Law Degree finals. I would have preferred to have been on the spot, although there was not anything that I could have done at the time. But I felt responsible for my charges even if I couldn't sit in the cockpit with them. I had at least forced the pilots to confront the problems of going down in the sea by getting them all into Binbrook's open-air swimming-pool in freezing weather earlier in the year to discover how quickly fingers become uselessly numb in very cold water. That might not have saved Bill Schaffner had he been around for it but it might have had some bearing on Ali's text-book survival actions.

The next two months went rapidly by, with two major air defence exercises, several rehearsals for a parade at which the Dacre Trophy for the best fighter squadron in No. 11 Group for 1970 would be presented to us, pushing hard to extract some night-flying from short nights, and working up for the annual inspection by Air Vice-Marshal Ivor Broom, the AOC. We were also busy getting aircraft serviced and ready for a detachment to Akrotiri, scheduled to begin on 29 July, to try our guns out for the first time.

About a week before we set out for Cyprus I got a salutary reminder of one of the disadvantages of losing sight of an opponent in air combat. The prime disadvantage – or incipient disaster in a hostile environment – is that an opponent may get into a firing position unseen. On this occasion Jerry Seavers and I were flying a 1 V 1 sortie. Pulling around in the wide circles that characterised the best that could be achieved in the Lightning, we ultimately both lost sight of each other and, as one should in an operational environment but perhaps not in a training one, we both kept turning hard. Suddenly we flashed past each other, canopy to canopy, less than twenty feet apart, travelling in opposite directions, both doing about 500 knots. Twenty feet closer could have produced an inexplicable loss of two aircraft, not to mention two pilots who should have known better.

We took nine Mark 6s, the T5 and a Mark 1A to Cyprus, getting there in good order and in one hop, thanks to the tanker fleet, and took over Battle Flight the following day from the resident Lightning Mark 6 outfit, No. 56 Squadron. With the arrival of an 85 Squadron Canberra on 5 August we started flying cine sorties on the flag. When a second Canberra arrived later in the month we were ready to begin a full firing programme. In anticipation of this Jerry Seavers and John Ward had been arguing about how best to harmonise the guns. Jerry, a product of the DFCLS during his Hunter days, and John of the post Hunter and therefore post-gun-firing IWI course, each had strong views. I let them argue it out and eventually they reached a consensus. The results we got in the first week of firing were not very impressive (a top score of 10%) and so the consensus shifted. But no great improvement resulted, and we had a final squadron average of less than 10%.

Akrotiri's annual Summer Ball took place halfway through our gun-firing programme. On arrival at the Ball the Station Commander, Air Commodore John Stacey, parked his car, as was his wont, in the Station Commander's slot outside the Officers' Mess. One of my pilots, the worse for a glass or two of Cypriot wine rather foolishly decided that it would be a bit of a joke to remove the Air Commodore's star from the plate on the car, move the car and hide it. Backing out of the parking slot, he ran over some previously unseen glass and punctured a tyre. John Stacey was understandably a trifle upset when he wanted to leave the party, noticed the missing star, and then discovered the puncture – incandescent in fact. The following day, Group Captain Operations, Mike Beavis (later Air Chief-Marshal Sir Michael and, in retirement, a friend), charged with making enquiries by a man convinced that his status and authority had been under attack, came to see me at the squadron to ask if I knew anything about it. I had not known anything until about an hour before his arrival when a somewhat shame-faced lad came to confess and to ask what he should do. I had suggested to him that he really ought to consider confessing to the Station Commander but added that there might be some danger in that action as John Stacey was well known for his wrath. He thought it best not to risk the wrath, and I must confess I was inclined to agree with him. I then had to try and persuade Mike Beavis, without actually lying to him, that it was highly unlikely that any member of 5 Squadron was involved. A couple of days later the Station was subject to a Taceval and, as 5 Squadron was tasked by John Stacey to supply most of its complement of airmen to mount guards in some very unlikely locations for over twenty-four hours, I had to assume that he had his suspicions.

Three days before we were due to leave Akrotiri the squadron engineers had got all eleven aircraft serviceable and ready for the off. To say thank you to them and to end a good detachment on a high note – not to mention cocking a snook at No. 56 Squadron, whose members had been less than hospitable to us as a visiting outfit – we flew our trademark figure five over the airfield. As 56 Squadron had lost a Lightning the previous day when one of its pilots experienced a fire in the reheat section and had had to eject, we should perhaps have been kinder. Unhappily for Barry Holmes, fate struck back via HQ 11 Group when the SASO selected him, in response to a request from the Command HQ at Episkopi, to stay behind and conduct the consequent Board of Inquiry.

Back home we were almost straight away into our own Taceval – happily without incident this time and happily accomplished satisfactorily. And then into several small exercises with the Navy as a lead-in to a major air and sea exercise scheduled for November. We wondered if all of this was an attempt by the Senior Service to disprove the RAF's assertion that we could defend ships from air attack within the cover of the UK air defence region. We were determined to prove that we could. The first exercise involved us in three days of PIs controlled by HMS *Antrim*, cruising about 100 nm north-east of Leuchars. The next was the defence of some ships about 200 nm north of Lossiemouth. Then, on 24 November the squadron was put on standby to deploy to Lossiemouth for the main thing – Exercise *Highwood*. Two days later, just to make life awkward, the Fire Integrity Programme struck again and the ground crew had to remove all No. 1 engine jet-pipes and perform some fiddly work on the fuel system.

On the 30th we flew ten Mark 6s into Lossiemouth and began an intensive eleven days of around-the clock flying. The pace was intense and it is doubtful that we could have kept it up without becoming dangerously fatigued had it not been for the nearby availability of V-force dispersal caravans, all nicely sound-proofed and blacked out and, regrettably, all long-since scrapped.

There were many individual brushes with minor panic, and many hasty fuel calculations as people found themselves at extended distances from usable airfields with no supporting Victor tanker in the immediate vicinity. Flying intensively can court disaster – an accepted risk during wartime operations but less justified during peacetime exercises. Luckily disaster did not strike 5 Squadron and the only RAF loss during *Highwood* was a Buccaneer that caught fire at the take-off point of the main runway at Lossiemouth. The ignition of the Lepus flares that it was carrying rendered the runway unusable for a couple of days but, by sheer good fortune, there was a persistently strong wind blowing during that period favouring the short secondary runway and this allowed us to keep operating. The Navy might have argued that the incident exposed a weakness in relying on shore-based aircraft for ship defence, but we could have taken off from the burnt runway and operated from elsewhere if it had been necessary.

The approach of the end of the training year saw us once again in the happy position of having all syllabus exercises completed and the required hours in the bank. I asked for a formally recognised stand-down to reward the troops for a lot of hard work during the year but perhaps this request was rather naïve. It was refused on the grounds that a stand-down could not be given to one unit alone. As it happened, this didn't matter much as I was able to ease most people away for a few days in the run up to Christmas.

The new year started with yet another bit of necessary work identified by the Fire Integrity Programme: the replacement of fuel system seals in all the aircraft. However, this didn't interfere unduly with the flying programme and we entered February with things going well – at least until the then on-going miners' strike began to affect us. Flying within the RAF was suddenly restricted solely to daylight hours because of the power cuts that were occurring as a direct result of the disruption of fuel supplies to electricity-generating stations. To try and get something extra out of the available daylight hours, and keep a reasonable rate of flying going, I persuaded Bill Maish to open the airfield for flying from 0630 hours while the strike continued. This was not popular with the support services on the Station but they did what was asked of them.

March was not a great deal better than February as it was not until well into the month that we were again able to operate in the dark hours. By the end of March we started to work up for another Akrotiri deployment, with cine work on the flag, only to have this programme disrupted at the beginning of April by yet more fire integrity stuff.

Over 6 and 7 April we flew the usual mix of 9 Mark 6s, one T5 and a Mark 1A directly to Cyprus, again courtesy of the Victor tanker force. As was standard practice, we had the over-wing tanks off the first pair and the aircraft ready for take-off within an hour of landing. I went along to the Station Commander's office to make a courtesy call. John Stacey had gone and had been replaced by Air Commodore David Craig. 'Have we met before?' he asked, in a sort of defensive half-question. Not only had he been my flight commander on 247 Squadron, but he and I had taken turns to drive each other to work on alternate days for the duration of the petrol shortage caused by the Suez crisis in late 1956. I was a little taken aback as I didn't think my appearance had changed so greatly in the sixteen years since then. However, he had barely asked the question before he realised who I was: the Short Service, not highly thought of, Flying Officer that he had known during my first six months or so on 247 Squadron. I couldn't blame him if he was thinking it extraordinary that that particular junior pilot had metamorphosed into a wing commander.

Because the weather in the range area was uncharacteristically cloudy for the first week, and we could not therefore clear the range area visually, we could not get cracking on the firing programme. I took the opportunity to push hard on the normal syllabus exercises and to make up the shortfall in our night achievements – the latter not entirely with the blessing of the occupants of Akrotiri's Married Quarters. Once we did start firing we were eager to see if the ideas that had emerged since our previous detachment, largely from discussions between the Mark 6 squadron IWIs about harmonisation and sighting, would give us better results than last time. Two new flight commanders, Tim Nelson and Tim Guvain, had replaced Barry Holmes and Jerry Seavers. As neither claimed any serious knowledge of gun harmonisation, John Ward's replacement, Mal Gleave, was left in undisputed charge of the harmonisation programme. Our final results were still far below those that had been achieved with the same guns on the Hunter (my best was a miserable 13 per cent) but there was an improvement, and it was welcome.

Shortly before we left for Cyprus we had learned from HQ 11 Group that we had won the Dacre Trophy for the second year running, and that a date for its presentation by Mrs Dacre had been agreed for the week after our planned return to Binbrook. As was usual on these occasions the squadron would have to mount a parade and, as this would require a fair amount of practice in marching and in rifle-drill beforehand, we had no option but to begin the process while we were in Cyprus. I knew that this was going to test sorely the good will of the ground crews, many of whom tended to go into holiday mode on detachment to sunny Cyprus, and most of whom would feel that supporting the demands of the firing programme was quite enough to fill their time. But they did it, and the detachment ended on a high note, with an all-ranks' party in the NAAFI club, an eleven-ship figure five formation fly-past followed by a 4 V 4 session of air-combat, and two days later, with the over-wing tanks fitted, an incident free air-refuelled flight home.

At the party I received something that I felt to be worth more than the two Dacres and the AFCENT Trophy combined. Late in the evening two squadron airmen, their confidence boosted by a lot of beer, lurched up to me. One simply stood swaying in front of me nodding his head as if to affirm something that his partner was about to say. The second poked me in the chest a couple of times to ensure he had my complete attention and then said: 'The lads gave them to you sir, didn't they? They gave them to you. We didn't believe you when you said you would only go for the hours you said. But you did. And we gave them to you, didn't we?' They most certainly had, and I couldn't help thinking that if the entire country's workforce could be motivated to work as hard and as selflessly as 5 Squadron's ground crews had done, and indeed as RAF ground crews have done over the years, Britain would have a sparkling economy. But, that aside, I was particularly pleased to know that my soapbox oratory on my first day had not been in vain.

We were met on landing back at Binbrook by Group Captain Don McClen, who had taken over from Mel Shepherd several months before. 'Have you thought about the Dacre parade?' he asked. 'You haven't got much time to prepare for it.' I had got to know and like Don when we were on the Lightning course together at Coltishall, and while he was in command of 23 Squadron concurrently with my spell on 11 Squadron. And, although I would not have presumed on friendship in any way while he was my boss, I felt I could get away with a tiny bit of cheek in response: 'It's OK Sir, we've done it before,' I replied. He laughed, and riposted: 'Well, you had better make sure you're perfect this time.' We did. We paraded and, later, we flew past with style – and I could not have been prouder of the officers and the men that I had been given the privilege of commanding.

When Esmé and I had first arrived at Binbrook, finding a school for Caroline in the surrounding area had posed a problem and, halfway through my tour there, the small privately run enterprise that we had found and sent her to had failed financially. At the same time Julia, at the age of ten, and rather more seriously determined than her sister to achieve some stability in her young life, decided that she wanted to board. Sending children away to school is not everyone's choice but it is an action that is almost inevitable if the academic turbulence that Service children can suffer as a result of the near constant movement of their parents is to be avoided. We had already had an unhappy experience with Caroline boarding at an independent school in Belfast after returning from Aden. The experiment had not worked as the constant change of schools up until then had put her well behind her contemporaries in age. However, we decided to bite the bullet again and boarded both girls, basing our choice of school at Whitby as much on the east coast location of fighter Stations as on anything else. That worked well while we remained at Binbrook. However, I was now going south at the end of my tour as squadron commander to attend a course at the National Defence College at Latimer in Buckinghamshire – and Whitby was beginning to look very much like the wrong choice.

I had my last flight on the squadron on 17 August – ending with an extremely satisfying high-speed zip at lowish level along a line between the hangar and the flight line building. When I landed, I was met by a group of the pilots, with the two Tims bearing glasses and a bottle of champagne which, when opened, had everyone falling about with embarrassed laughter as it was absolutely flat. The line-crew clustered around too, adding to the levity of the moment by presenting me with a pocket device for checking tyre-pressures, a tongue-in-the-cheek response to the fact that I had invariably insisted on having my aircraft's tyre-pressures checked before I flew it.

I left Binbrook with a great deal of regret. I had reached the end of my hands-on flying career; and, besides, I felt a distinct reluctance to hand over 5 Squadron and its air and ground crew to someone else. But I should confess that I also left feeling a great measure of relief that all had gone as well as it had while the squadron was my responsibility.

Notes

1 On Stations where squadrons were commanded by squadron leaders the Wing Commander Flying was very much the wing Boss. Where the squadrons were commanded by wing commanders this was not the case. The title was then 'Officer Commanding Operations Wing' and the incumbent's authority was diminished by the reluctance of some squadron commanders to accept him as *primus inter pares*.

CHAPTER FIFTEEN

Station Commander

The nine-month course at Latimer provided an excellent sabbatical for officers of my rank from the Navy and the RAF, majors (and some lieutenant-colonels) from the Army, and a few MOD civil servants. There were no foreigners. It was a chance, *inter alia*, to mingle in a very useful joint-Service way, see each slice of the military functioning in its own sphere (we went to sea with the RN, to Germany for a 'field-day' with the Army, and to various airfields with the RAF), exercise our brains on joint-Service problems, and get some bits of illumination on the ways of the MOD. It was also lots of fun.

On 1 July, some eight months into the course, I was both astonished and a little embarrassed to discover that I was being promoted to Group Captain. Astonished because I had only completed one tour as a wing commander and the default was at least two and a half. Embarrassed because I had received the award of the Air Force Cross in the Queen's Birthday Honours List published just a couple of weeks before, and now I was moving past my contemporaries, and some who had been my seniors. While I was still unaware of the competitive atmosphere that I later found to prevail in the higher – and thinner – reaches of the rank pyramid, and the jealousies felt by some if they saw a potential competitor coming up fast behind them on the inside rail, I sensed, quite rightly as it turned out, that my rapid rise would generate some adverse and envious comment. I was in the limelight, and I felt uncomfortable in it.

A few days after the promulgation of the Promotion List the Air Secretary, then Air Chief-Marshal Sir John Barraclough,[1] visited Latimer to speak to the RAF element about their postings. To my further surprise and acute pleasure I learned that I had been selected to command Leuchars with effect from late September. 'You'll need to fit in a couple of refresher flying courses,' he said, 'and you won't have much time to do them for we really don't want to have to delay the date we have set for the handover of command.' I tentatively suggested that a delay would be unnecessary, arguing that by the end of the course at Latimer I would have been less than a year away from active flying and could therefore go directly back to it with little in the way of refresher courses. I added that, as Leuchars had Lightnings and Phantoms, and I had plenty of experience of the first but none of the second, the ideal for me would be to go straight to the Phantom OCU at Coningsby for a short introductory course. And, I said, by avoiding the Jet Refresher Course at Manby and the Hunter follow-on at Chivenor, the Service would save public money. It may be that my point about economy, always a strong motivating force within the MOD, swung the day but, whatever the reason, I went directly to Coningsby for the last two weeks of August. I was made very welcome there by the Station Commander, my former squadron commander, now Group Captain David Blucke.[2] I had what was virtually a bespoke thirteen hours' familiarisation course on the Phantom FG2 – just about enough instruction to enable me to qualify to get into the air at Leuchars, fly safely, and pick up the intricacies of the aircraft as a fighting machine as I went along.

Before setting off northwards I had to visit HQ 11 Group for briefings from various members of the staff and to meet the AOC, Air Vice-Marshal Bob Freer and the SASO, Air Commodore Dave Simmons. The AOC began by asking if I knew a Wing Commander Keith Beck. Beck had been offered to the AOC by the Air Secretary's department as the next commanding officer of No. 43 Squadron and the 11 Group Staff had expressed misgivings about his lack of 'front-line' experience. SASO suggested that I might prefer not to have him. This was my first experience of an officer's career path possibly being adversely affected by staff doubt and I didn't feel at ease with it – though I realised that the management of 11 Group was actually being kind to me by offering me the option to turn down a possibly doubtful squadron commander. I mentioned that Beck and I had gone through flying training together but that I had formed no particular opinion of him then, which I hadn't, and added that I had not come across him since. This was hardly a ringing endorsement. However, as I felt that fairness required him to be given his chance to command, I said that I would be content to have him at Leuchars.

As a final item in my session with the hierarchy of 11 Group the AOC turned to the subject of refresher flying, or rather, my lack of it. I repeated the arguments that I had deployed to the Air Secretary but the AOC was not impressed. He told me that I was to select one of the aircraft types at Leuchars and fly only that. I thought this a bit unnecessarily restrictive but said nothing. Some five years later, when I was myself the SASO at 11 Group, I came across a note that Bob Freer had written on a file directly after meeting me. 'I don't care how good White thinks he is,' he had inscribed, 'he should have been made to do the full refresher courses; no one is to be allowed to avoid them in future.' Perhaps he was right but I felt, and feel, that there are times when the comfortable 'one-size-fits-all' approach needs to be questioned.

Things had changed quite a bit at Leuchars in the three and a quarter years that I had been away. Nos 23 and 43 Squadrons were still *in situ*, but 11 Squadron had been redeployed to Binbrook, and its former hangar, offices and parking apron had been given over to the shore support of HMS *Ark Royal*'s Phantom squadron, No. 892. Leuchars had become 892 Squadron's disembarked base, and the provider of accommodation for those of its families who had chosen to come north with it. Additionally, a rather odd unit, the Phantom Training Flight, had been formed as a sort of mini-OCU to convert naval crews to operate the Phantom. The PTF was nominally a RAF unit, commanded by a squadron leader, Andy Walker, who had, conveniently for the personnel people, switched from flying with the Navy several years before. The Flight was otherwise manned exclusively by naval aviators and ratings. To help the PTF to perform its task the outline of *Ark*'s deck had been painted on the threshold of the eastern end of the main runway, a Mirror Aided Deck Landing System had been installed, and a rapid rewind arrester wire had been stretched across the 'deck' at roughly the right position. The complement of sailors on the station fluctuated between two and four hundred depending on whether the ship was at sea or not. A Senior Naval Officer, Commander Mike Layard,[3] when I first arrived, had been appointed to the Station to see that all things relating to the dark blue went smoothly. They did, surprisingly so, given the Senior Service's distaste for the role of lodger on a light blue unit, and the loss of former size and strength that this pointed up. In fact, with the exception of one sailor on guard duty one night, the naval complement very fully and willingly supported the Station in all its endeavours and activities throughout my time in command, and it was a pleasure to have them there.

Given the AOC's stipulation that I fly only one type of aircraft at Leuchars I decided to stick with the Phantom. Besides, I needed a lot more Phantom hours before I could consider myself to be anywhere near competent in the aircraft. So I told Wing Commander Operations, Mike Gautry, that I would fly with 43 Squadron and the PTF and that he should fly with 23 Squadron. In retrospect, this arrangement was probably unfair to him as he had had minimal experience in single-seat aircraft and virtually none on fighters; he found the Lightning a little intimidating and, although he persevered, he clearly did not enjoy flying it. That is not to say that he was without spirit: he had attracted censure in a previous job by barrel-rolling a communications aircraft, the HS-125, in a moment of *joie de vivre en route* from Gibraltar to the United Kingdom.

The Phantoms in RN and RAF service[4] had been modified to take Roll-Royce Spey 202 engines. The engine intakes were a wider bore than those of the Phantoms produced for the United States military and consequently the fuselages of ours were not as originally designed. The changes took about 20% off the aircraft's original design performance. That not withstanding, the British version of the aircraft had very distinct advantages in the air defence role, particularly as this was now taken to include the defence of ships throughout the United Kingdom Air Defence Region. For a start, in the normal fit that 43 Squadron had adopted (two under-wing drop tanks) the Phantom carried some 17,450 lbs of fuel. To this could be added, without serious restriction to the operating envelope of the aircraft, a belly-mounted drop tank giving a further 3,960 lbs; the Lightning Mark 6's fuel load of 10,608 lbs was under half of this total.[5] Secondly, the Phantom had a man in the back to work the electronics – a division of tasks that certainly took a lot of pressure off the pilot and probably meant greater efficiency in tackling the more difficult targets, such as those evading hard in cloud, or employing electronic defensive measures, or doing both. And, thirdly, with its load of eight missiles, it had the potential to make very cost-effective use of its ability to stay airborne for a reasonable spell, even without air-to-air refuelling.

While flying single seat-fighters I had never felt the need for anyone in the back – in fact I think most people in the single-seat role felt a smug superiority at being able to do it all solo. But now that I was occupying an administrative and representative role, and only flying whenever I could escape from the various demands made on a Station Commander's time, I was content to have a helpful monitor in the back seat.

I wasn't aware what procedures for crew-cooperation had been adopted within the ground-attack Phantom force, or in any other multi-crew aircraft, but on 43 Squadron, the only FG2 squadron in the air defence role at the time, a concept of close 'team' integration had been nurtured. The squadron's idea of creating a feeling of equality in value and responsibility between the pilot and navigator was sound in principle, but it carried with it a risk of undermining the well-tried practice of giving sole responsibility for the safe operation of the aircraft to the captain. In single-seat aircraft the matter was simple: no one but the pilot had responsibility. In 43 Squadron, the responsibility was split by the team-concept because it required navigators to 'help', not merely advise, the pilots in the event of an emergency: the pilot would tell the navigator what was up (usually what was showing on the warning panels in the front cockpit) and the latter would get out the emergency 'flip-cards' and read from them. This lulled at least some of the pilots into feeling that it was unnecessary to work assiduously in the simulator to memorise emergency procedures. The same applied to some of the navigators who, not having to control the aircraft in the emergency situation, could feel that they would have no great problem in reading the necessary response from the flip-cards at the *moment critique*. I was not impressed with the response I got from some of 43 Squadron's navigators when practising emergency procedures in the Phantom simulator – and I don't think that this was because they were in a simulator and not in a real situation where adrenaline might have boosted their reactions. Lightning pilots practised to the point of having the emergency responses as second nature and, as a consequence, were seldom caught out. Possibly, the Lightning's propensity to catch fire spurred their interest in being prepared, and perhaps it could be argued that the Phantom's greater safety record justified the 43 Squadron approach. However, I was not convinced. My suggestion to Keith Beck that he make the point to his crews that teamwork must not replace responsibility did not produce much by way of noticeable change; however a stricter testing procedure in the simulator did.

Later, when I was the SASO at 11 Group, I had to deal with an example of split-responsibility in action. This merely reinforced my misgivings and made me realise that the team concept possibly extended beyond 43 Squadron. It involved a student pilot at the Phantom OCU who was teamed with a staff navigator for a night sortie. Towards the end of the flight the pilot reported an 'air-turbine over-speed' warning-light. The navigator responded by saying: 'One of the turbine warnings just requires you to throttle back, but the other requires you to shut down Number one engine fast – better shut down the engine while I get the flip-cards out and have a look at which is which.' Shutting down the number one engine shut down the electrics – the Phantom had no battery – and to restore them, and specifically, the lighting to the cockpit, required the auxiliary generator to be deployed into the airstream. In trying to do this in the dark the student pilot grabbed the emergency flap-lowering handle, and the flap-jacks, reacting to the pressure of the airstream above the maximum speed for lowering flaps, sprang a leak. The loss of the Number one engine generator lost him, among other things, stability augmentation and electrical nose-wheel steering – nothing too serious in themselves. However, the loss of hydraulic pressure meant that he would have to contend also with a heavy load on the rudder and hence difficulty in kicking the aircraft straight if he had to deal with any cross-wind component as he approached the touchdown point. Steering would still be possible using the toe-brakes on the rudder-bar. In these circumstances the recommended course of action was to lower the tail-hook and catch the threshold wire that by now was stretched across all runways where Phantoms operated. As it happened, on this occasion the damper on the tail-hook did not work as advertised and the hook bounced at the point when it should have caught the wire (the sort of thing known to everyone who flies as 'Sod's Law' or 'being nibbled to death by ducks'). The pilot was about to overshoot and try again – which was the correct thing to do – when the navigator, fearing that the swerving that the aircraft was doing as the pilot fought to steer it on touchdown was going to take them off the runway, decided that he had had enough and ejected.[6] The pilot had just opened the throttles for the overshoot but, thinking that the staff navigator must know something that he did not, followed suit. The aircraft gathered speed down the runway, veered off, struck some obstacles on the V-force dispersal at the end of the runway and ended up as a complete write-off. Now, I know that the pilot was inexperienced, and could have hoped for much more from the navigator, but I suggest that had he been required to memorise the emergency procedures on the basis that they were his sole responsibility he could have avoided the loss of this aircraft. The sad fact is that all he had to do when he first saw the warning light was to throttle back.

From the very beginning of my tour as Station Commander I found that life was never going to be dull. For example, the first night I was in charge, part of the Sergeants' Mess burned down. While answering a string of questions about the fire from Group the following day – questions that I was in no position to answer – and concurrently setting up a Board of Inquiry to determine cause, my PA came in to alert me to the presence in my outer office of a small group of irate locals who had come to protest about disturbingly loud music coming from the Airmen's Club each evening. I escaped from the call to Group and set about placating the noise delegation. They got my sympathy as I had heard the din the night before from my bedroom a mile away from the Club – a din that was probably quite a few decibels above the level that airmen working on aircraft were exposed to, and to counter which the MOD had provided expensive ear-defenders. I promised to see what I could do. A couple of days later I had an angry retired Admiral on the phone to protest about a Comet that he claimed had flown past below the level of his loch-side retirement home. I told him that Leuchars was not an air-transport base, but that I would pass his concern to the appropriate people; I didn't intend to hurry to do so as I couldn't believe that a four-engined strategic transport aircraft would be low-flying in the highlands, but I had to amend that belief when a Comet from the Royal Aircraft Establishment touched down at Leuchars an hour later.

My next, and rather more serious, protester was the Master of St Andrews University. St Andrews was just three miles away across the Eden estuary, a proximity that was unfortunate at the best of times. When a prolonged cold spell established itself in late October with an associated temperature inversion at a height of about 2,000 feet agl, from which sound waves readily reflected, I don't doubt that the noise of aircraft taking off and engines being ground-tested was particularly irritating. Unfortunately the Master made his first protest while lunching in London with a member of the Air Force Board. The latter telephoned me almost immediately afterwards to tell me that we must stop 'over-flying St Andrews' at once. His assumption that we were doing this was annoying as Leuchars' air traffic procedures had been designed to keep aircraft as far from the town as possible. He went on to suggest that I invite the Master to look around the airfield and to have lunch in the interests of mollifying him. I found it difficult to refrain from the shortest of responses as my predecessor had told me that he had tried this tack with the Master several times and had not had the courtesy of a single reply. The Master continued to protest for most of my first year at Leuchars, and continued to ignore all invitations. However, one night in the following year, when poor weather had in fact prevented flying, and no noise whatever was issuing from Leuchars, his wife telephoned me at two in the morning 'to show me what it was like to have one's sleep disturbed'. The next day I got a call from the great man's secretary extending an invitation to the Master's Lodge 'to explain what you are doing to avoid noise over St Andrews'. The invitation included my wife. When we got there, me equipped with all sorts of maps and diagrams with which I hoped to show the efforts Leuchars made to minimise noise, I was greeted warmly by the Master and ushered into a drawing room in which several senior members of the University staff were chatting, drinks in hand. Seeing my maps he smiled disarmingly and waved them aside. 'Never mind all that; no need for any explanations, just come and meet some of my colleagues,' he said. It was a pleasant drinks party and an unspoken apology for a rather inappropriate telephone call. I had no further protests from him – but he never did get around to answering any invitations.

Without question one of the great pleasures of commanding a flying Station is to be able to shove aside the files when nothing out of the routine of Station life is expected and to go and fly. Out-of-routine events at Leuchars, sometimes arising at very short notice, were more frequent than one might have wished and not always convenient. Visits were the most common of these and sometimes contained within them the unexpected – for example when a visit by the new SASO of 11 Group, Air Commodore John Curtiss, overlapped with a visit to 892 Squadron by an Admiral from the MOD. I had just handed SASO off temporarily to Mike Gautry, and, was giving the Admiral a welcoming cup of coffee in my office, when the crash-warning sounded and I was informed that a naval Phantom had declared an emergency. I bundled the Admiral into my car, raced to the Air Traffic Control tower and got there just in time to share with the SASO and the Admiral a grandstand view of one of 892 Squadron's aircraft making a bit of a mess of the runway.

Happily most visits were less dramatic and some merely involved the meeting and greeting of Royals and other VIPs who regularly used the airfield as a point of entry to Scotland. More time-consuming was the continuing requirement to entertain Admirals and Air Marshals on tours of inspection or other official visits. (I didn't understand at first why three Admirals directly concerned themselves with the naval element – until I learned that FONAC had responsibility for aircraft ashore, FOCAS had it for them when they were afloat, and FOSNI, who was just down the road, had responsibility for what happened in the sea area to the north of us.) Then, from time to time, one had to provide a briefing and lunch for visiting members of the Government or officials from the MOD and, occasionally, senior NATO acquaintances of C-in-C Strike Command who came up to be introduced for a day to the Royal and Ancient Club at St Andrews and be entertained overnight. Sounds bad but, fortunately there was time for flying, and nothing could match exchanging the office for a cockpit, and the earth-bound routines for the adrenaline rush of a spell on the high-wire.

I had got airborne in my second week in command, starting with a sortie with 43 Squadron's QFI and then moving almost straight away to the PTF to try out the naval version of the Phantom. From then on I alternated, depending on which outfit had an aircraft to spare, doing the usual air defence stuff with 43 Squadron and finding a lot of fun getting to grips with the naval approach to circuit work – at 500 feet as opposed to the RAF's standard 1,000 feet – and with the MADLS.

Staying in the green lights of the MADLS required a steeper approach on finals than was standard in the RAF and a landing that was deliberately firmer than light-blue pilots felt to be proper. The Phantom had a splendid little device that I had not come across before that greatly aided precisely correct approaches to the 'deck': the Angle of Attack Indicator. Instead of having to calculate a stalling speed for the weight of fuel remaining the pilot simply flew the recommended angle of attack, 17 units on the AAI on finals, increasing (with decreasing speed) to 19.2 units during role-out to wings level. The aircraft was also fitted with a stall warning vibrator, electrically actuated at 22.3 units, but this was more for use in combat than for the salvation of the inattentive in the circuit. All RAF Phantoms had the AAI, but as far as I am aware only the Navy and the PTF made use of the aural warnings of approach to the stall-angle that the AAI could produce as a supplement to the visual ones.

One Friday afternoon, at the end of week 'happy hour' in the Mess bar, one of the naval pilots suggested that I should take my MADLS practices to their logical conclusion and have a go at landing on *Ark Royal*. At the time that seemed like an entirely reasonable suggestion even though I knew it was in fact a challenge and a proffered opportunity for me to make a fool of myself on behalf of the light-blues. Mike Layard took it seriously as a means of promoting ever-closer relations between the two Services at Leuchars and cleared the proposal with his superiors. When I put the idea to Bob Freer during a visit to the Station in early March he wasn't very enthusiastic about it, but Mike Layard joined me in attempting to allay his doubts – and finally tipped the balance in favour of it by mentioning that an invitation from FOCAS was already on its way to me, and that it would be embarrassing to refuse it.

None of us approached the enterprise lightly. I concentrated on 'deck' landings at Leuchars throughout March, breaking off briefly to do a stint in the Q shed with 43 Squadron over Easter, and a spell with PTF firing 2-inch rockets on Tain range in the Moray Firth. In late March I had flown down to the Royal Aircraft Establishment's airfield at Bedford where a steam catapult was mounted on a concrete ramp and got myself fired off twice, landing twice into an arrester wire. I didn't manage much time in the air in April – just four hours, three of them at night with 43 Squadron. May was much the same: one hour at night with 43 Squadron and five on MADLS with the PTF. And I achieved just another four hours in June before my date with *Ark Royal*.

On the great day *Ark Royal* was steaming not far off Bognor Regis on a calm sea under a cloudless sky. The requirement for those who have not previously landed on a carrier is to produce three consecutive acceptable approaches before being allowed to 'touch down' and then, if that is satisfactory, to put the hook down and 'land' on the next approach. My first approach was satisfactory but I was waved off on my second and third ones by the man with the bats, the Flight Deck Officer. I was beginning to get just a tingle of concern when he let me approach almost to touchdown, and then to touchdown twice on the next two approaches. As I overshot on each occasion I was acutely aware that the upper surfaces of the 'Island' were covered with naval aviators, all watching to see if 'Groupie' would make it. My next approach was 'hook down' and to my great relief I picked up the second of the three wires. This was later, and of course, begrudgingly, acknowledged as not bad for an amateur. I don't at all doubt that in heavy seas, or at night, naval pilots earn their pay, but in the calm conditions that day the whole thing seemed easy.

My invitation was for an overnight stop aboard. However, before I left Leuchars that morning I received a signal from Group requesting my presence at a meeting at Bentley Priory the following morning. I therefore had no choice but to curtail my cruise, and just had time for a brief look around the ship and have lunch. On departure, I had a hard time manoeuvring the aircraft onto the right position for the catapult-launch. I only managed it by lurching around using the toe-brakes, all the time feeling just a touch of apprehension as I saw how close to the deck's edge I was being directed. The manoeuvring problem was entirely of my own making – as I realised when I noticed that my thumb was pressing the bomb-release button on the stick rather than the adjacent nose-wheel steering button. Me nervous? Perish the thought!

Some very sensible person had fitted the naval version of the Phantom with a wire that could be pulled out from the console just below the instrument panel and attached to the control column. When lined up for the catapult launch the pilot would pull the control column back until he got a signal from a sailor that the tail-plane had reached the right angle of incidence for take-off. He would then lock the wire. This simple device, plus a nose-wheel leg extension that could be activated by a switch from the cockpit, virtually guaranteed that the Phantom would fly itself off at the end of the catapult run. Having watched several Buccaneers take off while I was on the bridge, and seeing how they all sank below the level of the deck as their wheels left it, I realised what a very carrier-friendly aircraft the Phantom really was. I was glad of this when I was launched myself for I don't think that I can really claim to have been in control at the precise moment I was slung off the deck a matter of seconds after beginning to move.

As I flew homeward, glad to have done the carrier bit, I wasn't sure whether I should be irritated at being forced to miss a night on board, or be glad that Group's intervention was going to save me from a seriously sore head. As the meeting the following day turned out to be of little import and less urgency, and involved two uncomfortable overnight journeys by British Rail, mild irritation eventually won.

By August 1974 I felt that it was time to have a flight or two in 23 Squadron's Lightnings. A new AOC, Paddy Harbison, had taken over. Hoping that his predecessor would not have mentioned the order he'd given me not to fly more than one type, I told Paddy what I intended. He was quite content with this. I began with an instrument trip with 23 Squadron's IRE and gradually increased the frequency of my Lightning flying – though 'frequency' is perhaps not quite the right word as it suggests that I had rather more time to devote to getting into cockpits than I actually had. In fact, I achieved only thirty-three hours on the Lightning during my last fourteen months as Station Commander. During the same period I did most of my Phantom flying with 43 Squadron and, because PTF had gone to lodge at the Royal Naval Air Station at Yeovilton for part of that time, managed just six sorties with them.

For some time I had been urging the squadrons and the various sections on the Station to think about what we might have to contend with in war. I was not simply concerned about Tacevals – though clearly any realistic measures that we might take to enhance our preparedness for the unexpected would carry an advantage when we were NATO-tested. It seemed to me that it would be sensible to get everyone thinking about a 'worst case' situation. There are plenty of historical examples of the military being unprepared for surprise attacks, mentally as well as physically – and this has been particularly so when people thought they were at 'peace'. The NATO tactical evaluation system, and the tests of our ability to generate armed aircraft via NATO and Strike Command practice 'alerts' had done a lot to enhance our ability to react fast, but there was still a lot of evidence to suggest that people did not take their thinking far enough.

The conventional NATO wisdom was that we would have about a fortnight's warning of an attack on Western Europe by the Soviet Union. It was felt that this would allow time for negotiations and, if these failed to head off the threat, a gradual and, hopefully, non-chaotic progression to a war footing. There were various alert stages that would have to be debated in NATO capitals and in Brussels before being 'declared', and the cynics among us could not help wondering whether any of the agreements that would have to precede the declarations would be achieved in the available time.

My own doubts were reinforced during a lecture I gave early in my tour to the Scottish Police College about Leuchars and its place in the NATO scheme of things. The other speaker there was Professor John Erickson, an acknowledged expert on the Soviet Union, and especially on Soviet military doctrine. As I was giving the official line about warning time he spoke up from the audience.

'Tell me Group Captain, why do you believe that you would have any warning at all?' When I responded with an explanation of the various indicators that were thought likely to be available, from intelligence on the ground to evidence of preparations gathered from, among other things, satellites, he asked why I thought the right interpretations would be made and the correct conclusions drawn. 'Remember,' he said, 'that our Ambassador in Prague gave it as his firm conclusion that the Soviets would not intervene to suppress the Czechs during their bid for freedom in 1967; the very next day Soviet forces rolled across the border and the so-called Prague Spring was over.' It was a little embarrassing to be contradicted from the floor but I had to acknowledge that he did have a very valid point.

There were a lot of things that we needed to do to make sure that we could function, and continue to function, effectively at Leuchars in the event of trouble. There was a need to prepare to defend against sabotage in the run up to war, quite apart from the requirement to do what we could to reduce the effect of any attack on us from the air. The great problem was lack of cash for adequate defences against any would-be Soviet saboteurs (or indeed against any acts of terrorism by the IRA). Of course, we could position sentries at the gate as a visible suggestion that we were alert, and we did; and, thanks to a local Territorial Army engineer unit that was willing to come and practise the erection of barbed-wire defences, we managed some of that form of protection. We liaised with the local police about the possible threat from Russian special forces (*Spetsnaz*) in the run up to war – and the IRA in peace – pitching up with hand-held surface-to-air missiles. I organised the cleaning and patching up of the concrete blast-wall protected dispersals that had been built at Leuchars in the early 1950s and never used – rather unkindly labelled 'Embry Follies' after the man who happened to be C-in-C Fighter Command at the time – and required the squadrons to operate from them during alert exercises. We reinforced a number of buildings with sandbags and, when a building or a vehicle was scheduled for repainting, used drab green paint. And we persuaded Strike Command to 'loan' us an arrester wire that was in storage for use, if the need arose, at any poorly equipped deployment airfield that might have to be used at short notice overseas; we put this at the centre point of the subsidiary runway (too short for normal landings) thereby giving us a chance to recover aircraft should the main runway be put temporarily out of use by enemy action in war – or, indeed, by an aircraft in emergency during normal every-day operations. Happily our improvising did not have to be put to the test in wartime conditions – but it was not wasted as our various measures unquestionably earned us a point or two when we came to be 'Tacevaled'.

One of the highlights of the Leuchars year was the annual Open Day. This involved a fair degree of hard work for OC Operations Wing during the course of the months leading up to it – and close control of the flying display during the day itself. Apart from the flying programme, there were static aircraft displays to be organised, catering concessions to be allocated, publicity to be seen to, crowd control measures to be agreed with the police, and security to be thought about. Traditionally, the Station used the occasion to offer hospitality to people who had helped us in one way or the other, or whose goodwill we wished to have – the Master of St Andrews University would have been one in the latter category, and he would have been very welcome had he come. However, on reviewing the numbers, which had been continuing to grow each year, I felt it was time to do a bit of weeding. The problem was not one of cost, but of accommodation. The 'VIPs' had always been given lunch in the Mess and then invited to 23 Squadron's crew-room to watch the flying display. Lunch was easy, but the crew-room, on the upper floor of a former air traffic control tower, and ideal as a viewing platform, had limited space. When I began to get telephone calls from local worthies telling me 'something must be amiss as we have not received our invitation yet', I realised that my culling was likely to do more harm than good. I decided that all I could do was to leave the list as it was and apologise for the crush on the day.

The weather for the display was perfect. Enthusiasts came from as far away as Southampton – Caroline and Julia had surprised me earlier in the year by reporting that they had seen a poster on Darlington railway station advertising the event as they were on their way home from Whitby. The Flying Scotsman locomotive steamed into the airfield on our private spur from the main line. Pipe bands marched up and down, competing for a trophy. And most important of all, the display went off smoothly and safely, closely controlled by Mike Gautry. A crowd of some 80,000 had been entertained and sent on their way happy with what they had seen – one person particularly happy, having won a car in our prize draw. I was simply relieved to have it over.

I continued to fly when I could during the rest of 1974 and into 1975, glad to hog the longish sorties that the Phantom produced, and to look for the real pleasure of flight in the Lightning. When April – and Easter – came round I once again took a turn at holding Q, and my recompense for sitting in the 'shed' for twenty-four hours was a three and a half hour Phantom sortie during which we chased after, and intercepted, two Bears halfway to Iceland. At the time there was plenty of action to keep the QRA crews happy – in fact, Leuchars' aircraft had made some 360 interceptions of Soviet aircraft during 1974. The only slack period had been towards the end of the year, which was unfortunate, as Independent Television News had asked the MOD if they could send a cameraman to us to be flown in a Phantom to film an interception of a Russian aircraft. He sat in 43 Squadron's crew-room for a fortnight waiting for one to turn up and none did. The people at ITN became increasingly unhappy about having him hanging around unproductively and kept telephoning the MOD to complain. Eventually Paddy Harbison rang me to ask what we might do about it. As there was really nothing that we could do to get the man the pictures he wanted (without the cooperation of the Russians) I asked, tongue in cheek, if Paddy had thought about ringing Moscow and asking for some help. 'How could we do that?' he fired back, in a voice that suggested he wasn't immediately sure whether I was being serious or making a joke. Then he laughed, and asked if I knew the number, and all was well. Actually, if anyone behind the Iron Curtain had had a sense of humour a call might have provoked an interesting reaction.

At the end of April all changed at Leuchars. Throughout the month machines and materials had been arriving for the task of digging up and resurfacing the main runway. This annoying but necessary disruption to the Station was scheduled to begin in May, last through the summer, and hopefully be complete in good time to allow the airfield to be swept free of loose stones, dusted off and sorted out for the 1975 Open Day. Plans had been made for the resident flying units to be detached while all this was going on: 23 Squadron to Wattisham, 43 to Kinloss, and 892 and the PTF to Yeovilton.

The day after the last aircraft had departed, and noise at Leuchars had reduced to that of the machines being set up to deal with the runway, I got a letter from the Secretary of the Royal and Ancient Golf Club asking me if I might consider stopping flying for the duration of the Open which was to be held that summer at St Andrews. Normally all I could have done would have been to explain the impossibility of closing down and give an assurance that we would redouble our normal efforts to minimise noise. On this occasion I was happy to assure him – without immediately saying why – that there would be no aircraft noise whatsoever while the Open was on. When I got a rather handsome note of thanks and an invitation to lunch at the Club I felt I had to telephone and tell him the truth. I still had a rather good lunch though.

Leuchars was normally open twenty-four hours a day, and every day of the year. Two things required this rate of working: its operational role in meeting the Northern QRA commitment, and its status as a Master Diversion Airfield. Quite apart from the noise generated by our own aircraft on a daily basis, we also had that of aircraft from elsewhere. And, it didn't stop at weekends: we were a popular destination for fly-in visitors, particularly golf-playing members of the USAF stationed in Europe. As a result, neither Mike Gautry, with his responsibility for keeping the runway open come ice or snow in the winter, or emergencies of any sort at any time, nor myself, with overall responsibility for safety, security, welfare, and what have you, could ever feel totally relaxed or be off-duty. The runway closure, therefore, allowed us to relax a little and take some leave without worrying unduly about what might be going on in our absence. Of course, the normal work of administration, planning and essential social intercourse went on, but the burden of this too was lightened, and sufficiently so to enable me to find time to get down to Wattisham or up to Kinloss to spend time and fly with the deployed squadrons. I didn't go to Yeovilton because of the journey time involved and so had to content myself with simply keeping in touch with the PTF by telephone. I spent the summer doing many more hours in the car than in an aeroplane but still managed about eight hours a month in the air.

Esmé and I had had an invitation from Jerry Seavers and his wife to go and stay with them at the HQ of the USAF Tactical Air Command in Virginia, where he was on an exchange tour. With the runway repairs well under way I was happy to take this up. The night before I was due to start on this promising break I attended a Ball at the United States Navy's facility at Edzell, some forty miles north of Leuchars. While there, my RAF driver succumbed to the hospitality of the US ratings' Mess, and when it came time to leave I found him to be so drunk that I had to throw him in the back of the car and drive myself. Approaching Leuchars I found the sentry at the main gate, a sailor on this occasion, sitting on the floor of the sentry box asleep. Furious, I called out the guard, had both the driver and sentry locked in the guardroom, and tore a strip of the guard corporal for his failure to see that the sentry was alert. First thing in the morning, before setting off on leave, I telephoned Charlie Ram, Wing Commander Engineering, and told him to charge the driver and remand him to Bruce Hopkins, 23 Squadron's boss, who would be acting Station Commander in my absence. Bruce would be able to use the full force of a Station Commander's legal authority to deal with him. I also telephoned Mike Layard and suggested he deal with the sailor. Perhaps this was undue interference on my part with the course of justice but I felt that the driver had forfeited his right to remain in the RAF trade category of driver, and the sailor ought to be made to realise that guard duty was a serious responsibility. I was not very pleased when I returned from the States to find that the driver had simply been Reprimanded. This mild punishment contrasted dismally with the fourteen days in Colchester military prison that Mike Layard had awarded the sailor.

We had an enjoyable fortnight in Virginia, doing a lot of sailing on Chesapeake Bay, totally relaxing without responsibility. However, at a cocktail party given by the C-in-C of Tactical Air Command for a visiting group of senior NATO officers, responsibility returned. I was taken aside by one of the visitors, the current RAF Air Member for Personnel, Air Marshal Sir Neil Cameron. He told me that he would be sending back to me the annual report that I had completed on one of 43 Squadron's officers at the end of the previous year. 'I've got a problem,' he said, 'his father cannot understand why, with eight year's seniority as a flight lieutenant he has not been promoted and is pressing me for an explanation. Have a re-think about what you have written.' When I got back from the United States a newly raised Form 1369 was waiting on my desk under a short covering letter from 11 Group explaining that the one that had been forwarded in the normal way with the squadron commander's assessment and my own comments on it had had coffee spilled on it. I was requested to have the new one completed and returned to Group. I gave Keith Beck the new form telling him simply that somewhere up the line it had been thought that we had reported on this particular officer over-harshly. I said nothing to influence what he might write and was pleased to find that he did not change his original assessment. I had no intention of doing so either. Some weeks later I had a letter from the father of the 43 Squadron officer concerned, a very exalted and much admired former Chief of the Air Staff, asking me if I might explain why we thought so little of his son. I responded as fully and as clearly as I could and, almost by return of post, got a very gracious reply from the great man thanking me for my candour. By contrast, Neil Cameron, who went on to become in turn Chief of the Air Staff and Chief of the Defence Staff, never spoke to me again.

Back from leave, I began hustling the people doing the runway, probably irritating them with my questions about progress – but I was concerned to urge the importance of the Open Day, preparations for which were already under way. By late August the new surfaces had all been laid and then, to my consternation, circular plugs were lifted from them for analysis of the quality of the asphalt, and time slipped maddeningly by until it had been confirmed that this was fine, and the holes were filled in. Then came repainting, the replacement of runway lighting, and a slow clearing and removal from the airfield of the mini-factories for mixing and preparing materials and all the other bits of contractors' machinery. With about ten days to go all was clear and the runway was handed back to the RAF – a bit tight in time but enough. I organised the entire Station complement to emerge from offices, hangars, the armoury, bomb-dumps, stores, Messes and dark corners, to walk the station surfaces, bin-bags in hand and pick up everything that should not have been lying about. Jet engines have been destroyed by objects sucked off the ground – objects that had come to be referred to throughout the RAF, inaccurately, as FOD, the acronym for Foreign Object Damage. Everyone pitched in willingly, many of the airmen, airwomen and officers obviously quite intrigued to be walking the holy surfaces of an airfield for the first time.

Mike Gautry had planned to include formation fly-past demonstrations by our own squadrons in the Open Day flying programme, as on the previous year. I briefed each squadron commander as to what I wanted from them – essentially, as decent a show as they could produce while adhering to the rules and endangering neither the public nor themselves. As formation aerobatics were specifically prohibited unless especially authorised by the Air Force Board, the squadron commanders could plan to do little more than turn as tightly as possible around the airfield, displaying changes in formation as they went past the crowd. The Lightnings had the ability to add interest by doing the Lightning party piece. The Phantoms were not quite as spectacular and so Keith Beck, unknown to either Mike Gautry or myself, decided to add a 'Canadian Break' as his finale. The traditional – and normal – fighter 'break' involves a run in to the airfield at speed with aircraft arranged in echelon away from the intended direction of turn onto the downwind leg. Over the airfield each aircraft peels off in turn, usually at intervals of one or two seconds, in order to achieve separation downwind. The high-speed approach was an old wartime practice designed to minimise the risk of an enemy 'jumping' a formation as it returned to land. The hard turn that the break involves knocks the speed off quickly to that required for lowering flaps and landing gear, and thus contributes to getting the formation on the ground in minimum time. A Canadian Break requires the last numbered member of the echelon – number five in the case of 43 Squadron's display formation – to go first, rolling away from and pulling underneath his fellows. The rest follow suit, one after the other. The whole thing takes quite an act of faith as each member of the formation, after number five, has to roll without being able to see the one that has gone immediately before him, and therefore has to hope that everyone is doing the thing correctly. The 43 Squadron formation started practising the Canadian Break while still at Kinloss but, after a couple of trips Keith Beck abandoned the idea, largely because of the expressed unhappiness of number three in the formation.

As soon as the squadrons were settled back at Leuchars I got them to show me what they were proposing to do. The 43 Squadron formation finished an entirely satisfactory display with a normal break and I cleared them formally to repeat on the Open Day what I had seen them do. I knew that Keith Beck intended to fly another couple of formation practices and accepted this as entirely normal. What I didn't know was that he had decided to try the Canadian Break again. He did so at a couple of thousand feet; the pilot flying number three lost his nerve as he rolled underneath on the first practice and somehow contrived to enter an incipient spin. His navigator, spurred by the proximity of the ground, ejected. He followed suit, and the aircraft crashed.

At the subsequent Board of Inquiry I argued on Beck's behalf for, despite 11 Group's initial misgivings he had commanded his squadron up to that point entirely satisfactorily. I suggested to the Board that there was room for doubt as to whether the Canadian Break should strictly be classed as an aerobatic manoeuvre, and that this doubt should raise in turn a question as to whether the squadron commander could be considered to have deliberately contravened orders or merely misinterpreted them. The Board took the view that while there was indeed room for some doubt, the manoeuvre was sufficiently risky to require anyone wishing to try it at low level to seek advice and authority for it. I could not disagree with that logic. My argument may or may not have affected decisions at Group and Command, but the outcome, a Reprimand delivered by the C-in-C Strike Command, was more than fair to him; Keith Beck could well have lost his squadron.

During the Open Day all went well with the display – apart from a ghastly moment when I thought that a naval helicopter was going to hit the control tower full of VIPs while showing its paces. Nos 23 and 43 Squadrons did what was required of them and did it well. Our principal guest, the Chief of the Air Staff, Sir Andrew

Humphrey, seemed well pleased with it all, at least until he and I had a short conversation about the loss of the 43 Squadron aircraft. 'That accident was unavoidable Alan, was it not?' he asked. 'It wasn't one of those silly ones that shouldn't have happened?' At that point I was conscious of Paddy Harbison, a pleasant and normally supportive man, moving away from us as if to distance himself from anything I might say to the CAS, or possibly from blame by association. I had known Andrew Humphrey since Aden. He had been C-in-C Strike Command when I commanded 5 Squadron. I had entertained him on several occasions overnight in the Station Commander's house at Leuchars. But, as I replied 'I'm afraid, Sir, that it was indeed a silly accident and it most certainly should not have happened' I knew that I could not expect much sympathy from him. In fact, as I learned later, when he heard that Beck had been treated, in his opinion, too leniently, he told his successor as C-in-C Strike Command, Splinters Smallwood, that 'someone should be sacked'. Happily for me Splinters did not follow that suggestion through. A year later Keith Beck was out of the RAF as a result of some misguided actions on his part; I couldn't help thinking how pointlessly irrelevant this made my attempt at Leuchars to save his career, and put myself unwittingly in the firing-line by doing so.

Shortly after the crash, and compounding the air of gloom that had descended on 43 Squadron's crews, a rather sad human tragedy struck. The teenage son of one of 43 Squadron's flight commanders, hitch-hiking into St Andrews on a Saturday afternoon, was offered a lift by one of 23 Squadron's pilots. The latter, driving faster than was prudent, crashed his open sports car just before reaching the town and the teenager was killed. The driver was breathalysed and found to be over the limit, the result of a session in the Mess bar over an extended lunchtime period. The boy's parents were distraught and almost beyond consolation. To compound matters, not much sympathy was evident from above. In fact there was a distinctly chill air blowing down the chain of command as people considered the possibility of seriously adverse publicity arising from the likelihood of a serving officer being charged with manslaughter. My concern, however, was primarily for the boy's parents – and there was a secondary one: countering the consequent *frisson* of upset within 23 and 43 Squadrons, and the rumours of heads rolling, principally my own, that were beginning to go the rounds. The Station had to continue to function smoothly and efficiently.

I had my last two flights as Station Commander on 16 October when I decided, imprudently as it turned out, to fly down to RAF Benson, the nearest suitable airfield to Strike Command HQ, on the morning of my scheduled farewell interview with the C-in-C. As the interview was to be at 1000 hours, a more sensible travel scheme would have been to have taken the overnight sleeper from Leuchars. However, the date of the interview had been fixed after 892 Squadron had made firm arrangements to dine me out on the night of the 15th, and so I had asked 43 Squadron to produce a Phantom for an early morning take-off. The weather forecast had given fog as a possibility in southern England but the risk hadn't seemed serious enough to force a change of plans.

On the morning of the 16th, however, the reality was much worse than the forecast had suggested: the whole of southern England was blanketed by heavy fog. As this was expected to begin lifting as the sun began to make its effect felt, I took off hopefully. Sod's Law prevailed, and the nearest airfield to High Wycombe that I could get into was RAF Wyton, about fifteen miles north-west of Cambridge. The Station Commander there loaned me a car and driver and, having telephoned the C-in-C's office to say that I would be a trifle late, I set off across country. I arrived over an hour late. Given this discourtesy to a very senior man, coupled with the recent misfortunes at Leuchars, Splinters was remarkably courteous and kind in his farewell good wishes.

Notes

1 For a period, Air Secretaries were appointed at this rank level. The idea was that such senior officers would be immune to any importuning or pressure to afford privileges of any kind to protégées.

2 Sadly David Blucke was killed a few months later when the Phantom he was piloting, and a crop-spraying aircraft, collided in mid air.

3 As Captain Layard, Senior Naval Officer aboard the *Atlantic Conveyor* during the Falkland conflict, he had to swim for his life when that ship was sunk by an Exocet missile. He retired as Admiral Sir Michael.

4 The RN version was designated the FG1; the RAF version was designated the FG2. Both were based on the US Navy F4-J and were designated by McDonnell Douglas, the manufacturers, as the F4-K and F4-M respectively.

5 The Lightning over-wing drop tanks could add 4,160 lbs. However, they had been designed for ferry use only and severely restricted the aircraft's manoeuvrability. With fuel in them, for example, the aircraft was limited to 3.5 g.

6 Rocket-propelled seats, such as those fitted to the Phantom, were now so efficient, and so largely avoided damage to the spine, that few felt inhibited about using them, even at ground-level!

CHAPTER SIXTEEN

Grounded

Some months before we left Leuchars Esmé and I had decided that we ought to try to get a toe-hold in the housing market. Constant movement at home and overseas, the advantages of being on Stations at which one was serving, and a basic lack of capital had previously kept us from making any attempt to do so. However, rapidly rising house prices, and a desire to provide an overdue static base for the family, suggested we should delay no longer. During one of my trips to Wattisham to visit 23 Squadron I had been offered a mooring at the mouth of the River Deben. Although we didn't have the slightest hope of buying a boat and a house at the same time, this was a sufficiently attractive offer to decide us to begin looking for a house in the area. We eventually found a place on the outskirts of an attractive village in the rural outback of Suffolk and went well over budget to buy it – so much so that for the next few years we were very short of spending money indeed.

We moved directly from Leuchars to the new house and spent December settling in. At the beginning of January 1976, leaving Esmé and Julia (who had insisted in giving up boarding in favour of doing A levels locally) happily ensconced in it, I went to join the year-long course at the Royal College of Defence Studies in London. As it was not practicable to commute daily from the village I found myself a room for use from Monday to Friday, boarding with a dear old lady who let me know very quickly that she would not have taken a lodger had her husband not had the indecency to die just as he was about to take up an ambassadorial appointment.

The RCDS course comprised people from some twenty countries: seventy officers of one-star rank and above from navies, armies and air forces, twenty members of various diplomatic and civil services, and some high-ranking policemen. As it was going to be conducted at a more reasonable pace than I had known for some time it seemed the ideal thing to follow a hectic spell in command. Reasonably paced or not, it was a prestige course and a considerable privilege to be on, particularly for a Group Captain.

In February I got a letter from Paddy Harbison telling me that Leuchars had been judged the best Station in Strike Command for 1975, my second year as Station Commander – a bit of an irony considering how close I came to being sacked. A month later I was summoned to go and see the Assistant Air Secretary, Air Vice-Marshal Alec Maisner. When I got to his office, wondering what he might want me for, he invited me to sit down and, without any preliminary chat, told me that he was required to express to me the Air Force Board's displeasure that I had not acted to curb excessive drinking by the 23 Squadron officer who had had the car accident. He added that this officer had been recorded to have had a serious drink problem during his basic flying training and that this should have alerted me to keep an eye on him. Had I been given an opportunity to say anything in advance of this censure I would have pointed out that only the keepers of his records, the Directorate General of Personnel, would have known of any previous mention of a problem, and nothing had been disclosed to me. I could also have pointed out that his drinking habits at Leuchars had not been noticeably different to those of many of his peers on the squadrons. I didn't leave Alec Maisner's office feeling admonished; I left feeling saddened by this example of disregard for the firm principle of English law that no one be condemned unheard. I also couldn't help thinking of those lines by a character in Act 1 of Brenden Behan's play 'The Hostage': '…. I was courtmartialled [sic] in my absence and sentenced to death in my absence, so I said they could shoot me in my absence.'

It was, of course, hardly the most serious of condemnations and I let it pass. However, when the Air Secretary, now Air Chief Marshal Sir Neville Stack, pitched up at the College in September to give the light blue element their postings his opening statement to me really did take me aback. 'You were selected for substantive promotion in July,' he said, 'but the Board felt that in view of the incidents at your Station you should not be seen to be receiving the accolade of promotion.' I thought this an extraordinary statement; had it not been delivered I would have been none the wiser about the promotion, and so I could only interpret it as an addition to the admonishment already delivered by Alec Maisner. 'However,' he continued cheerfully, 'I want you at the end of the year as an Acting Air Commodore in the appointment of Director of Operations (Air Defence and Overseas) in the MOD.' This took some of the sting out of not receiving 'the accolade of promotion' and, as it meant that I would be getting acting rank after just three and a half years as a Group Captain I felt I really had little to complain about. Besides, I could always hope that I would be 'substantiated' in the rank of Air Commodore as soon as the Board considered my sins to have been expiated. All these positive thoughts notwithstanding, I was left with something of a bad taste in my mouth.

The RCDS year turned out to be exceptionally enjoyable, full of good things that made it memorable. There were lectures by ministers, ambassadors, the Chief of the Defence Staff, the head of the Metropolitan police, and a myriad of other experts in their fields – and we were able to fire awkward questions at them all. The highlight for most of us was the overseas tour that took parties of course members on five-week long educative jaunts to various parts of the world. My party went to North America, visiting such diverse locations in Canada as Quebec, Montreal, Edmonton, Calgary, Vancouver, Yellowknife, and Inuvik, an Eskimo settlement in the far and frozen north. We started in the United States at Los Angeles and went on to Atlanta, Denver, Williamsburg, Detroit, New York, and ended up in Washington. We were feted and treated as VIPs wherever we went, and indeed, this was the case throughout the entire year – which was lovely while it lasted, but it did make it rather difficult to come back to an ordinary working environment when it ended.

It didn't help that the working environment I was destined for, the Ministry of Defence, Main Building, Whitehall, was a vast and depressing edifice, from the 'greasy spoon' canteen in the basement to the offices tucked away on the seventh floor. Dreary uncarpeted corridors, their walls painted in one-colour Works Department magnolia, ran on both sides of it, parallel to Whitehall on one side, and to the Thames on the other. In the centre of the building were two enclosed wells clad in dirty white tiles into which the winter sun did not penetrate. My office, and the nearby offices of my staff, were off the Whitehall corridor on the fourth floor. My boss, the Assistant Chief of Air Staff (Operations), or ACAS (Ops) in the jargon of the place, was on the next floor up. Three and four star officers and equivalent-level civil servants occupied the few decently appointed offices in the entire building on the sixth floor. Some months after I took up my appointment, the lifts in the Westminster end of the building were taken out of service for a week for essential maintenance work. Meeting the new Chief of the Air Staff, Air Chief Marshal Sir Michael Beetham – who had very recently taken over the post from Air Chief Marshal Sir Neil Cameron – at the bottom of the stairs one morning just as he was starting the long climb to the sixth floor, I tried a bit of humour to break the silence between us. Pointing at the stairs I said: 'It must be tough at the top, sir.' He either didn't catch my rather feeble attempt at a pun, or was remarkably fit, for all he said was 'Not in the least' and bounded off upwards.

It took a little time to become familiar with the conventions of the Main Building and to discover that power did not always run straight up and down the military hierarchical structure within it: due allowance had to be made, among other things, for the influence of the civil servants who, as a rule, had the advantage of remaining longer in their posts than their military counterparts. I quickly realised how beneficial it would have been to have served an apprenticeship in the Ministry at a junior level before being exposed to the place in the glare of a higher level of responsibility.

When I took up my appointment in the building the ACAS (Ops) was my one time flight commander, David Craig. David was still the rather shy, reserved, mild-mannered, gentleman that I had known on 247 Squadron. A highly intelligent man, and a lot more experienced in the ways of, and astute about coping with, Whitehall than I was ever likely to be, he exhibited, despite his shyness, a steely resolve and a determination to press the best out of all who worked for him.

For most of my first year I was busy with little more than the routine of my role: advising on matters of air defence policy, chairing a committee charged with introducing computers to the operational side of the RAF, seeing that all reports of UFO sightings were compared with the recorded and retained air defence radar-scope pictures (a time-wasting task that had been allocated to the ADGE people at some time in the past), trotting over to Brussels to attend the odd NATO air defence meeting, and liaising with the USAF at Ramstein and the Italian Air Force in Rome about setting up an Air Combat Manoeuvring Range off the coast of Sardinia.

My Directorate had also become responsible for the rump of the once large Overseas Department. Before my time this had been reduced to a staff of one wing commander and three squadron leaders charged with holding and amending the contingency plans produced by the Commands. Normally these officers had very little to occupy them but, when something threatened that might require a contingency plan to be put into action a brief could be very rapidly required on the sixth floor. The first time this happened during my tenure the wing commander was on leave and the squadron leaders were unable to produce what I needed quickly enough for a meeting called at short notice by the Vice Chief of the Air Staff, Air Marshal Sir Peter Terry. He wanted to discuss options in response to some threatening trouble in Africa and was not impressed by my failure to have all the facts of the pertinent plan at my fingertips, and let me know it. I should of course have recognised earlier the dangers of not being instantly able to service the desire of top men to be ahead of the game at all times, and I hastened to close the stable door by bringing the Overseas lot under the supervision of Group Captain (Air Defence), at that time my old saviour from the tedium of target-towing, Brian Cox. Unfortunately, as far as Peter Terry was concerned, I had let the horse bolt.

About a year before I was appointed to the air defence role in the MOD a small Working Party had been set up under Air Commodore Dickie Wirdnam, one of my erstwhile course-mates at Coltishall. This was tasked to determine how best to make the existing (analogue) air defence radars compatible with a planned (digital) communication system that was designed to provide high-speed links between the various elements of the UKADGE, NADGE, the operations centres at 11 Group and HQ Strike Command, and the airfields. The Working Party had obtained authority to commission a feasibility study by an electronics firm and had committed

£4,000,000 to this. The study had been completed and the firm involved was proposing a box of tricks to be fitted to the air defence radars at a total cost of £29,000,000. I thought this to be a waste of money, as it did absolutely nothing to enhance the radars' capability. A better use of that sum, I felt, would be to spend it buying modern mobile radars. Marconi had just brought onto the market a highly capable digital mobile radar that incorporated a whole new approach to countering jamming. The quoted price for one of these, including transporters and support vehicles, was £2,500,000. For £29,000,000, I reasoned, enough of these could be bought to replace our existing main radars, and have a few to spare. Not only would detection capabilities be enhanced in a jamming environment, but there might also be a better chance of radars surviving conventional attacks; the static radars at known locations would be at serious risk (the Type 85s, for example, had huge scanners mounted on large brick buildings). I therefore wrote a paper recommending that new mobile radars be purchased as an alternative to fitting the old with conversion kits. I suggested that these could be based in peacetime at the existing sites and be dispersed to previously surveyed but undisclosed rural sites if and when hostilities threatened, and moved as required during any hostilities to enhance their chance of survival from conventional attack.

Dickie Wirdnam did not like my proposal and David Craig was somewhat dubious about it. Understandably Dickie resented the thought of wasting all the work already done, and the money already spent. David argued that changing plans that had already been the subject of a preliminary request to NATO for assisted funding might be a dangerous mistake, and counselled caution. Moreover, the members of my ground environment staff, all having served time on the existing radars, were emotionally opposed to the suggestion that any of them – particularly the Type 85s – should be replaced. In response to David's point, I argued that a more dangerous mistake might be to wait until someone in NATO looked at the vulnerability of the existing radars, or asked what improvement we were likely to get in their capability by spending £29,000,000 on them. And I argued with my ADGE people the matter of the vulnerability of the Type 85s (and the Type 84s), the performance of yesterday's technology against the new, and the cost of the 'fix' against lack of enhancement, but without converting many of them.

David Craig moved on to a new post while we were still trying to get some idea of how any change to the plan might affect the request for NATO funding. We failed to get a clear-cut answer and so I deployed my arguments again to his successor, Tim Lloyd. He agreed to put the proposal to VCAS for consideration and it eventually went to the Air Force Board.[1] I fear, however, that somewhere along the way the identity of the originator of the idea was lost. Certainly VCAS seemed not to know where credit might be due. During the farewell interview I had with him before leaving the MOD he told me that he thought that I should have achieved more during my time there. He ended, almost as if he felt the need to soften his message a little, by telling me that he recognised that I had had little staff experience and that he saw me as 'a commander rather than a staff officer'. Of course he was right as far as my preferences went, but I was a little piqued by the implication that I could not hold my own in staff circles. And he was possibly also right in another sense: shortly before I was posted I had contradicted CAS on a point about air defence in front of his Air Force Board colleagues – an action that alone would have marked me down as being much too tactless, or perhaps too foolish, to be a successful 'Whitehall Warrior'.

I left the MOD at the end of 1978 after two years in the hothouse of the Main Building and with eighteen months' seniority as a substantive Air Commodore. Substantiation had come nine months after I had been told about the 'the accolade of promotion' and so, in essence, I had been docked a year's seniority by administrative action. Not a great loss, but somewhat irritating nonetheless.

In January 1979 I went from the MOD to HQ 11 Group at Bentley Priory as the SASO. Bentley had been the HQ of Fighter Command from 1936, when the Command was formed, until 1968 when Fighter and Bomber Commands merged to form Strike Command. It was from Bentley that Dowding had directed the Battle of Britain. The old Priory building, in which every subsequent C-in-C, and latterly AOC, had occupied Dowding's unchanged office, and sat at his original desk, had recently been declared structurally unsafe and

was about to undergo a major refurbishment. The AOC and the
SASO were now accommodated in adjoining offices in a modern
structure in the grounds of the Priory. The current AOC, Peter
Latham, was a delightfully relaxed man enjoying his final tour in a
pleasant role before retiring. Once the dashing leader of the Black
Arrows his main interest now, after sailing, was making and
mending clocks. I could often hear him through the thin wall
between our offices filing away at a clock component, something
that he tended to do whenever he got bored with the paperwork on
his desk. As he was well into his tour when I got there, and had
clearly decided that he had done his bit as far as visiting the Group's
airfields and radar sites was concerned, I got pretty nearly *carte
blanche* from him to go visiting myself – and I did so whenever I
could, knowing that anything that cropped up when I was away
would be well looked after by George Black, currently Group
Captain Operations at the HQ.

The only problem about going out and about was the journey
time to even the nearest of the 11 Group airfields, Wattisham and
Coningsby. For visits to the Group's more widely scattered units,
particularly the radar sites in the far north, it was possible to a get
one of the Devons based at Northolt. Once, for a visit to RAF
Brawdy, I managed to get myself picked up from Northolt by Hawk
and deposited back there at the end of the day. That – one-off
opportunity as it turned out – gave me a opportunity to have a go
at a very flyable little aircraft, so very clearly out of the same stable
as the Hunter. The fact that the man in the back seat was happy to
let a middle-aged, and not very current, staff officer fly the aircraft
into tight little metropolitan Northolt, and land there, says
something for his imperturbability and a lot for the ease with which
the aircraft handled. Unfortunately the Devons had to be shared
with all-comers from the various headquarters around London and
so quite a few miles had to be done by car.

On one of my early outings I drove up to Coningsby intending to
get airborne in a Phantom and, hopefully organise, for my next visit,
a short conversion course on a Spitfire of the Battle of Britain
Memorial Flight. However, my hopes of flying on that day were
dashed by some really foul weather. The airfield was declared 'Red'
shortly after I got there and it was forecast to remain closed by low

cloud for the next few hours. There was nothing for it but to be content with a chat with some of the OCU instructors and students, have a look around various sections, and have lunch in the Mess with the station executives. I didn't get very far with the Spitfire either, as the Flight was not having an easy task keeping its few aircraft flying and clearly didn't want to widen the small circle of pilots authorised to fly them; I had no real justification for pressing them, and didn't.

I was about to climb into my car for the journey back to Bentley when I had a bit of good fortune. Peter Latham telephoned to ask me to go on to Leuchars to represent him at a memorial service the following morning. I can't recall what it was that forced a change in his plans but he had cancelled his own transport arrangements and had asked Leuchars to try to get a 43 Squadron Phantom into Coningsby to pick me up. The weather at Leuchars was good, and not bad to the west of us so, even if the pilot could not get under the cloud-base at Coningsby he could divert to somewhere like RAF Waddington and I could drive to him. The Leuchars' aircraft did get in to Coningsby, flown by one of my old 5 Squadron pilots, John Spoor, now on 43 Squadron. He was pleased to have been given the opportunity to throw me about in the Phantom and I was, subsequently, glad to have him do it. As soon as he had refuelled we got airborne, with me in the back surrounded by navigational gear but no stick or throttles, wishing that the aircraft had had dual controls. Letting down for an approach to Leuchars John announced that he was going to burn off some fuel to get down to landing weight, banged in the re-heats and pulled the aircraft into a sustained tight turn at pretty near maximum g. As I was determined to show him that I was still able to 'hack it' I wasn't going to admit to any discomfort in the rear seat, still less that my 'Highcockalorum back' was telling me that it was no longer up to heavy loading. When he straightened out I was rather relieved – and almost able to stand upright when I climbed out of the aircraft. In the Mess bar later it was the greatest of pleasures to meet and mingle with Leuchars' current crop of youngsters, some of whom I knew from the past. That at least was – temporarily – rejuvenating.

Apart from trips out, which I always welcomed, particularly to the airfields, but even to the far fringes of the ADGE chain, to

Fylingdales for which 11 Group had administrative responsibility, or to the underground Operations Centre (the bunker) at HQ Strike Command (to man the AD cell whenever exercises were in progress), life in the HQ went by with no particular alarms or excursions. Peter sought no initiatives or changes to the established routine, and the members of the staff went about their responsibilities with the minimum of prodding or interference from me. The progress of the squadrons towards achieving their annual tasks was watched and charted, Taceval results analysed, flight safety requirements emphasised and, at the end of the year, the destination of the Dacre decided.

About half way through my first year at Bentley, Peter Latham got a telephone call from the MOD to say that the owner of a large piece of silver, some three feet high, and intricately worked with models of early aircraft had indicated a desire to present it to the RAF, and the Air Force Board, noting that 11 Group did not have a gunnery trophy, thought it might be appropriate for us. As the Dacre Trophy had originally been awarded for air-gunnery results at a time when all fighter aircraft had guns, and had been in a sense misappropriated when the gunless Lightning came into service, we sought the views of the widow of its donor, Mrs Elizabeth Dacre, and found that she was quite happy for its present use to continue. We passed the word to London that we would be glad to have an award for the results of air-to-air firing, and in due course a handover ceremony for the new trophy was arranged at the RAF Club. During this it emerged that the donor, Mr Seed, a splendidly archetypal Yorkshireman of advanced age, had been conned some years before into thinking that he was buying the Schneider Trophy – a fact that he related with wry humour. It was an astonishing piece of surreal art – not everyone's idea of aesthetic good taste, but we accepted it graciously and gratefully.

Formal guest nights in the Priory were a frequent and pleasant part of life at 11 Group and, during my first year, it was still possible to hold the annual Bentley Battle of Britain cocktail party in it. This had always been a splendid occasion, from the end of the war onwards, and successive AOCs of 11 Group had been determined to maintain the tradition that had started under the auspices of Fighter Command. There was unquestionably something special about the setting, with guests moving out onto the balustraded terrace, from which Dowding had gazed at the fires of blitzed London, to watch a fly-past provided each year by a Spitfire and Hurricane of the Battle of Britain Memorial Flight.

The Priory Mess was not available on my second year owing to the refurbishment programme which, sadly, was seriously set back by a fire that broke out one evening in June, and which spread with such spectacular ferocity that it looked likely at one stage to destroy the entire building. Fortunately the fire was confined to the central core of the Priory. The main walls were left intact and in due course – after my time there – all was faithfully restored as per the original by some uncharacteristic sensitivity and spending by the Department of the Environment.

Peter Latham went off into retirement in early 1981 and was replaced by Peter Harding. Not long afterwards George Black departed for HQ 38 Group and was replaced by Mac McEwan, one of my former compatriots on 145 (R) Squadron at Chivenor. Peter Harding was a determinedly new brush, fresh from one of those NATO appointments reserved by the Air Secretary for officers marked for high places. He was keen to find out what made 11 Group tick – and what did not. He wanted to be briefed about everything, and to get cracking on visiting the various elements of his parish. I was happy to organise the first but the second placed me very firmly behind the counter minding the shop while he was away.

As it happened this didn't matter much for I badly screwed up my back during a squash game about a month after his arrival. It had been giving me recurring problems since that silly game so many years before but now, suddenly, it needed serious attention and I had to suffer the indignity of being carted off to hospital on a stretcher. But worse, I was forbidden even to think of sitting on an ejection seat for the time being. The incident gave Peter Harding the opportunity to quip, as I was being dined out on posting from Bentley, that my departure on a stretcher had been the worst case of writer's cramp he had ever seen.

I was posted from Bentley in February 1981 to HQ Strike Command as Air Commodore Plans. On arrival I was given a run down on the appointment by the chap I was replacing, John Field. He told me that I was going to find it an interestingly odd staff position: Air Commodore Plans answered directly to the Deputy C-in-C (at the time Air Marshal Sir Peter Bairsto) whereas the other air commodores on the Air Staff were directly subordinate to SASO, himself subordinate to the Deputy C-in-C. Air Commodore Plans also sat in on the formal weekly meetings that the C-in-C held with his Deputy and the two-star members of the HQ staff. My attendance at these was going to expose me to close scrutiny by the top management at Strike Command, but I was not unhappy with that.

My staff comprised two group captains, seven wing commanders and seven squadron leaders. Group Captain Plans, Chris Sprent, had been in command of Coningsby when I first took up my appointment as the SASO at 11 Group; he gave me a thorough introductory briefing on my second day in the job. From what he said about planning responsibilities, one anomaly seemed to stick out like a sore thumb: my team and I were responsible for just about everything within the Command that required a little forethought and a plan of action or organisation, other than contingency planning for action abroad. That was under the control of a group captain in another – distant – part of the Air Staff building. Having had my fingers slightly burned in the MOD by failing to anticipate the need to bring the Overseas Staff under close supervision, I felt a trick was similarly being missed here. However, I thought it best to put aside the idea of proposing change until I found how things actually worked in the HQ.

My other group captain, Barry Blakeley, had been the Station Commander of Boulmer for part of my tour at Bentley, so he too was a known quantity. At Strike his principal responsibility was to oversee the introduction and development of (what was then called) Automatic Data Processing in and to the HQ. I was happy to leave him to this, aided as he was by a representative of the equipment manufacturer, and simply contented myself with reviewing the schedules that had been agreed for getting the system up and running, stepping in only where it appeared I could help speed things up.

The Plans job was quite a busy one, demanding on time, and offering few reasons for getting out and about. As in Aden, I had to accept the dearth of opportunities to go flying, and get on with my primary responsibilities – and I added to these after a few months by putting forward my views on the desirability of bringing contingency planning under Air Commodore Plans and having this accepted. However, things ticked along without too many intractable problems clamouring for instant solutions – but I did lose a bit of sleep each week before the C-in-C's meetings as I was determined not to be caught out by any of the questions that invariably came my way during it.

I had been allocated an excellent Married Quarter at High Wycombe and this allowed Esmé and me to entertain quite decently – something that I realised with hindsight we had not done adequately during my time in the MOD, and thus had lost opportunities that others took routinely to network and impress. I had got to know through mutual friends when I was at Bentley, the then Lord Mayor of London, Sir Peter Gardsen, and we invited him and his wife to dinner shortly after we set up house at High Wycombe together with the C-in-C, Air Chief Marshal Sir Keith Williamson. The following day, clearly intrigued by my acquaintance with the top City dignitary, and impressed by the fact that Sir Peter had made the effort to drive out to High Wycombe through threatening flurries of snow, Sir Keith asked me how I knew him. I was about to make a joke of it and tell him that I saw my future to be in high finance, when suddenly it struck me that the C-in-C really knew very little about me – although he too had been a fighter pilot our paths had not crossed – and his question probably reflected natural curiosity about an unknown quantity on his staff. This thought reminded me that both he and Peter Bairsto had spent some time quizzing Esmé when they had first met her at High Wycombe, and I suddenly wondered if allowing ourselves to become socially invisible while I was at the RCDS and the MOD may have been more damaging than we had thought. Buying a house may be a great investment, but if the process makes a serving officer so hard up that he has to park his wife in it and live apparently apart he may be sending out the wrong signals.

In February 1982, after I had been in the job for a year, Peter Bairsto surprised me by suggesting that Esmé and I might like to accompany him and his wife to Germany for a few days. He explained this by saying that he felt that I ought to be aware of what had been done in Germany to 'harden' the airfields as there was a possibility that this process would be funded for the fighter airfields in the United Kingdom in the near future. We stayed in Germany with the Deputy Commander, John Sutton, in the Deputy Commander's impressively fine house in the grounds of the RAF hospital at Wegberg, a couple of kilometres from the HQ at Rheindahlen. Peter and I had a full Command briefing, looked over a couple of airfields, and went out in the field (frozen at −21°C) to spend a few hours with a RAF Regiment Rapier surface-to-air missile unit. I was particularly impressed during our visit to the airfields by the hardened aircraft shelters and hardened crew accommodation, sealed and pressurised to withstand chemical and biological weapon attack. Experiencing that tiny slice of RAF Germany was enough to make me feel again my earlier regret that I had never had a posting there.

Back at High Wycombe I returned to business as usual in the plans department. By late March, however, the HQ was alerted to the activities of a party of Argentineans in far away South Georgia and we began to monitor this, wondering whether it would involve any tasking by us. Concurrently there was growing concern in Whitehall as to what Argentinean intentions in the South Atlantic might be. Then, on 2 April, Argentinean forces landed on the Falkland Islands and we manned up the operations bunker for full twenty-four hour a day cover.

Shortly before the invasion occurred the Prime Minister, Mrs Thatcher, had been considering with Cabinet colleagues, advised by the single-Service Chiefs (the Chief of the Defence Staff was abroad), what response could or should be made if the Falklands were invaded. Two nuclear submarines had already been despatched southward by the Secretary of State for Defence, John Knott, in response to the Argentinean actions on South Georgia. On the eve of the invasion the Chief of the Naval Staff, Admiral Sir Henry Leach, robustly assured Mrs Thatcher that, if it became necessary, retaking the Falklands would be feasible. Within hours of the invasion happening, he was charged to prepare a task force to sail south to give us the option of taking them back. He was also instructed to send a third nuclear attack-submarine hard in the wake of the first two.

The CAS, still Sir Michael Beetham, had already tasked ACAS (Ops) to look at all possible options for RAF participation in any action to recover the islands. Following the decision to assemble the task force he had telephoned CNS to ask what the Navy might need from the RAF. CNS had been fighting a battle in Whitehall against cuts in the Navy's strength then being proposed as part of a current Defence Review. The Falklands operation presented a heaven-sent opportunity to prove the value of retaining a deep-sea capability and to show that the cuts were a mistake. To this end he was determined to keep operations to retake the Falklands exclusively dark-blue. He asked simply for three Hercules C 130s for logistic support of the task force; Sir Michael told ACAS (Ops) to bring the whole of the RAF transport force to standby.

At Strike Command we watched the build up. We listened to intelligence briefings. We acted as and when asked. However, although few of us realised it at the time, we were being somewhat marginalised. Executive power was being moved to Northwood. Northwood, on the north-west fringe of London, had been the HQ of the former RAF Coastal Command since 1938. It now housed three NATO HQs[2] plus two single-Service ones, that of C-in-C Fleet, and that of Strike Command's maritime-air Group, No. 18. C-in-C Fleet and AOC 18 Group, currently Admiral Sir John Fieldhouse and Air Marshal Sir John Curtiss respectively, also wore the NATO hats. They worked closely and well together and it was natural, therefore, when the Admiral was given command of the Falkland enterprise, that the AOC should be his Air Commander. Sir Michael Beetham, convinced that the RAF would have a crucial role to play, whether the Navy liked it or not, saw John Curtiss as the best medium for getting the RAF view across. He therefore short-circuited the normal command structure by authorising AOC 18 Group to deal directly with the other Groups likely to be involved.

It was fascinating to watch the whole thing come together. The first step for the Government was to get American permission to use the airfield built by the US Army in 1942 on the British-owned island of Ascension, a halfway stage in the 8,000 nm trip to the

Falklands; this was freely given. The next step, for the RAF, was to move equipment and supplies to Ascension to be loaded on those task-force ships that had been got under way speedily without first returning to UK ports; included in this move were six Harrier GR3s and their pilots from No. 1 Squadron, and four Chinooks and their crews from No. 18 Squadron. There was also a need to position aircraft on the island capable of providing surveillance cover for the task force as it moved south. The Nimrod maritime surveillance fleet did not have the range to go the whole distance beyond Ascension; only the Victor K2 tankers, capable of carrying a considerable weight of fuel, their crews well practised in refuelling from each other in the air, could initially do the long-range reconnaissance task. By 20 April, eight Victor K2 tankers were positioned at Ascension (and on the 22nd four of them refuelled a fifth on a flight to South Georgia to support an attempted British landing there). Action was rapidly initiated to equip the Nimrods and the Hercules fleet, and some Vulcans,[3] with an air-to-air refuelling capability.

Sir Michael Beetham had had the possibility of mounting a bombing mission in mind since the decision to retake the Falklands was made, and this was eventually approved by the Cabinet. On 1 May, two Vulcans were launched from Ascension, one as a spare, and one to bomb the airport at Port Stanley. They were supported by thirteen Victors. The difficulties encountered by the crews of both aircraft types, and the manner in which they overcame them make an epic tale.[4] The raid, by an aircraft long past its prime, followed subsequently by five more single aircraft raids, was a success. Although only one bomb, dropped on the first raid, hit the runway fair and square, its effect was to deny the use of the airfield to Argentinean offensive aircraft for the duration of the conflict; had Exocet-armed aircraft been able to land and refuel at Stanley, and consequently attack the two carriers (parked well to the east and out of range from the South American mainland) the outcome of the Falkland conflict might well have been very different.

Three of the four Chinooks sent south were lost when the ship carrying them, the *Atlantic Conveyor*, was sunk. The one Chinook that survived flew with remarkable intensity and remained unbelievably serviceable. Happily the Harriers had transferred to HMS *Hermes* before the *Atlantic Conveyor* was attacked and throughout the conflict they were heavily tasked by the Navy to fly ground attack missions. Subsequently reinforced by more No. 1 Squadron aircraft (by way of a nine-hour air-to-air refuelled flog from Acsension) and some extra pilots, the small Harrier force acquitted itself extraordinarily well; that (and the fact that 24% of the Sea Harrier pilots serving on the Naval squadrons were RAF) deserved more recognition than was accorded by RN publicity when all was done and dusted.

The Argentinean forces on the Falklands surrendered on 14 June, and while things were far from over for our people on the islands, on the ships, at Ascension or involved in one way or another within the United Kingdom, life at Strike Command settled back to normal. The staff in and out of the bunker may not have had direct control but we had been able to help in a number of ways, and we had felt part of every phase. And, having been privy to the things tackled and achieved by the Victors and their crews throughout the Falklands period, I came away from the bunker with total admiration for a force that I had previously simply set behind and suckled from.

A month before the surrender Peter Bairsto had called me into his office, and to my total – and unbelieving – delight, had told me that I had been selected for the post of Deputy Commander, RAF Germany. I was due to take this up in July. I can't be sure whether he had been aware that I was possibly being considered for this when he took me visiting in February but, as he also said that I had been considered for the post of AOC 11 Group, and that he had suggested that I should have a respite from air defence and have a chance to experience something different, it is a fair assumption that he did. It is also a fair assumption I that I owed my coming promotion to the rank of Air Vice-Marshal to him, and through him, to Keith Williamson.

I had never given much thought to the less obvious factors that affected careers in the Service, and the things that might influence the fits and starts of an individual's movement – or lack of it – upwards. I had no reason to do so until I slowed almost to a halt as an Air Commodore. The confidential reporting system in use in the RAF gave scope for adverse comment without the need to spell this out to the person reported upon. Defenders of the system argue that any such comment in one report stands out when a sequence of reports is looked at and thus undeserved disparagement can be discounted. However, I have seen mild dispraise create sufficient doubts in the minds of members of a promotion board to cause them to defer the promotion of an individual from the list they were considering. And there is nothing quite as damnatory as the thing one sometimes saw: faint praise. Although there were careful guidelines issued with the Forms 1369 in the interests of achieving a reasonable level of objectivity, and most reporting officers strived for this, likes and dislikes inevitably played a part in determining the way in which some reports were written. But, taking a person's ability and effort as read, the most important thing that anyone can hope for in any hierarchy is that he or she has the good fortune to work for people sufficiently sure of their own qualities and abilities to recognise and unstintingly commend good qualities in their subordinates. I was lucky to have worked for a few such. It is perhaps invidious to mention just five but I owe much to: Sir Michael Le Fanu in Aden, an admiral of the first water; John Nicholls at Leuchars, a fighter pilot through and through; Don McClen at Binbrook, a man of such outstanding ability that I do not doubt that he would have reached the top-most rank had not illness and marital upheaval disabled him; Air Chief Marshal Sir Dennis (Splinters) Smallwood, who supported me as C-in-C Strike Command; and Peter Bairsto, known affectionately by all who served under him as the 'Bear', and recognised by all as a shrewd, occasionally irascible, particularly demanding, but scrupulously fair boss.

Notes

1 The Board bought the idea and the concept was trialled though the 1980s. Two types of mobile radars were purchased, designated the Type 91 and the Type 92. The Type 84s were decommissioned in 1989, the Type 85s in 1991. The end of the Cold War and the concomitant political desire to achieve a 'Peace Dividend' led to a reduction in the number of mobiles in service.

2 HQ Allied C-in-C Channel, HQ C-in-C Eastern Atlantic Area, and HQ Allied Maritime Air Force Channel and Eastern Atlantic Area.

3 The Vulcan force had not used air-to-air refuelling for about twenty years. To restore it now required some serious engineering work and a lot of crew practice.

4 Well told by Rowland White (no relation) in his book *Vulcan 607*.

CHAPTER SEVENTEEN

Deputy Commander

I went to Germany in July 1982 glad to be back in charge of something other than a desk, and delighted to be at the heart of the NATO 'front line'. RAF Germany was commanded at the time by Air Marshal Sir Thomas (Jock) Kennedy, a delightful man whom I had first met on the RCDS course. As C-in-C he also held the NATO appointment of Commander Second Allied Tactical Air Force, an organisation with a Headquarters staff but no forces under direct command in peacetime. As Jock was heavily engaged in the delicate diplomacy required to ensure that 2 ATAF might actually coalesce into an effective fighting whole should war threaten, he was happy to leave his deputy to run RAF Germany as fully and as freely as any AOC running his Group. As far as I was concerned this was a very satisfactory arrangement.

HQ RAF Germany was co-located, in the vast complex of Rheindahlen, with HQ BAOR and two NATO units, HQ Northern Army Group and HQ 2 ATAF. The Command had four active airfields in West Germany (Wildenrath, Bruggen, Laarbruch, and Gutersloh) and one at Gatow in the British Sector in West Berlin. When I took up my appointment there were two Phantom squadrons and a Bloodhound SAM squadron at Wildenrath in the air defence role; four Jaguar squadrons at Bruggen; two Buccaneer squadrons at Laarbruch; and two extra-large Harrier squadrons and a Puma helicopter squadron at Gutersloh. There was also a communications squadron at Wildenrath equipped with twin piston-engined Pembrokes. The main purpose of Gatow was to provide an airhead for the resupply of the British garrison in Berlin, but it also housed a very useful listening post that enabled RAF intelligence to tune into what was going on in the air in East Germany; and it had two Chipmunks on strength to enable us to exercise our right to fly within the Berlin Control Zone.

It has always been traditional within the RAF for the commander to fly – and I was perfectly happy to pursue this and have a go with as many of the squadrons in the Command as I could. To start with I chose the easy option, the Phantom FG2. Nobody mentioned refresher flying this time, but we went about it sensibly via a very full check-out in mid-August by one of the squadrons' QFIs. He pronounced me fit and throughout my tour I flew when I could with both Phantom outfits, Nos 19 and 92 Squadrons, taking advantage not just of my familiarity with the aircraft but also of the fact that Wildenrath was only 14 kilometres down the road from the HQ. However, I had a slight problem whenever I went to fly, and this applied throughout RAF Germany: most of the aircraft were in hardened aircraft shelters and in the gloom of these the only way I could tackle the start-up checks in the cockpit was to put on my half-moon reading glasses; this was not the image of a fast-jet pilot that the young ground crews were used to and I could see an element of incredulity on their faces at the thought of some geriatric aviator foolishly trying to recapture his lost youth.

Wildenrath was also just 135 nm from the nearest point of the Inner German Border, as the German Government euphemistically called the 'Iron Curtain', and the plethora of airfields and especially prepared highway strips on the other side of it in Eastern Germany. That is, between seventeen and twenty minutes' flying time for a low-level intruder, or half that for a supersonic high-level one. These times, and the probability that the NATO air defence radars would not see much in the electronically induced fog of war, put the emphasis on setting up agreed CAPs rather than holding readiness states on the ground – the more cost-effective way of employing fighters. This situation was on the point of improving dramatically when I got to Germany with the appearance in theatre of USAF-owned Airborne Warning and Control aircraft, and with plans well advanced for NATO to procure its own. The AWACs introduced a new level of capability to the air defence world, with their ability to see low-level targets at ranges bounded only by the distance of the horizon at the heights they chose to fly and the capability of their radar.

But all this was for the future and, while I was there, we mostly practised interceptions from Wildenrath's CAP lines, an exercise often made more interesting by the open season that prevailed on the continent on all passing military aircraft. That said it was intensely irritating to be seen off constantly by Belgian F 16s capable of pulling inside the Phantoms' radius of turn and onto our tails with depressing ease.

It was quickly obvious to me that Tacevals were even more fiercely prepared for by the RAF Germany Station Commanders than they had been in the UK, with self-generated call-outs and exercises forming a pretty frequent component of the normal station routine. I didn't want to discourage this as it produced a competitive focus for people in every section of each base and kept everyone at a very effective pitch of readiness to counter the real threat if it came. However, very shortly after I became Deputy Commander I found it necessary to counsel a bit of caution and remind people not to push safety aside in the interests of realism.

Before my arrival a Phantom had shot down a Jaguar and, almost before I had found my way around my office, the results of the Board of Inquiry into the incident landed on my desk. The facts were that the Station Commander at Wildenrath had called an alert exercise and the Phantoms had been produced and armed in response. As the exercise was almost complete he was telephoned by a Taceval team, springing an unrelated surprise evaluation on an air defence radar station, to request him to supply some aircraft to test its controlling capability. He did so without first having the aircraft disarmed. On take-off the navigator of one called out, as was the standard practice on everyday training sorties, 'Check Master Armament Switch live' and the pilot, forgetting for some inexplicable reason that the aircraft was armed, put the switch to live. They were ordered to intercept the Jaguar and they did so, all too successfully. I felt it best in the circumstances to convene a court martial so that the Phantom crew would have the opportunity to be represented legally and deploy whatever defence they might have.

During the proceedings a defending barrister, who had done his homework well, pointed out that while the Command Flying Order Book allowed flights with live missiles provided they were 'made safe', the reference to making safe was a hang-over from Lightning days. The Redtop missiles, to which the book had once referred, were entirely safe unless deliberately made 'live' by plugs that the pilots had to insert in them on the ground; the missiles carried by the Phantom had no similar safety device and the Master Armament Switch was relied on in lieu. Whoever had had the job of rewriting the Command Flying Order Book whenever the Lightnings were replaced by Phantoms in RAF Germany had lazily changed the names without amending the text to suit the changed circumstances. The HQ RAF Germany staff officer responsible had been guilty of outrageously poor work – and cannot have been adequately supervised. This did not exculpate the foolish firers but it did mitigate the punishment that the Court might otherwise have awarded.

To draw a line under the whole matter and protect the Station Commander, Roger Palin, from any administrative action that might possibly be demanded from London *pour encourager les autres*, I had him in my office and formally delivered a Reprimand to him. I explained to him that the reason I was doing this was because he should have foreseen the possibility of such an accident occurring in the heat of an alert exercise and, if live weapons were to be carried, a cautionary briefing should have been delivered beforehand. I am not sure that he entirely appreciated my reasoning but, reflecting on it all later, particularly when he reached the rank of Air Chief Marshal, he could hardly hold to the belief that the Reprimand did him any harm.

Getting airborne in an aircraft with which I was comfortably familiar was one thing. However, I was forced to accept that it was not going to be so easy with anything other than the Phantom. I had thought at first that I could do a lot of the paper work that came across my desk after normal office hours in order to find time for flying, but that was naive for I soon found that about five evenings each week were going to be taken up by the round of entertaining and being entertained that was the inescapable routine of the job. And then there were the official commitments in a variety of forms that took me away from the desk. Many of these were of course a pleasure, and some a considerable pleasure. For example, a month after I arrived in Germany, I was invited to represent the C-in-C at the annual regatta of the British Kiel Yacht Club, an entity that had emerged from the aftermath of victory in 1945 via the requisitioning of premises and yachts that had belonged to the *Luftwaffe*. It had been kept alive by the establishment of a Royal Engineer diving school with enough spare capacity to run the club. I went up to Kiel throughout my tour and sailed in the club's boats whenever I could get away.

Another pleasure that Jock Kennedy passed my way was the task of representing him at the RAF Germany skiing championships at Val d'Isere the following January. This was followed in March by some skiing at Garmisch on the border with Austria. But one pleasure – and privilege – that I particularly enjoyed was visiting Berlin. A delightful house, once owned by the wartime *Luftwaffe* fighter ace Adolph Galland, had been procured for British use soon after the war ended. This was maintained and staffed for use by the C-in-C RAF Germany whenever he was in Berlin (courtesy of the 'Berlin Budget', money made available by the German Government to fund the Allied garrisons in West Berlin). Jock was happy to let me use it and I did so whenever I could. West and East Berlin with their dividing wall, the history of the town, its atmosphere, and its reminders of the Nazi era, produced a compelling atmosphere. Two particular bits of living history exemplified this: the boxing ring in the 1936 Olympic Stadium, where Joe Louis hammered Max Schmelling, was still there exactly as it had been during those Games; and the cellar in the former Supreme Court building still had hooks in the ceiling from which those tried in the building for the conspiracy to assassinate Hitler were hanged by piano-wire. I was clearly going to have to squeeze my flying into odd moments but, could I cavil if I could not find time to go solo in everything in the Command? Hardly. And in any case, as long as I could get my hands on the controls, would it matter if I flew with another pilot aboard to satisfy qualification and currency requirements? No.

My predecessor, John Sutton, had warned me that I would be required to open an air display each September at a small grass airfield called Auf dem Dümpel. This was near Bergneustadt in the hilly, wooded, country about 40 kilometres east of Cologne. The President of the airfield's flying club had had the initiative some twenty years before to call on the then C-in-C RAF Germany and persuade him to support an open day at Auf dem Dümpel. He also had had the guile to invite the C-in-C to be the show's patron in the interests of promoting continuing support. In due course this annual commitment was delegated to the Deputy Commander. As John Sutton had also said that he had attempted some German words when he opened the display I felt that I could do no less. So, some weeks before the event I did what he had done: I had what I intended to say carefully translated into good German and reproduced on tape in the interests of getting the accent absolutely right. I listened assiduously to the tape and, on the day, was confidently ready. Unfortunately, the Club's President pre-empted me by saying very largely what I was about to say as he introduced me over the loudspeaker system to the crowd. On my following two occasions as patron I made no attempt to pose as a German linguist.

We got lots of other requests for aircraft to participate in air displays throughout Germany, and we were generally able to provide them. However, I received one request that I felt it politic to turn down. The officer commanding the British Army brigade in whose area the Möhne dam lay telephoned to ask me if I could organise an over-flight of the dam by the Lancaster bomber that the RAF still kept in flying condition. He thought it would be just the thing for the brigade's open day. I thought that he might have understood that the Dambusters' raid did not have the same resonance among the locals as it had had with British filmgoers. Even though very nearly forty years had passed since the end of the war, memories were still a little raw down-stream from the Möhne.

Towards the end of September I went up to the Sennelager military training area, a vast acreage of farmland, abandoned buildings and forest, on the northern side of the Teutoburgerwald near the garrison town of Paderborn and not far from Gutersloh. This, now much used by the British Army in Germany, had been the scene of military manoeuvres since before Bismarck became the first Chancellor of the new German Empire in 1871. My purpose was to visit the Harrier Force deployed 'in the field' at Sennelager, and to combine this with a commitment to show the Harriers to a group of European parliamentarians who were having a look at some of the forces that would be assigned to 2 ATAF in war. I got there the day before the parliamentarians and had time to look around, have a thorough briefing from Gutersloh's Station Commander, Group Captain Dick Johns,[1] on the various options available for deploying the Force in war, and have a flight in a Harrier T2. I was impressed, first of all, by how far the RAF had come since my time in Chiang Mai in procuring good equipment for functioning away from base. The Harrier Force had some magnificent gear, from good tents to an impressive array of support vehicles. To add icing to the camping-equipment cake some earlier Harrier Force Commander had procured, rather like General Montgomery before him, a comfortable caravan for use when deployed; Dick Johns very kindly housed me in this for the night I spent with the Force, and it was luxury indeed. Unfortunately, the one thing that had not been improved was the standard of field latrines; our holes in the ground at Chiang Mai were infinitely preferable to the over-full Elsans I found at Sennelager.

The Harriers were parked under pine trees just off a metalled road running through the woods around it. We strapped in for my flight under the trees. Squadron Leader Burwell, the pilot taking me up, did his checks, then the camouflage netting over the aircraft was removed, and we were pushed out onto the roadway for a rapid start-up (away from the risk of setting the 'hide' alight). Take-off was a matter of running for a hundred yards or so along the roadway.

Once airborne I was given control and had an enjoyable thirty-five minutes throwing the Harrier around at low level and having a bird's-eye view of the Sennelager area. My impression of the aircraft was that it was very similar in performance at low level to the Hunter, perhaps a little less stable, and somewhat lighter on the controls. However, I was not offered an opportunity to try my hand at hovering or any of the things special to the Harrier. I had to hand control back for the landing, which was adroitly accomplished, vertically downwards, on to a pierced steel-plate laid out in a clearing at the side of the road from which we had taken off.

The short take-off and the vertical landing capabilities of the aircraft were certainly impressive and with these attributes, and the weapons now available for the Harrier force such as the SNEB rocket pod, cluster bombs, and soon, hopefully, laser-guided bombs, ground attack had certainly advanced since I was on 20 Squadron. The head-up display in the GR3 represented an improvement in weapon-aiming as well, and the inertial navigation system, provided there was time available for it to be aligned properly, was a very useful aid to getting accurately to the chosen IP. Above all, the Harrier force offered survivability in an environment where attacks on airfields would unquestionably be given the highest priority. Provided the plans for resupply in the field could be made to work in the disruption and fog of battle, the Harrier would certainly have a vital role to play in helping stop Soviet tanks if they ever rolled across the IGB. Unfortunately, as Gutersloh was a bit too far from Rheindahlen for a quick nip out of the office, the Harrier was one RAF Germany aircraft in which I could hardly hope to have more than a very occasional trip.

However, the distance between Rheindahlen and Bruggen did not pose the same problem and I felt that I should have a go at getting to solo stage in the Jaguar. I had my first flight in early October with the officer commanding No. 17 Squadron, Wing Commander Peter Johnston. I followed this with four conversion sorties over a two-day period some five weeks later with the squadron QFI, Squadron Leader Holder. On 12 November I was sent off by myself for a low-level trip, having been given one final warning to avoid rotating for take-off at too slow a speed. I had not noticed any particular problem but apparently the Adour engines did not have the power to overcome the drag that could be induced if the nose was lifted too high in an attempt to get off the ground. I set off in a north-westerly direction, skirting the Ruhr and on into the north German plain, gingerly using the Jaguar's moving-map display to tell me where I was. This was a considerable luxury for an old Hunter – and even Lightning – pilot and more than made up for the absence of a navigator in this single-seat aircraft; however, being an old Hunter pilot, I still monitored my progress carefully using the map in my hand.

The Jaguar was designed for fast low-level penetration of enemy defences and, accordingly, the ride through the turbulence that is inevitable near ground level was a lot smoother than I remembered it having been in the Hunter. At height it was somewhat unstable, as I found when I later flew one down to the NATO weapons' centre at Decimomannu in Sardinia to visit one of the RAF Germany squadrons on detachment there. As there was no autopilot, and it didn't seem possible to trim successfully for level flight, I found I had to watch my height constantly and work away at countering the aircraft's continuing attempts to depart from it. Because it was possible to pre-dial 'way-points' into the aircraft's computer and thereby report with an accuracy that I hadn't previously known in a single-seat aircraft, it was possible to fly on civil airways. This was just as well, as most continental countries were tending to phase out – other than in designated training areas – the right of military aircraft to navigate freely as had once been the case above the level of civilian flights. The other requirement for flying airways – which the Jaguar also had – was the height responder facility on the Identification Friend or Foe kit. The accuracy that this device provided had its penalties however. As I checked in on passing over an airway reporting point at Nice, en route to Decci, a female voice asked me to report my height. When I replied that I was at Flight Level 330, which is 33,000 feet with the standard millibar setting of 1013.2 dialled into the altimeter, she came back immediately with 'No you are not, you are at 32,800 feet'. Given that International Air Traffic rules require aircraft on specific headings to be at specific flight levels, separated by (at the very least) 1,000 feet of height difference, and given the Jaguar's friskiness in pitch, I felt that a passing 200 foot deviation from my required flight level was not at all bad. But I had not allowed for a bit of Gallic feminist point scoring.

Bruggen represented the serious side of our Cold War defences. Four Jaguars were kept permanently on standby there, each loaded with two tactical nuclear bombs slung under their wings. The hardened aircraft shelters in which they were housed were themselves inside security fences guarded by armed RAF police in watch-towers and at the electronically operated gates across the taxiway leading out of the readiness dispersal. The police had orders to shoot any pilot attempting to taxi out if they had not received the requisite and required coded clearance. By my time in Germany the RAF had been handling nuclear weapons for over twenty-five years without risk or mishap. Orders and instructions were clear and tight, and ground-handling equipment proven – or so we thought.

One evening I was telephoned by Bruggen's Station Commander, John Thompson, to say that he had a problem: a bomb being returned from servicing at Aldermaston (nestling in its specially designed carrying-case) had not been properly secured on the low-loader lorry that was transporting it from the delivering Hercules to storage in the Bruggen bomb-dump (the Hercules had been late in arriving, the Station Armament Officer had been called away to deal with something else, and the corporeal driver, on duty longer than he thought he would be, decided that he could get away without strapping the case onto the low-loader as was clearly required by regulations). The bomb, or rather the carrying-case with the bomb in it, had slid off the low-loader as the driver turned a corner and had hit the ground. The case had burst and some slight damage appeared to have been done to the casing of the bomb. To cover the possibility of a leakage of radiation John Thompson had sensibly called a 'practice' incident to enable him quietly to establish a cordon on the Station at a safe distance. The laid down procedures required me to acquaint the British Embassy at Bonn immediately of any type of nuclear incident, no matter how trivial, and this I did. The following morning I went down to Bonn to have a word with my point of contact there, the Minister, Christopher Mallaby. Christopher, later HM Ambassador in Bonn, and after that in Paris, was primarily interested in knowing how quickly we could remove the problem from Germany. He was not very happy when I told him that nothing could be done until experts had been whistled up from Aldermaston, and had had time to determine if the bomb could be moved safely. There followed a fraught period while it was painstakingly pored over and the warhead carefully X-rayed. Nobody was taking any chances and there were a considerable number of consultations between the experts on the spot and Aldermaston. Finally, after some three weeks of testing and teeth-sucking the bomb was deemed safe for moving, loaded onto a Hercules and shipped out. As it turned out, there never had been any risk of radiation leakage. However, nerves in the Embassy stayed a little frayed until I was able to report that the bomb was well out over the North Sea; the real fear was perhaps not so much of a leakage of radiation, but rather of a leakage to the German Press. The subsequent Board of Inquiry into the incident recommended disciplinary action against six servicemen.

Incidentally, the especially designed cases in which the bombs were transported had been tested for strength as a condition of their procurement. The requirement was that they survive undamaged a drop of twenty-five feet onto a concrete surface. They had passed this test perfectly but no one seemed to have thought of testing them with a mock-up in them of the heavy article they were designed to contain.

I paid my first visit to Berlin in December, flying up the access corridor from Braunschweig in a Pembroke at 3,000 feet. Visibility was good and it was very interesting to see, assembled on the airfields that we passed over or near, some of the Russian military strength that was deployed close to the Iron Curtain. The corridor, one of three agreed in 1945 when the western allies and the Russians were still friendly, led into the Berlin Control Zone, a circular cylinder centred on Berlin of 35 nm diameter stretching from ground level to 15,000 feet. Flights within the Zone were coordinated by one of the very few four-power cooperative ventures that had survived much beyond 1945, the Berlin Air Safety Centre. There was an agreed right of flight throughout the control Zone for all four former allies, and some thirty years after my last flight in a Chipmunk I had one over Berlin, crossing into the Russian Sector at 1,000 feet at the Brandenburg Gate, flying down the Unter den Linden before having a scenic tour of most of East Berlin. Even at that height it was possible to see how tatty that slice of city was in comparison with the thrusting, prosperous-looking, busy bit on the western side of the wall.

The original post-war agreement allowed military and civilian flights along the corridors but restricted the latter to a few nominated airlines, in our case British European Airways – and later British Airways – only. The originally agreed top height of the corridors, 15,000 feet, probably seemed very reasonable in 1945, but in the jet age the airlines wanted the advantage of flying higher both for fuel economy and to avoid subjecting the paying passengers unnecessarily to turbulent conditions nearer the ground. However, the Russians were unwilling to change the terms of an agreement that they had willingly reached in the heady aftermath of victory.

At the beginning of February 1983 I flew out to the United States in an RAFVC-10 to visit one of Germany's Jaguar squadrons detached, as part of an on-going programme to Nellis Air Force Base, for live weapons training. I was met by John Thompson and members of the squadron, taken to check into my Las Vegas hotel, and then 'down town' for a meal. The fact that it was three o'clock in the morning by my body clock did not deter them at all. The USAF had established at Nellis, and in the Nevada desert, an extremely effective weapons-training complex. There was an 'Aggressor Squadron' that studied Soviet tactics, and flew aircraft painted in Russian colours and with Russian insignia; they were the 'enemy' with a mission to disrupt the ground attack and bombing sorties mounted by the visiting squadrons. F 15s were provided to fly escort to the weapon-delivering aircraft, the latter all carrying live munitions to fire or drop on the ground ranges. And there was the pinnacle of sophistication for air combat training – an Air Combat Manoeuvring Range whose radars could record combat exercises in detail and whose sensors, using responses from pods mounted for the exercises on the participating aircraft, could record the participants' heading, height, speed, g, and angle of attack at any and every moment during it. The end product was a definitive record of results for use during debriefing – and a resultant improvement in tactics and pilot skills in combat.

I was given a ride in a two-seat F 15, one of four escorting a flight of six RAF Germany Jaguars carrying live bombs to drop when they reached the target area some sixty miles up-country. We flew at 3,000 feet watchfully waiting for the Aggressors to pounce on the Jaguars and, when they did, found ourselves immediately in a glorious swirling low-level dogfight. The F 15 was a joy to throw about and absolutely splendid at low-level, high-speed, high g manoeuvring. I was an instant convert to it and desperately wished, as so often RAF pilots had wished over the years, that the British Government would splash out for the odd up-to-date bit of kit from the States – and avoid tinkering and modification on the rare occasion that it did buy anything!

In April, Jock Kennedy departed, destined for the Air Force Board as Air Member for Personnel. He was replaced by Air Marshal Sir Patrick Hine – the same Paddy Hine who had dragged me away from my law books at Andover nearly twenty years before. I don't know whether he was concerned that past friendship might be detrimental to a professional working relationship between us, but from the beginning he was, and remained, unwilling to allow himself the close relationship with his deputy that had been Jock's style. However, he was the boss and I adjusted to the new regime. Happily one thing did not change: although Paddy was determined to visit every corner of his parish, and get airborne whenever he could, he did not cavil at my well established practice of getting away from the office for some flying myself and in May I was back in the Phantom, even getting a weekend trip in one, via a stop at Brindisi, to Akrotiri.

The next opportunity I had to venture into East Berlin was in late June. This time I travelled from West Berlin by car via the Glienicke Brücke, the agreed crossing point for military vehicles and, according to a number of Hollywood films, the spot where captured spies were exchanged. The occasion was a cocktail party given by the members of the British Mission to the Commander-in-Chief, Russian Forces in Germany (BRIXMIS) in its Mission House. These Missions – the French and Americans each had one as well, and the Russians had reciprocal ones with the western three – had been set up in 1945 for genuine liaison purposes. However, as each had the right to travel in the others' areas of control they had gradually developed over the years into useful little spying teams.[2] And, of course, each was subject to restrictions and close observation when on the opposite side of the IGB to their own. In East Germany, our people were often subjected to downright dangerous interferences. For example, their vehicles would be forced into 'accidents' on the road, and on one occasion I had to protest as Duty Commander (a duty which the Chief of Staff, BAOR and I held in turn) via the head of SOXMIS, the normal conduit to the Soviet authorities, after two members of BRIXMIS had been injured when their car was forced into a ditch.

Our side did not set out to injure but we were not above a few tricks, such as when we got the West German police to arrest a SOXMIS crew for 'illegal parking' and, while they were detained, carted away their car and stripped it to see what sort of recording and camera equipment were in its hidden compartments. That naturally brought a protest from SOXMIS and another lengthy exchange of correspondence. At the cocktail party, however, all was sweetness if not light, and I had a lengthy spell trying to converse with the Chief of Staff of the Soviet Air Forces in Germany, Major General V Myescheryakov. He seemed a pleasant enough man but, as he had what I took to be a political minder at his elbow at all times, he was not very forthcoming and carefully avoided putting forward any views on any of the subjects on which I tried to open a serious conversation. When, finally, I suggested to him that it was a bit ridiculous for two former allies to be lined up against each other across the IGB, and that perhaps we were unnecessarily fearful of each other's intentions he said, glancing at his minder: 'We are frightened of nobody.' Good patriotic stuff, but death to the pursuit of a meaningful discussion.

Having had a few trips in the Puma, and found how willing No. 230 Squadron was to fly one to Rheindahlen whenever I asked, I felt that I should show willing in return and learn to fly the aircraft. I spoke to Dick Johns about the possibility of organising a short course and this was arranged for mid-August in a very easy and convenient way: I was picked up by a Puma on each of three mornings from the grass just outside the fence that surrounded the Headquarters and put through a trimmed-down syllabus of six training sorties by the Squadron's QFI, Flight Lieutenant Brewerton. My only previous experience of helicopters, apart from sitting down the back end of several on various transit flights, and following winching from dinghy drills at sea, comprised one flight in the cockpit of a Whirlwind many years before with my old QUAS instructor Harry Dodd at the controls. I recall thinking then how impossible it seemed to be to deal with and coordinate the demands of stick, rudders, cyclic pitch and twist-grip throttle. However, technology had moved on and in the Puma a computer made things much simpler by keeping the engine output matched to the demands made of the main blades, and the tail-rotor in balancing tune. Thus, while there was still a lot to learn, including how to cope with the computer off-line, getting to grips with the modern machine was not as difficult as I had expected. At the end of the sixth flight we landed at Bruggen, shut down, and I was sent solo. All I had to do was start up, lift the machine of the ground a few feet into a hover and, having ascertained that everything was working as advertised, fly across the airfield and land. I found myself feeling again something of the apprehension about being able to do it as I had felt on my solo trip in the Chipmunk – and much the same exhilaration when I had accomplished it. Having spent so many years rushing at speed down runways to get airborne, and decelerating along them on landing, the ability to lift into the air and put down again almost anywhere was somehow very appealing. While I wouldn't have wished to have started out on helicopters, and missed all the years on fighters, I was now more than ready to use any reasonable excuse to fly the Puma.

Out of the blue I got an invitation to go and meet the SOXMIS people at their West Germany mission house at Bunde, in the BAOR I Corps area. I went up by Puma and landed on a hockey-pitch sized patch of grass surrounded by quite tall poplar trees within a rather dreary looking compound enclosed by barbed wire. There was an office building, a Mess building and a few houses for the use of those SOXMIS personnel who chose (or were allowed) to bring their wives with them. Outside the compound, and down the road a little, a British military police-car was parked, permanently on stand-by to follow any sorties out of it. The seven members of the SOXMIS team were lined up to greet me, Brigadier General Golitsyn (the head of mission) saluting and smiling broadly as I climbed down from the chopper. After he had introduced me to his officers, and shown me around, we got down to a session of informal talks, amounting initially to little more than a discussion of the complaints about which we had previously corresponded with each other, and ending with mutual assurances of good will and a promise by the General to ask the 'East German Police' to respect the rights that the Russians had given us in 1945. I wasn't sure what to make of that promise but, as it had been the East Germans who had been giving us most grief I gave him the benefit of the doubt; it was just possible that the East Germans were acting, not as surrogates, but on their own malicious initiative.

Talks over, the General led the way into the dining room of the Mission Mess and my heart sank at the sight of a table piled high with food. I knew that before we started eating we would almost inevitably have to follow the Russian tradition of toasting each other, and everything we could think of – and we did. A couple of hours later, having eaten our way through the mountain of food and talked some more, I climbed aboard the Puma, started it up and, determined to make a good exit from the poplar tree confines of the compound, lifted us into the sky like a rocket. The 230 Squadron pilot – with me to satisfy currency requirements – was rather alarmed by the rate of ascent and made to reach to restrain it, doubtless concerned that I might override the computer-controlled synchronisation between blade angles and power. However, as the Puma was designed to lift the weight equivalent of sixteen fully equipped soldiers, and was empty, no harm ensued.

I flew the Puma whenever I could through September and October and, in December, had an introductory trip in a Chinook of No. 18 Squadron. The squadron had deployed to RAF Germany in June and had been working up with No. I British Corps since. As it had not yet built up to a full complement of aircraft post Falklands – and was only slowly achieving it – I felt it best to leave the crews to their work-up for the time being, content myself with looking in on the outfit whenever I was up at Gutersloh, and continue to fly with 230 Squadron.

I also had the opportunity to get a ride in an Army Gazelle from time to time whenever I needed a speedy transit from Rheindahlen to some distant site and 230 Squadron could not oblige. The Gazelle pilots were mostly SNCOs, which reflected an employment policy quite different to that of the RAF. The Germans, too, had NCOs in the cockpit: once when I got a lift in a *Luftwaffe* 'Huey' with my good friend and former Messerschmitt 109 pilot, Major General Hans Flade, the Chief of Staff of 2 ATAF, we were flown – very competently in thick cloud – by a corporal. I had always been somewhat ambivalent about the RAF's policy of commissioning pilots and navigators. Perhaps it was a good recruiting lure to offer short-service commissions widely, but I think we might have missed some useful people by fishing in a pool narrowed by looking for 'officer qualities'. Against that, it seemed wrong to have the mix that we had during the Second World War when officers and NCOs were often exposed to the same risks and responsibilities in the air, but at different pay and accommodation scales on the ground.

Another change under way in the Command during the autumn of 1983 was the replacement of the Buccaneers at Laarbruch by Tornados. The first Buccaneer Squadron to disband and reform with its new aircraft was No. 15, followed a month or so later by No. 16. I had had no great desire to learn to fly the Buccaneer, an aircraft that had been developed for the Navy, and was by now well past its prime, but I had felt for some time that I had better show some willing and had eventually organised a trip in one. I was taken up by Laarbruch's Commanding Officer, Group Captain Graham Smart. Graham, anxious to show me what the aircraft could do in terms of its low-level under-the-radar penetration role, had arranged for a pair of Phantoms to mount CAP and we occupied ourselves for about thirty minutes with runs against them and a bit of hard evasive turning. All very well for Graham with his hands on the controls in front, but not very interesting for me in the back. I was sitting low in a control-less compartment my vision impeded, as it had been on the Phantom trip from Coningsby to Leuchars, by apparatus that I didn't even know how to turn on. And then we set off for a few passes on a bombing range. Hitherto I had simply been a little bored in the back but now, with negative g on each dive on the target and high positive g on each pull-out, I began to feel decidedly unwell. I had never felt like this when I was doing much the same thing in Hunters, but then I was in current flying practice with the aviation equivalent of 'sea-legs', and I was doing the flying (which was probably what kept me hale and hearty in the F 15 out of Nellis). It was acutely embarrassing having to hand over a sick-bag (fortuitously left in the aircraft by a previous occupant) to the airman who saw us back into dispersal at Laarbruch. It was almost as if the aeroplane was paying me back for my disdain for it. One positive thing did come out of the trip, however: for the first time in my flying life I began to appreciate the courage and stoicism of navigators and other aircrew who don't have any chance of getting their hands on the thing that really matters – the stick. Happily it doesn't take long, back on firm ground, to recover, and by the time I was on the way back to Rheindahlen the colour had returned to my face, and the only thing I was suffering from was the loss of some dignity at Laarbruch.

The evening ahead included dinner at Flagstaff House, the

residence of the C-in-C BAOR, General Sir Nigel Bagnall. The Prime Minister Margaret Thatcher was staying overnight with him and he had invited a cross-section of senior staff from the combined HQs to come and meet her. She was seated for dinner on the General's right, by his deaf (gunner's) ear. I was seated immediately on her right and, from the moment she realised that he was having difficulty hearing her, and for most of the time we were at the table, I had her attention. Our conversation began rather blandly with the PM asking me what I did and what I thought of life in Germany. She then asked me – she had obviously been well briefed about BAOR – if the wives of RAF men in Germany were as disgruntled as Army wives were about spending so much of their lives there and missing out on the opportunities that the United Kingdom provided for gainful employment (it was not in fact a serious problem for us as RAF personnel, on the whole, spent much less of their lives in Germany than the Army people did). She felt, she said, that surely wives would prefer to be with their husbands rather than be unaccompanied as was happening so frequently when units were sent to Northern Ireland. That led us on to the topic of the 'troubles' in the Province and, when she discovered that I hailed from there she asked if I had any views on the possibility of the two sections of the community ever reaching agreement on anything. I suggested that it might well be possible but not quickly, and it would first be necessary to find a way to weaken or placate the Republican desire to make Northern Ireland part of the Irish Republic. However, I went on, before any offers were made to either side both should be starved a little of the unemployment benefits that enabled so many to be full-time terrorists. I even suggested, slightly mischievously, that it might be worthwhile trying to concentrate minds in the Province by announcing an intention to remove all troops on a given date, say, in eighteen months from any such announcement. 'But we did that in Aden,' she immediately parried, 'and that produced nothing but chaos.' 'Ah, but Aden was quite different,' I countered, adding rather pretentiously that I was there at the time. 'The two terrorist groups in Aden, unlike the Irish, wanted the same thing. They were simply determined to out-do each other in nastiness to the British in order to win support locally. An impending end-date in Ulster might make negotiations with both sides possible and profitable.' I banged on at some length about the nature of the tribal divisions in Northern Ireland, doubtless telling her what she already knew, and probably boring the pants off her, but she was gracious enough to listen.

In February, a test pilot from Boscombe Down brought a Hunter T7 out to Germany to give us a look at the work being done on Forward Looking Infra Red, a device for picking out heat emitting sources on the ground. He also had with him a couple of sets of helmet-mounted Night Vision Goggles. I had not had any experience of either, and when I went up with him for a low-level flight on a pitch-black night I was impressed by both. There was still some work to be done on FLIR but it was easy to see that it had considerable potential. I was aware that Night Vision Goggles were already in service but to me they were novel, and it was a new experience to approach an unlighted airfield and runway, seeing both in a sort of ghostly greenness, and be able to carry out a landing as easily as one did by daylight. While hurling an aircraft at the ground in the dark in a steep dive was never going to be comfortable,[3] on the strength of this short experience it was easy to be convinced that both devices were going to make a real difference to ground attack work in the future, and most particularly to close air support.

1984 continued at a fast pace with commitments of one sort or another both inside the HQ and away from it. There was plenty to do and very little that wasn't a pleasure. In late February, for example, I travelled to Bad Kohlgrub, near Oberammergrau in the Bavarian Alps to visit the RAF Germany Winter Survival School for a couple of days. As well as exposing aircrews to the rigours of camping in the snow in self-built shelters, and then subjecting them to interrogation sessions conducted by professional Service interrogators, the school offered participants a chance to learn to ski. Although the first two items had to be endured, the skiing was a pleasure and ensured that there was never a shortage of people wanting to go on the school's courses. I ducked out of the interrogation bit, however.

In March I travelled to Switzerland at the invitation of the CAS of the Swiss Air Force, a delightfully pleasant man whom I had hosted on a visit to RAF Germany the previous autumn. Among the highlights of this trip was a look at one of the underground hangars that the Swiss had sunk into the sides of mountains and equipped to survive several months of nuclear ravage across Europe. I also watched Swiss Hunters practising live air-to-ground firing at a range high in the Alps, and a Swiss Air Force anti-aircraft gun unit firing live shells at towed targets in another section of the Alps, somewhat surprised that both activities were possible in a country that I had always thought to be short of space and full of people pursuing out-door activities. Before leaving I was given the chance to try my hand at a Pilatus P7, a rather nifty and fully aerobatic two-seater training machine that British Aerospace, acting for the manufacturers, was keen to sell to the RAF.

In April I began again the annual round of Air Officer's Inspections of our five airfields plus the RAF Hospital at Wegberg, the administrative unit supporting the HQ, RAF Rheindahlen, and the RAF unit at Decimomannu. They all came and went with due formality, some excellent hospitality, and a chance to chat with people across the rank structure. At Wegberg I was reminded that I had banged on about the rank structure in relation to discipline some six months before when the commanding officer of the hospital had remanded one of his nurses to me on a Charge. She was a flight lieutenant in the Princess Mary's Royal Air Force Nursing Service who had joined the gliding club at Bruggen, been instructed by a corporal, succumbed to his charms, and was later found in bed with him in a caravan by a couple of Bruggen's patrolling RAF Policemen. During the process of hearing the Charge she was accompanied by another woman, as is the standard requirement. The latter was a substantial lady who seemed to be glowering at me throughout the proceedings, and particularly fiercely when the 'offender' started to weep. This happened when I pointed out to the nurse that the Royal Air Force Act conferred on officers the power to order those under them – perhaps, in the circumstances, I should have said subordinate to them – to carry out actions that might well be hazardous and, in war, could even result in their deaths. Unless discipline was nurtured and enforced, I went on to explain, such orders might not be followed *in extremis*; and sleeping with a person to whom one might have to issue an order, particularly an unpleasant one, was hardly conducive to the level of discipline necessary in a military context. All very ponderous stuff but I felt it necessary to say something in an egalitarian and sexually liberated age that might get through to her. I caught sight of her during my inspection of the hospital, hesitating in a doorway, almost as if she was torn between wanting to hide and wanting to speak. We didn't speak but the woman who had accompanied her, a squadron leader matron, did make a point of seeking me out to tell me that until they had heard my harangue about discipline neither had appreciated the responsibilities involved. I had thought she was going to take me to task for being harsh to one of her girls, or even to point out to me that a nurse was hardly likely to need to issue hazardous orders. I was very happy that I got both assumptions wrong.

By July I had been Deputy Commander for two years – normally the most that one could hope for in any senior command appointment. However, the MOD was in the middle of another round of cuts and joint-Service rationalisations and a temporary freeze had been imposed on postings for people of my rank level and above until it had been completed. I had been told in February that my next appointment would most likely be as Commandant of the Staff College at Bracknell, but that this could be contingent on the outcome of the MOD review. And, Jock Kennedy had warned me later in the year that once this had been completed, he might well want me to move quickly. As it turned out, he did: the freeze ended in early September, my posting to Bracknell was confirmed, and my date of departure from Germany was fixed for two weeks later. I agreed to a request that I get swiftly to Bracknell to take over from my predecessor there as soon as possible.

I embarked on a whistle-stop tour of visits to the various units in the Command, and even managed a trip to Kiel to enjoy for the last time the British Yacht Club's autumn regatta. I also squeezed in a helicopter ride to Auf dem Dümpel to open the air show for a third time, and take my leave of my friends there. I had not done too well in 1984 as far as flying was concerned; apart from the T7 ride, the swirl around in the Pilatus P7 in Switzerland, an introductory flight in a Tornado GR2, and a few sorties in Pumas and Phantoms, but I really had no cause for complaint. I had one final flight on 4

September; it was, as my first flight in Germany had been, in a Phantom on a low-level PI trip in the Ardennes area south-west of Aachen – once again being duffed up by Belgian F 16s!

My tour in RAF Germany had given me the greatest pleasure. The military environment was fascinating; the job outstanding; the opportunities to fly a wide variety of aircraft types, unique. I had waited a long time to be posted there. And it had been worth the wait.

Notes

1 Gutersloh's Station Commander also had the role of Force Commander of deployed Harrier squadrons in war. Dick Johns went on to become CAS.
2 The BRIXMIS team found their most productive source of information to be from papers and documents carelessly discarded in Russian waste dumps.
3 See Chris J Bain's account on pages 3 and 4 of his book *Cold War: Hot Wings*.

CHAPTER EIGHTEEN

Turning Finals

Esmé and I left Germany travelling in a Hercules – by choice. We had two cars to get back to Britain and very luckily I had found a lift for them – and us – on an aircraft returning empty to RAF Lyneham from Gutersloh. The Hercules, as many military personnel could attest, is a very uncomfortably noisy aircraft. But I was more than grateful for the ride, noisy or not, and for the convenience accorded me by its operators. Within half a day of leaving Rheindahlen, we were on the M4 heading for Bracknell.

The following day, with hardly time to catch my breath, I was being walked around the College by the Deputy Commandant, Air Commodore Joe Hardstaff, by way of introduction to it as Commandant. I was glad to be there – I had got a lot from my time at Andover and, since those days, had been totally sold on the value of the Staff College course to the RAF. I was sure that that I would enjoy being back in that academic environment, and possibly at the same time, be able to make a reasonably useful contribution to it.

However, as I paused during my introductory tour to look at the photographs of previous Commandants hanging in Bracknell's entrance hall, the idea of making a contribution there suddenly seemed rather presumptuous. Almost all of the men portrayed had gone on to fill top appointments, many of them becoming Chiefs of the Air Staff. I would be following a long line of very acute and capable predecessors and it was entirely probable that there was little left that I, or any subsequent Commandant, could hope to do by way of making useful changes. But, simply functioning as a figurehead was not my style; I would have to see what I could get my teeth into.

Nor was it my style to think that I would automatically follow the upward path of past Commandants as evidenced by the rogues' gallery in the entrance hall. If Bracknell turned out to be half as pleasurable as RAF Germany had been it wouldn't matter if I did not. I would retire happy. That said, it would be totally dishonest to deny that it was very satisfying to the ego to have been given the opportunity to follow so many distinguished predecessors into what was obviously a highly regarded appointment.

Bracknell now ran four separate courses simultaneously. The first that an officer did was a correspondence course that could be taken over a period of eighteen months. This had replaced the examinations that were previously the necessary prerequisite for selection to the rank of squadron leader and for selection for the original year-long Staff College course. The next step in the scheme of staff training was a month-long Junior Command Course, long since removed from Ternhill and now at RAF Henlow, which introduced junior officers to leadership skills, public speaking and some practical applications of Air Force law. The third level was a month-long Junior Staff Course held at Bracknell, attended by squadron leaders, and concentrating largely on the disciplines of staff work at their level; with thirty people per course and ten courses per year this allowed a useful number of young officers to be given some preparation, for junior staff appointments.[1] The fourth level was the time-honoured year-long Staff Course, still with the same objectives and wide spectrum of mentally stimulating activities, updated and contemporary, and changed just a little to accommodate the fact that it was now attended mainly by officers of wing commander rank (or equivalent from the other, and foreign, Services). I reviewed everything, well aware that the courses had been massaged and developed over the years, but I felt I ought to have a little twiddle on the knobs just to establish who was in control. I added a bit on logical thinking and reasoning to the curriculum of the Junior Staff Course and, for the next main course starting in January, added to the amount of time devoted to discussions on international terrorism, and created some opportunities for formal debate on topical matters, but I was otherwise happy to leave things undisturbed. The staffs of the various courses breathed a collective sigh of relief when they realised that there was not going to be a major upheaval, and got on with what they were already doing well.

I spent over two years at Bracknell in a thoroughly absorbing role, meeting, talking with and entertaining members of the Air Force Board, Commanders-in-Chief from the three Services, members of the Government and the Opposition, members of military delegations from abroad, captains of industry, and a variety of other interesting people who came to lecture. I went with the courses on visits to Service establishments in Britain, toured USAF bases in Germany, went to sea with the Navy, and travelled to lecture to Staff Colleges in Canada, Italy, Germany, Pakistan[2] and the United States. I didn't have many opportunities to fly – and I could hardly have expected to – but I did manage regularly to bag a RAF Gazelle helicopter for flights between Bracknell and Henlow on my visits there to lecture to the Junior Command courses, and I had one nostalgic trip in a Lightning on a fleeting visit to Binbrook.

Each year the three single-Service Staff Colleges got together for a fortnight to give the students an opportunity jointly to look at, discuss and work at joint-Service operational problems and the support they required. The venue for this was the Army Staff College at Camberley – with a formal dinner for all participants held towards the end of the fortnight in the Painted Hall at the Royal Naval Staff College at Greenwich (an occasion made memorable not only by the sheer splendour and historical associations of the Hall but also by the loud and enthusiastic rendering by some 300 British students – to the bemusement of the foreign ones – of a collection of last-night-of-the-Proms type songs from 'Rule Britannia' through 'Hearts of Oak' to 'Land of Hope and Glory').

During the joint-Service fortnights each of the single-Service Commandants hosted, in turn, the various visiting speakers. On two succeeding years it fell to me to look after, among others, the Opposition spokesman on defence matters, Mr Denzil Davies. On both years, following his talk to the combined student body about the Labour Party's defence policy, he was given a hard time during the question periods, and it was obvious that he was ill at ease defending the Party's anti-nuclear policy. During lunch on his second visit I asked him why Neil Kinnock persisted with that policy when he must know that it was hardly a vote winner. His answer was either disarmingly frank, or an attempt to deflect the question with a joke: 'Neil can't change it,' he said, 'Glynis wouldn't let him.'

About six months before the end of my nominal two years at Bracknell I had a telephone call out of the blue from Jerry Seavers asking if he could come and see me. I had had no contact with him for about five years apart from an annual exchange of Christmas cards. The last time he had called me was to ask if I would defend him at a court martial that he had been warned he might have to face. He was at that time in command of a Jaguar squadron at RAF Coltishall. While leading a formation of four aircraft to Denmark for an air-exercise there, and trying to stay below a lowering cloud-base, he had breached the minimum height of 500 feet allowed for low-flying over Holland. A member of his formation had felt that he had taken them dangerously low and had reported this to higher authority. As it turned out, he was not court-martialled but was rather peremptorily removed from command of his squadron. All he would say on the telephone was that he wanted to put a proposition to me. Intrigued, I invited him to come and stay overnight.

I was aware that Jerry had retired from the RAF a couple of years after losing his command, had gone to work for the Sultan of Oman's Air Force as a squadron pilot, and had progressed to command Thumrait, the Omani Air Force Jaguar base. When he came to stay, and we had got the preliminary social chit-chat out of the way, he told me that later that year he was to be replaced by an Omani officer and had been considering what he might do when this appointment rendered him redundant in Oman. He had researched the prospects of selling an airborne target-towing and ECM training service to the Omanis and to other Middle Eastern military forces and was convinced, largely by the Omani reaction to it, that the idea had distinct possibilities. He felt that Paphos airport, Cyprus, at that time seriously under-utilised, would be a well-sited base from which to operate the service into the Arab world. He had prepared a business plan, and had made some preliminary and encouraging enquiries in the City about the possibility of finding finance for the venture. He reminded me that I had once mentioned that I was thinking of living in Cyprus when I retired and was wondering if I had decided to do this. If I had, he went on, he wondered if I would be interested in joining him in forming a company there to pursue his idea. I was indeed increasingly attracted by the idea of retiring to Cyprus, an idea whose origins went back as far as the 247 Squadron detachment when I had discovered both how much I liked the place and how comfortable my skin became in a warm climate. Moreover, as both Caroline and Julia were by now married and well settled, there was no family obstacle to retiring abroad.

I was more than interested in his proposal as a post-retirement pursuit. The prospect of running a flying operation, with all the possibilities that movement around the Middle East in one's own aeroplanes might open up, was very appealing. If I was not in line for any further promotion I would have to leave the RAF at the standard age for retiring of fifty-five, a matter of a year away. This timing was acceptable to Jerry. However, if I was in line for further promotion before my next birthday, then I would not be retired on it and, as there were a couple of appealing appointments at the next rank level on the verge of becoming vacant in the months ahead, either of which I would have been happy to find myself appointed to, I was inclined to make no decisions prematurely about retirement. Besides, appealing as Jerry's idea was, he was offering very little more than birds in the bush. I told him that I was very interested but could not commit to a specific date for joining him.

Time passed and others filled the appealing appointments. Then one afternoon after work, about a month before I had completed two years at Bracknell, I got back to the Commandant's house to find C-in-C Strike Command, now Air Chief Marshal Sir Peter Harding, sitting in the drawing room having a cup of tea with Esmé. 'Just called for a chat,' he said. As he had not done that before, and as Bracknell was off the beaten track between High Wycombe and Whitehall, I thought it a bit odd. When we had dispensed with the teacups and settled down to a gin and tonic he said 'I've just been looking over the plot with David and I am afraid that there isn't a three-star job coming up in the near future.' I assumed that he was talking about David Craig, the CAS, but, as I hadn't been aware that Peter Harding was on the point of succeeding him, I didn't immediately realise that he was speaking as a man with an already significant influence on future senior appointments rather than as one simply conversing about how things were in a reducing Air

Force.'We feel that people caught by such circumstances should not have to retire at fifty-five,' he continued.'So, if you're happy to stay at Bracknell for a further nine months there'll be an appointment available for you.'

My mind worked fast. Staying on at Bracknell was an attractive thought. However, I was pretty certain that no three-star command appointments would be vacant within the time scale that Peter was talking about, and the prospect of a staff desk somewhere did not compete well with the prospect of going to the sun and launching a flying business.

'No thank you, I wouldn't be happy to do that,' I heard myself saying. He stared at me as if I had taken leave of my senses – and perhaps it could be argued that I had. I was tossing away, among other things, the knighthood that came automatically with three-stars – and the prospect of an enhanced, possibly even four-star, pension. As lightly as I had joined the Air Force, I was leaving it. And, as far as Peter was concerned, I was cavalierly turning my back on an offer for which most would have been grateful and throwing back in his face his kindness in coming to put the proposition to me. He said that he was sorry that the idea did not appeal, finished up his drink, gathered up his things and went.

Well, that was that. I left Bracknell on 15 January 1987, via a VC-10 out of Brize Norton, bound for retirement in Cyprus with some leave and a 'Resettlement Course' to take me up to my official date of retirement of 11 March. Walking around the College before I went, saying farewell to the members of the staff, I paused in the Officers' Mess dining room, my eye caught by the badges of RAF Commands mounted on the surrounds of the band alcove. There were fourteen. All had been in existence when I joined almost thirty-three years before. There were now just three. A Service that had emerged from the Second World War with over a million men had dropped by 1950 to 200,000 and, by the time I retired, to 93,000. As I write it has dropped almost to 40,000.

In the 1920s the RAF had had to fight for survival, principally against the Air Arm of the Royal Navy, a fight waged largely in Parliament and in the press. Now that times are again harder than ever, and despite all the joint-Service amalgamations that have taken place since the formation of the Ministry of Defence in 1961, the 'Rationalisation' of jobs across the single-Service dividing lines, and the privatisations of supporting services, the canard of the abolition of the RAF and the division of its assets between the other two, comes up again from time to time. The only arguments ever deployed for the abolition of a third Service have been financial ones; the military case is and always has been thin. In the 1920s Lord Trenchard stated the alternatives clearly: '…the air could be used simply as a means of conveyance…(or) to carry out reconnaissance for the Navy and Army… or there could be an air service which will encourage and develop the air spirit… to make it a force that will profoundly alter the strategy of the future.' The 'air' did prosper and develop and there could have been no greater acknowledgement of this than that made by the military historian John Terraine. In writing about the RAF's role in the Second World War he described the Service as 'The Right of the Line',[3] and anyone with any knowledge of the military will know what a mighty compliment to the independent RAF that was.

Young officers should continue to be taken up through the ranks of their own separate Services as at present, but should as a matter of course fill a variety of joint-Service appointments as they progress. In this way they would become familiar with the needs of all three Services as well as being aware of the particular requirements of their own. They would then later know how to argue for the balance that must be achieved between the wants and the requirements of all three Services in the face of constant and instinctive Treasury pressure to reduce.

What a reduction in RAF strength 'peacetime' has brought – and what a consequent reduction in top posts and thus in job prospects for young thrusters. However, if I were a young man I would do the whole thing over again, prospects or not. And I would wholeheartedly recommend a career in the RAF to anyone in spite of the shrinkage that has been a continuing part of the past sixty or so years, and which may continue – for the time being – in spite of the increasing menace of Islamic fundamentalism and the threatening spread of nuclear weapons to those who may feel few restraints on their use.

Notes

1 In 1984 there were over 4,000 squadron leaders in the RAF. Around 400 officers were promoted to the rank annually.

2 In Pakistan, among other things, I was invited to lay a wreath at the grave of Muhammad Ali Jinnah, revered there as the founder of the country. I was also generously given a comprehensive tour starting from Karachi and going as far north as Peshawar (where I found, in the Officers' Mess of the Pakistan Air Force base, framed photographs of No. 20 Squadron, RAF, still hanging on the ante-room wall).

3 The English Army faced apparently hopeless odds before the Battle of Crecy in 1346. In drawing up his men for the battle King Edward III gave his eldest son, the Black Prince, 'the place of honour and greatest danger, commanding the vanguard on the right of the line'.

Glossary

AAI	Angle of Approach Indicator	CRDF	Cathode Ray Direction Finder
AAFCE	Allied Air Forces Central Europe	DF	Direction Finding
ACM	Air Chief Marshal	DFCLS	Day-Fighter Combat Leaders' School
ADEN	Armament Developments Enfield – 30-mm cannon	DFLS	Day-Fighter Leaders' School
ADGE	Air Defence ground Environment	DME	Distance Measuring Equipment
AFCENT	Allied Air Forces Central Europe	ECM	Electronic Counter-Measures
agl	Above ground level	EOKA	Ethniki Organosis Kipriakou
AI	Airborne Intercept (radar)		Agonos (National Organisation
AOA	Angle of Attack – angle at which a wing is meeting the airflow		of Cypriot Struggle)
AOC	Air Officer Commanding	FAC	Forward Air Controller
APC	Armament Practice Camp	FEAF	Far East Air Force
ATAF	Allied Tactical Air Force	FGA	Fighter Ground Attack (aircraft)
ATC	Air Traffic Control	FLIR	Forward-Looking Infra Red
AVM	Air Vice-Marshal	FLOSY	Front for the Liberation of
AVPIN	Isopropylnitrate – Highly inflammable liquid used to fuel the engine starter turbines in the (later) Marks of Hunters and Lightnings		Occupied South Yemen
		FOCAS	Flag Officer, Carriers and Amphibious Ships
		FONAC	Flag Officer, Naval Air Command
AWACS	Airborne Warning and Control System	FOSNI	Flag Officer, Scotland and Northern Ireland
AWF	All Weather Fighter	FR	Fighter Reconnaissance
		FTS	Flying Training School
BAOR	British Army of the Rhine		
bhp	Brake horse power	g	Acceleration due to gravity
BOAC	British Overseas Airways Corporation	GCA	Ground Controlled Approach
		GE	Ground Environment
BRIXMIS	British Mission to the Commander-in-Chief Soviet Forces in Germany	GOC	General Officer Commanding
		Gp Capt	Group Captain
		HAS	Hardened Aircraft Shelter
CAP	Combat Air Patrol	HE	High Explosive
CAS	Chief of the Air Staff		
CDS	Chief of the Defence Staff	IGB	Inner German Border (border between West and East Germany)
CENTO	Central Treaty Organisation		
CFI	Chief Flying Instructor		
CFS	Central Flying School	IFF	Identification Friend or Foe
chaff	Very small lightweight metal strips released in bundles to confuse radar	ILS	Instrument Landing System
		IP	Initial Point (from which an attack run is started)
C-in-C	Commander-in-Chief	IRE	Instrument Rating Examiner
CNS	Chief of the Naval Staff	IRT	Instrument Rating Test
CO	Commanding Officer	ITCZ	Intertropical Convergence Zone
COS	Chief of Staff	ITN	Independent Television News

ITS	Initial Training School	RAAF	Royal Australian Air Force
IWI	Interceptor Weapons Instructor	RAF	Royal Air Force
JEngO	Junior Engineer Officer	RAuxAF	Royal Auxiliary Air Force
JPT	Jet-Pipe Temperature	RAFVR	Royal Air Force Volunteer Reserve
Knot(s)	Nautical Mile(s) per hour	RNAS	Royal Naval Air service
		rpm	Revolutions per minute
LSL	Landing Ship Logistic	RP	Rocket Projectile
		RT	Radio Telephony
Mach	Mach (number); strictly, the ratio of the velocity of an object to that of sound in a given medium. An aircraft travelling at Mach 1 is doing so at the velocity of sound in air	SAM	Surface to Air Missile
		SASO	Senior Air Staff Officer
		SEATO	South East Asia Treaty Organisation
		SEngO	Senior Engineer Officer
MADLS	Mirror-Aided Deck Landing System	SNEB	Pod mounted air-to-ground rocket projectiles
MEC	Middle East Command	SNCO	Senior Non-Commissioned Officer
MPC	Missile Practice Camp		
MOD	Ministry of Defence	SOP	Standard Operating Procedure
MQ	Married Quarter	SOXMIS	Soviet Mission to the Commanders in Chief BAOR and RAF Germany
MRS	Master Radar Station		
NAAFI	Navy, Army, and Air Force Institute	STI	Special technical Instruction
NADGE	NATO Ground Environment	TA	Territorial Army
NATO	North Atlantic Treaty Organisation	TACAN	Tactical Air Navigation (equipment)
NLF	National Liberation Front	Taceval	Tactical Evaluation
nm	Nautical Mile. One nm = 2,025 yards =1.15 statute miles = 1.552 kilometres	TAF	Tactical Air Force
		TTF	Target Towing Flight
NVG	Night Vision Goggles	UAS	University Air Squadron
		UFO	Unidentified Flying Object
OC	Officer Commanding	UHF	Ultra High Frequency
OCU	Operational Conversion Unit	UKADGE	United Kingdom Air Defence Ground Environment
ORP	Operational Readiness Platform	UKADR	United Kingdom Air Defence Region
PAI	Pilot Attack Instructor	USAF	United States Air Force
PI	Practice Interception	USMC	United States Marine Corps
psi	Pounds per square inch	USN	United States Navy
PT	Physical Training		
PTF	Phantom Training Flight	VCAS	Vice Chief of the Air Staff
PUP	Pull-Up Point	VHF	Very High Frequency
Q	Shorthand for Quick Reaction Alert	WW2	Second World War
QFI	Qualified Flying Instructor		
QRA	Quick Reaction Alert		
QUAS	Queen's University Air Squadron		

BIBLIOGRAPHY

Some suggestions for further reading:

Action Stations Revisited; The Complete History of Britain's Military Airfields, Michael JF Bowyer, Crécy Publishing, 2006

Aden Insurgency – The Savage War in South Arabia 1962–67, Jonathan Walker, Spellmount, 2005

Air Power and Colonial Control 1919–1939, DE Omissi, Manchester, 1990

Air Wars and Aircraft: A Detailed Record of Air Combat from 1945 to the Present, Victor Flintham, Arms & Armour Press, 1989

Berlin Wall, The, Frederick Taylor, Bloomsbury, 2006

Brief History of the Royal Air Force, AP 3003

Britain's Armed Forces Today: 4 – Royal Air Force Germany, Paul Jackson, Jane's Publishing, 1984

Britain's Secret War: The Indonesian Confrontation 1962–66, Will Fowler, Osprey Publications, 1966

Cold War, Hot Wings, Chris J Bain, Pen & Sword Aviation, 2007

Cold War – A Military History, The, David Millar, Blackwell Publishing, 1999

Collapse of British Power, The, Corelli Barnett, Eyre Methuen, 1972

Downing Street Years, The, Margaret Thatcher, Harper Collins, 1993

Dry Ginger, Richard Baker, WH Allen, 1977

End of Empire and the Making of Malaya, The, TN Harper, Cambridge University Press, 1999

Endure no Makeshifts: Some Naval Reflections, Henry Leach, Leo Cooper, 1993

English Electric Lightning, Martin Bowman, The Crowood Press, 1997

English Electric Lightning – Volume Two: The Lightning Force, Stewart A Scott, GMS Enterprises, 2004

Fighter, Len Deighton, Cape, 1977

Fighter Combat in the Jet Age, David C Isby, London Harper Collins 1998/ Jane's Air War 1

Fighter Pilot, Paul Richey, Jane's Publishing, 1980

Having Been a Soldier, Lt Col Colin Mitchell, Mayflower, 1969

History of Singapore 1819–1988, A, CM Turnbull, Oxford University Press, 1989

History of Modern Indonesia since C. 1300, MC Ricklefs, Macmillan 1991

History of No 20 Squadron, The, NJ Roberson, Printed by Palka-Verlag, Weeze, 1987

Last Post – Aden 1964 to 1970, The, Julian Paget, Faber & Faber, 1969

Middle East in Revolution, The, Humphrey Trevelyan, Macmillan, 1978

RAF Harrier Ground Attack Falklands, Jerry Pook, Pen & Sword Aviation, 2007

Right of the Line, The, John Terraine, Hodder & Stoughton, 1985

Royal Air Force and Two World Wars, The, Sir Maurice Dean, Cassell, 1979

Seventy Days to Singapore, Stanley Falk, Hall 1975

Singapore Burning; Heroism and Surrender in World War II, Colin Smith, Penguin Books, 2005

Source Book of the RAF, The, Ken Delve, Airlife Publishing , 1994

South East Asia Past and Present, DR SarDesai, Westview Press, 1997

Splash One – The Story of Jet Combat, Ivan Rendall, Weidenfeld & Nicolson, 1998

Thailand – A Short History, David K Wyall, Yale University Press, 1982

Trenchard, Andrew Boyle, Collins, 1962

View From Steamer Point, A, Charles Johnston, Collins, 1964

Vulcan 607, Rowland White, Bantam Press, 2006

INDEX

Page numbers in *italics* refer to maps. Subheadings under the author's name appear in approximate chronological order.